D0244463

MISSION PARADISE

A WORLD WAR TWO MEMOIR

By

MARJORY RAE LEWIS

Published by New Generation Publishing in 2015

Copyright © Marjory Rae Lewis 2015

First Edition

The author asserts the moral right under the Copyright, Designs and Patents Act 1988 to be identified as the author of this work.

All Rights reserved. No part of this publication may be reproduced, stored in a retrieval system or transmitted, in any form or by any means without the prior consent of the author, nor be otherwise circulated in any form of binding or cover other than that which it is published and without a similar condition being imposed on the subsequent purchaser.

www.newgeneration-publishing.com

 New Generation Publishing

ACKNOWLEDGEMENTS

With thanks to my family and friends for their support,
encouraging me to write down my story.

To Cicely Hill for reading the first draft, her praise and telling me
that it made her laugh out loud and it made her cry.

To Christine Allen for her valuable work with the computer.

To Heather Godwin, for her faith in me and her constant help and
Michael Morpurgo's spark of interest that ignited my determination
to get into print.

In memory of

my Mother and JC whose exceptional courage brought them together and made them friends.

FOREWORD

This is a true story. The Second World War was a time of separation. City children were evacuated to the countryside to protect them from air raids. Young men and women were called up into the armed forces to fight in far-away places. There was apprehension and sadness.

It was also a period of coming together as England became a refuge for those lucky enough to evade Hitler's oppression often at considerable peril. They were ready to resist the monstrous incursion of their homelands. It was an opportunity for mixing with people one might never have known in more peaceful times.

It is also a love story. The unconditional love of a mother for her children, the self-sacrificing love of a patriot for his country and it was the rapture of first love and awakening sexuality. Hope and love were powerful driving forces in a world that seemed as if it was going to end.

All together it is a glimpse of the social life of the time.

I have a faculty for burying an emotion in my heart
and soul for forty years, and at the end of that time
exhuming it as fresh as the day it was interred.

Thomas Hardy

MISSION PARADISE

A WORLD WAR TWO MEMOIR

PART ONE

REAWAKENING 1965

'Les seuls vrais paradis sont les paradis qu'on a perdus'
PROUST

At the quayside the salt wind loosened my hair and whipped my cheeks with shining health. Overhead the sun tried to penetrate the haze. Soon the clank of chains and capstans turning, the mewling seagulls, the commands and lapping water set me tingling. It made me feel young once more, with all the exuberance of a schoolgirl.

I was on my way to Brussels at last, the city for which I had a special affinity. Only two hundred and forty miles from London, but for twenty years it had seemed as far away to me as it must have done to those wartime Lysanders acting by moonlight as ferries for 'secret consignments' between the two capitals. People think nothing of the journey today, yet as I was making it, I felt something of that earlier insecurity. It had long been my desire to come here, to indulge those emotions I had for years suppressed, to draw conviction from their reality and, especially, to meet Rose with whom I had been fitfully corresponding since 1945 – for reasons my mother would have understood.
"Do you remember the Belgians?" I could hear her. "And that Christmas?" as if I could ever forget.

From the moment I joined the summer crowds at Victoria, the tourists, school and college parties, groups of friends and lovers, at each stage of the journey had jolted my memory and spurred on my imagination. Long-haired boys and girls in jerseys and jeans, possessors of a new freedom, a more liberal code of living and loving, both widened that gulf I had set out to bridge yet at the same time narrowed it, for I still remained a witness of both worlds.

My mind needed little provocation to turn back to the war and, as we sped across Flanders, the landscape drew it all into focus. It was this same land with its doll's house cities grown up around medieval Cloth Halls and Belfries which Caesar once conquered - 'The Belgae in the North are the bravest of all Gaul', I had learnt at school. I did not dwell on the Roman Conquest. In spirit I was out there in the sunlit fields, among the pollarded willows bordering the canals and the tall regiments of poplars. In my mind's eye I saw only modern armies: the blockhouses and the gun emplacements which were there before the new, neat houses came to be built on land stained poppy-red by the blood of two world wars.

Brussels, just as full of ghosts was bustling with importance as might any capital city of Europe today. Every brick and cobble surviving from 1940 had existed through events so near to my heart that it gave me a feeling of pride to see them mellow in the sun and to feel them hard and enduring under my feet. The spirit of the old city and its long, dead heroes seemed to have roused themselves in welcome. I felt no longer alone. I sensed love around me, as if one of those gentle souls smiling down on me had put a protective arm around my shoulder. Today Brussels belonged to me. I had a place. At last into Belgium's heart had come my heart - rivals once. We had a lot in common, this little heart-shaped city and I. For all her importance, her hard-won freedom and independence, was she not in some small part indebted to me?

***

After I had been there two or three days Rose began to open up and speak intimately of events which had afflicted us both. I had been waiting for her to introduce the subject and she brought over a shabby cardboard box and came to sit beside me on the settee in front of the window. Outside the fast metropolitan traffic raced up and down the wide avenue. Smelly fumes of exhaust occasionally wafted in through the open casement on the warm summer breeze gently fluttering the curtains behind us. Rose put on her spectacles and with a nervous, serious preoccupation began to sort through the papers in the box, stopping every now and then to read again and refresh her memory of some detail before handing them over to let them speak for themselves. A quietness, a closeness and an overwhelming sadness overcame us both. For Rose and me, comparative strangers until now, this meeting had quickly affirmed our friendship. She had her memories and I had mine and somewhere along the way they had briefly converged. With this beautiful woman whose warmth and smile had given me a glimpse back to those days of promise, and in whose eyes I saw a spark of that kindred fire which had once burned me with an improbable love, I knew we should be able to exchange our recollections as intimately as sisters.

Presently she handed me a letter drawing my attention to a small paragraph. I saw that her eyes were full of tears. I took the paper with a shaky hand and scanned the words in silence, unable to take in much of their message written in

3

French, for which, after years of little practice I needed special concentration. At that moment any questions would have stuck in my throat and even one glance exchanged would have spilled my tears gathering just below the surface. The writing was familiar, too painfully familiar. I saw at once that this letter was almost identical to one I had received, written in pencil on the same impersonal paper and showing similar ravages of frequent handling. Faded, tear-stained, opened and refolded so many times that brittle and antiquated in my hot hand it tried to concertina back into the seclusion of its creases and the words themselves, unless one knew them by heart, were nearly too faint to be legible. The summer heat, the oppressive lack of any easy and appropriate comment, plus the weight of our suppressed emotion became stifling. Again and again I tried to read the passage she had ear-marked for me but could only take in three words - *'une petite fille'* concise apt and surprisingly clear; and my tears, sympathetically encouraged by my friend, trickled down my face and fell in silent drops on to the paper magnifying odd letters and words to make them speak out more clearly than the rest. I thought of the one who had written the letter and of my mother who, with such light-hearted pride, had made that significant introduction all those years before.

After a deep sigh to convince myself I was able to breathe, I told Rose it was impossible to take in everything at once and she replied that she would leave the box with me to investigate as I pleased. Tactfully she set about her jobs while I sifted through the rest of the contents which had been lovingly and proudly preserved. I was eager to fathom the box's treasures but also afraid of what I might unearth in the process. Amongst the letters there were photographs and tiny snapshots small enough to conceal in a deep pocket. Some were very old-fashioned as one might have expected, but others more surprising, retaining their freshness and clarity and could almost have been taken yesterday. These I found particularly unnerving for it was here that everything fell into place and the dream, which I had kept to myself for most of my life because of the nightmare it became, turned into reality. At last we found ourselves talking easily, exchanging memories which until today I had found impossible to share with anyone. Once I delved through the box and unshrouded the corresponding compartment of my soul it was all there just as it had been, as bright as the day it had been abruptly shut away. I wanted to relive the rapture with the anguish, those green, golden days of innocence and illusion. 'How can I meet you without the war,' I read in English. I had with me a collection of letters and mementoes - like Rose's, bundled into a cloth bag lovingly sewn with childish stitches. From the first they had to be hidden away. No wonder that I should feel some guilt as the story was beginning to free itself. But I am racing ahead. Every episode had some relevance and must be accounted for if this visit were to have effect.

***

AWAKENING 1940

My dear, plucky, ambitious mother was good at going over the past. I think she found security and strength from what had been accomplished and was safely passed over. She referred to every period which had gone before as 'The Good Old Days' and she recalled them with feeling and precision. As a rule she never liked to dwell on sadness and would make a determined effort to cast it from her mind until, enhanced by age and rarity, she would dig it from the past and polish and revere it like some prized antiquity. She would begin to talk increasingly about the war as it receded in time. It was to have significance in the lives of us both.

Given to aphorisms and cliché - the more pithy and succinct the better - and a fair amount of superstition, she taught me early that love between a man and a woman was the most beautiful thing in the world. 'Love makes the world go round' was her maxim and that we had been pretty children because she and my father had been in love when my brother Robin, born two years after me, and I had been conceived.

No-one could have predicted my parents as destined for one another. They had met by chance on a railway station. My mother, the elder daughter in a family of Italian extraction, was established as a fitter in a firm of Court Dressmakers in Mayfair at the time. My father had a private fortune and was born of wealthy Scottish parents in Italy. My mother always spoke about my father's origins with great reflected glory.

The age of my infancy was referred to as Modern Times. Paris was the centre of chic and fashion, the Court of St. James the Mecca of High Society, and most of the large, fine, but ill-heated houses in London's prime residential districts were still maintained as private dwellings. Our first years were happy and the nearest we came to a normal, carefree childhood. My mother had a rich store of memories covering this period and quite a few photos to bring them to life.

When I was almost four my father, in an endeavour to conserve his dwindling fortune during the Depression, bought a derelict house and market garden in Jersey which he was setting out, with me for company, to restore with his own hands. One winter, tired out with worry and overwork, he succumbed to an attack of pneumonia and died before my mother could reach his bedside.

To this day I can remember the haunting loneliness of imminent death as I lay awake sensing the crisis of that night - the grown ups shifting noiselessly along the landing all through the small hours, a thin strip of light outlining my bedroom door on which my eyes remained fixed. I knew by instinct that if it went out all would be well, and then the ice-cold feeling of rejection the next morning when I was restrained from going into my father's room for my usual cuddle by the motherly lady who had come to take charge. "Your Daddy's gone to heaven, my darling," she said, gently bending down to gather me up in her arms, and I saw stars reflected in her bright beads.

The first move my mother made after my father's death was to take over smart business premises in Knightsbridge, within the neighbouring district of Belgravia, which were for a few years to become the centre of our world; a world of titled ladies and debutantes, tea-gowns and court dresses, tiaras and ostrich plumes, a world already doomed. I grew up to recognise a Paris Model before I understood the function of a brassière. Chanel, Worth and Schiaparelli were familiar names.

My mother threw herself wholeheartedly into her profession. She was by nature an artist, and had never been happy confined to a domestic existence and she was a great success with her dresses. She was making clothes for some of the wealthiest socialites of the day and she made a lot of money which she spent lavishly.

As her business life encroached upon the time she could spend at home so she compensated by a whirl of activity on our behalf. We had music and dancing lessons, parties galore with the appropriate clothes to go with them, and when the summer holidays came we went to stay with our German Nanny's parents in Nazi Germany. Always with a feeling of better things around the corner, we moved several times during the pre-war years and we suffered as a result. To have lost one parent was bad enough, but denied the undivided attention of the other and a stable home had its effect on my brother and me and, needless to say, it drew us close and we loved our mother with a concentration that made it difficult for anyone to come in and take her place.

At the outbreak of the Second World War my mother was approaching fifty and years in business had changed her. A woman alone in the world of commerce where with her independent spirit she was determined to be the equal of any man - she was always telling us she was both father and mother - had made her competitive and rash. Hand-in-hand with her impetuosity went a streak of immaturity, even a childishness that saved her from hardness and was one of her most endearing attributes. We were on holiday in Jersey when war was declared. Our mother liked to come and look again at the lovely old house our father had been restoring and, with a handkerchief to her nose as she cuddled us close - nostalgia had become for her the supreme emotion - she told us again about the 'old days' and our father's exalted beginnings. She looked upon us children almost as if she had had no hand in our creation, considering herself plain, unrefined and unlovable, while retaining a persisting illusion that we were just the opposite. We moved in a close-knit trio. She took us to see Walt Disney's Snow White and Errol Flynn in Robin Hood and she made it fun walking back in the blackout holding our hands. She pretended we were a family of moles burrowing underground in the same way as she had tried to comfort us as tiny children during a thunderstorm by insisting the thunder was the three bears growling in heaven and the lightning the good fairy keeping them in order. She had the most fertile imagination in the world and could tell the best stories. It was not until the war, the period in which I started to grow up, that I really began to know my mother and, contrary to her delusions, I could tell that in many ways I was like her and, because she was as she was, so I became as I was.

I think she realised that war would mean the end of her world as soon as we stepped off the boat-train at Waterloo station. Coming back to sad, blacked-out London with the war already a week old was a different proposition from the last carefree days of our holiday. There were discomforting signs cropping up all over the place:

AIR RAID SHELTER, FIRST AID POST, EMERGENCY
WATER SUPPLY

All around us were troops on the move and loose crocodiles of children labelled and already weighed down with winter clothes, providentially chosen a size too large, to last until 'further notice'. Their anxious smiles masked an inner bewilderment Robin and I knew well. For once we were smug. There were no plans for us to leave home and we kept possessively close to our parent as she hailed a taxi to take us there.

In the patriotic rush in which everyone was now swept up most of my mother's customers had exchanged their fine clothes for practically-identical uniforms with only the badges V.A.D., W.V.S. or A.R.P. to distinguish them. War had no place for Haute Couture. With a heavy heart she dismissed her staff and closed down the workrooms. Her indecision did not last. True to form, she made an extraordinary move that most people without her outrageous courage would have described as foolhardy to say the least.

She left us one morning with the daily woman - Nanny, fearing internment, having soon departed to marry her English fiancé - I had noticed before she went out how unusually excited she appeared, for one burdened with bringing up two growing children with most of her income suddenly non-existent. I remember her return some time later, her dark eyes sparkling with the elation of a child as she brandished an official-looking document before us. Spreading it on the table, she scanned the paper for the relevant details.

"Look - see here, oh yes - here we are! See what it says," she read aloud, her words tumbling out in breathless excitement.

"Look - the Duke of Westminster!" she picked out slowly with her finger, "The landlord - and Mrs. Alice Letitia Rae the tenant!"

She looked up watching for our reaction and by her insistence we gathered it must be evidence of some important transaction, though neither of us was conversant with terms landlord and tenant.

"What is it?" we said, "What does it mean?"

"It means, my darlings - we are going to move, that's what it means, and we shall be living practically next door to Lady Lever," she impressed on us gathering us, both together, in her arms.

"It's an absolute bargain. Isn't it marvellous? Me and the Duke of Westminster - I can't get over that."

For a few days I was expecting the Duke of Westminster to have at least the necessary grace to move in with us.

A house in London with the prospect of air-raids had been enough to daunt most people. Those with money made arrangements to evacuate whole households into the country. Many beautiful houses in the centre of town were left empty and landlords, rather than having them falling into disrepair while they waited for the bombs to demolish them for good, now offered them to let at peppercorn rents.

Some weeks after the war had started we moved into our mansion in Belgravia, the same postal district as Buckingham Palace and the heart of embassy land. Six bedrooms and three bathrooms for a family of three seemed a little extreme when economy was the order of the day, even if we were only paying a nominal rent for them. But true to character there was method behind this madness and our mother set down her plan of campaign a few days after we had settled in. It was her intention, she said, to take in 'paying guests', as she described them in her endeavour to keep it a stylish-sounding undertaking; but in that callow period of my life I could think of no worse indignity than my home being inhabited by strangers as if they had every right to be there, except perhaps for the Duke himself.

"With a first-class address like this we should only get the best people,"

She tried to pacify me, and I was just about old enough to understand that to whatever hardship she might debase herself ostensibly on our behalf she was, in fact, realising one of her loftiest ambitions, war or no war. My mother was full of confidence for this new venture and with the situation on the Western front giving the illusion of no war at all, we began to make plans for our first wartime Christmas.

Lady Lever, one to have moved her household into the country, had been one of my mother's best customers. She had also known my father in the 'Good Old Days'. On the strength of this she made frequent trips to town to keep in touch. She often remarked that Robin and I must be the only two children left in London. It therefore came as no great surprise when, early in 1940, she invited the two of us to spend the 'duration' with her and her husband on their country estate in Hampshire. My mother looked upon this as a heaven-sent opportunity to provide for our welfare and safety. Our protests did nothing to change her mind. We children would be well-looked after, in an even more ambitious coterie than she could aspire to and, of more immediate concern, we would be off her hands thus enabling her to get on with the serious business of running the guesthouse, keeping things ticking over until she could re-establish herself in the world of fashion. "Just what Daddy would have wished," she stressed to make it a more acceptable undertaking. And she began to paint such a glowing picture of life with the Levers that we were quite won over, especially as she promised to telephone regularly and to visit us once a month.

***

Robin and I arrived in Winchester one darkening winter day before tea and Lady Lever was there to meet us at the station. As soon as we left the platform where I observed the ticket collector respectfully tip his cap as to no-one else and found the chauffeur waiting with the car, I recognised this to be the adventure of fairy-tale dimensions my mother had promised and a challenge, now I had got this far, I was eager to undertake. Constant change had developed in me a vain, chameleon-like wish to merge with any group without drawing attention through non-observance of some quirk of fashion or lack of savoir-faire. We sat on the back seat of the car beside our new fairy Godmother, the Canadian bearskin draped snugly over our knees, and as we moved off I felt like Cinderella on the way to the ball though, thanks to my mother too proud and clever to allow us to be at a sartorial disadvantage, nothing was necessary in the way of any outward transformation. There appeared no immediate evidence of war here, no sandbags, no barrage balloons. Were it not for our gasmasks and the shades on the lights one could have believed we had left the war behind. We soon reached the open countryside which I only knew in summer, and with the daylight fast going there was an eeriness creeping over the land; dark hills looming to where the first stars were bright in the sky. Suddenly we turned off the main Roman road through two-ever open gates and we were there, crunching to a halt in front of the big white front door surmounted with gleaming brass.

Kingsworthy Court was set back from the gates at the top of a wide circular drive, screened from the road by a thick Yew hedge and a small wood. It was one of the largest houses in the village, built in the style of Queen Anne, with two round bays either side of the front door. As we alighted from the car to walk up the three shallow steps, the door opened as if by remote control and there was Buttons in the guise of Thompson the butler, waiting to take her Ladyship's coat and bring in our luggage.

From the first it was a golden house, built of brick which the soft southern rain and the sun, which bathed its walls from dawn until late into summer evenings, had weathered and mellowed into warm shades of ochre and russet. The bloom of the facade was further enhanced by the pristine white of the paintwork surrounding the windows and picking out the dentils under the eaves. It faced the sun and the downs with nothing to interrupt the view and in summer bees hummed and busied themselves in the sweet-smelling honeysuckle and roses which covered the walls.

When finally that first night I was tucked in bed, clean, powdered and rosy, in my new silk nightdress chosen by my discerning mother to be in keeping with my splendid bedroom with its own bathroom adjoining, Lady Lever came and planted a warm kiss on my cheek, the first of those that were to continue nightly for the next three years. In the darkness and the very audible absence of the roar of London's traffic I thought of my mother and father, how he had been born into luxury but it had been of little lasting comfort while my mother, because she had not consented so readily to our coming here to be brought up in the environment she considered to be our birthright.

Sir Hardman and Lady Lever were an ageing couple. They had no children of their own but were diligent in the task they had taken on themselves and quickly found us a place in their hearts. Lady Lever, Canadian by birth, was gracious and methodical with a liberal outlook on life. She did not appear to be bound by the more restrictive conventions of the English upper classes and believed implicitly, often to our tongue-tied embarrassment- Nanny seeming to have held the opposite view - that children should be heard as well as seen and, to our simple surprise, she was not above shopping in Woolworths. Fastidious about her appearance, she was tall and slim and dressed in the height of fashion. She used a surprising amount of bright lipstick for one I looked on as so ancient and a superfluity of light, almost white, face-powder. The skin of her long scrawny neck had exactly the same translucence of a fowl, freshly plucked and floured ready for the oven. Her thick white hair was curled in front and drawn back into a heavy bun on the nape of her neck. Her body still retained the sylphlike quality of a young girl's. Her limbs, however, had been fat in proportion and with age, had grown flabby so that loose flesh overhung her neat feet in their habitual high-heeled shoes and at her wrists around her watchstrap. Her home was well run. The bulk of the housework had been completed by the time we came down in the mornings but the servants, out of sight but always alert, were ready to pounce unnoticed amongst the first sign of disarray amongst the cushions or the selection of magazines and newspapers neatly arranged on the side table in the study. There were fresh flowers everywhere over which Lady Lever took time and trouble herself. Soon after my arrival she initiated me into the serious ritual of arranging flowers.

She did not consider it necessary for girls to be educated to the same high standard as boys. Girls got married and their instruction from puberty onwards should therefore concentrate on refining those accomplishments likely to attract the most eligible spouse. Impeccable outward appearance being all-important.

"After all, my dear, that is how you will be judged by the rest of the world," she would say.

Yet Lady Lever often confided to me that it was the women who ruled the world by the influence they exercised over their menfolk. "If only Hitler had a good woman behind him we wouldn't be in the mess we are today," she would declare, dusting her hands apart as if she herself might have been just such a woman to shape the world's destiny.

Any aspect of life she found distasteful or beyond her control she ignored while that which came within her jurisdiction she tackled briskly and cheerfully. Appreciative of her wealth and position, she believed in God and St. Anthony and went to church regularly to give thanks for her good fortune and the recovery of her lost property. Robin and I found her Canadian accent a shock at first; it reminded us of the films and it never failed to make us smile when she addressed her husband as 'Sammy' or more often 'Sammy dear'. But despite her private conviction of woman's superiority she was careful not to undermine his authority and tactfully regarded him always as master in his own home, even though he was shorter than she and in delicate health.

Extremely wealthy by his own efforts, Sir Hardman Lever KCB Bart. very much a man of the tough political and business world - he had at one time been Financial Secretary to the Treasury in Lloyd George's time - took a guarded and serious view of life. He held conventional, even old-fashioned beliefs as to a woman's role in the order of things. It was certainly not to rule the world. That was exclusively a man's prerogative. An extremely shrewd, perspicacious and logical brain, he did not pray and went to church once a year, and then only to please his wife for whom he felt profound admiration and deep romantic love. Rather did he poke fun at clerics and intimidate the Rector when he came to tea. "Sammy dear, that was naughty," his wife gently reprimanded after one such occasion when, incensed by what he termed later as 'sickening humbug' from one who by the very nature of his calling was supposed to practise self-restraint, he had literally snatched the jam-pot from the bewildered man - too liberally indulging himself - with the irate reminder: "I say - steady on! it's rationed don't you know."

Bald, with a greying fringe of dark hair encircling the back of his head, he had large honest and expressive eyes under two prominent examples of what he termed his 'superorbital bosses'. He was a keen shooting and fishing man with a large assortment of sporting tackle to hand inside the lobby by the front door. It was an advantage once food was rationed. But he was essentially humane and took more than a game interest in the wild creatures who sought succour and shelter in the garden. He could recite many well-known ballads and large passages from Shakespeare, usually managing to call to mind quotations pertinent to most incidents in his daily life. With no son of his own he quickly took Robin under his wing, leading him out and about when he made his twice-daily inspection of his new world of wartime retirement, the chickens, the greenhouses and the kitchen garden. But, like many children, we didn't fully appreciate our good fortune until later, and most of the time regarded Sir Hardman with his fanatical obsession with clocks and punctuality, as a kindly but tetchy old bore. Nothing annoyed him more than to be kept waiting at mealtimes when his anger would manifest itself in shrinking sarcasm. "Forgot to wind your watch, did you?"

So our first months in Hampshire passed comparatively easily. We were after all evacuees and, like the rest of them, busy fitting ourselves into a new mode of life with a different set of rules. The chalk countryside with its flints and clear trout streams proved a source of constant discovery. We gathered kingcups and bullrushes in the water-meadows and took back jars of frogspawn to put in the water-lily pond. We went walking for its own sake - kicking up the leaves as we went along: the long lanes and hedges concealing and revealing their treasures - craftsman-built nests, webs threaded with beads of dew, puddles as blue as the sky. We learnt the names of the wild creatures as well as hearing from Sir Hardman himself how to interpret the changing moods of nature and forecast the weather, some little country jingle to fit most meteorological conditions ever lurking on the tip of his tongue. There was hardly time for homesickness, though I missed the barrel-organ that played outside my bedroom window and the red-coated Chelsea pensioners who paraded the street in summer. Our mother kept her promise to make regular contact, but once the break from home had been smoothly effected, our guardians, more alive to the serious times through which we were passing, pointed out that the telephone was best kept for emergencies.

***

'How can I meet you without the war, without the invasion of Belgium?'

May the 10th, 1940 was my birthday and a friend of my mother, Secretary to the Speaker, had promised me a visit to both Houses of Parliament as a treat to celebrate the occasion. As there had not yet been any air raids in London I was allowed to keep the engagement and went up to town the day before. I had been looking forward to the trip very much, not particularly as an educational outing, but to get home again, to see my mother and to have just that little extra attention lavished on me that special day. The morning was warm and cloudless; a glowing mistiness suggested it would become even hotter as the day wore on. There was a particular poignancy in the summer starting early as I knew that overnight the war had taken a turn for the worse. I could tell by my mother's face and the way she kept clicking her tongue against the roof of her mouth.

I was happy to be in London again. Overhead the sun rose brighter through the haze, shortening the long morning shadows, and drying up the last of the moisture left by the shopkeepers in their early efforts to freshen up their fronts. The barrage balloons glinted with silver in the smoky blue of the sky. Then all at once, outside Sloane Square underground station, propped beside the flower seller with her display of violets, roses and asparagus fern, were the newspaper placards with their shocking headlines:

BELGIUM HOLLAND LUXEMBOURG INVADED

Belgium was a land we only passed over on our way to Germany. It had never been worth a visit on its own account. All I knew of it was the port at Ostend where we boarded the train to speed us to the frontier and Nanny's parents. The country was flat, small fields divided by poplar trees and canals, a windmill here and there, and odd-shaped spires as we approached the cities.

The newspaper boy was doing a brisk trade. The sun minimised the sense of foreboding. 'Allies answer call for aid - Leopold at head of army,' a long-faced man read out. The battle was getting closer! A puff of cool air sent a chill unexpected shiver down my spine.

***

After Dunkirk and the fall of France, the Levers took things very seriously. Sir Hardman came to church on the National Day of Prayer and on Sunday evenings beckoned us up on our feet respectfully when the BBC played 'God Save the King' at the end of the long and growing list of National Anthems as more and more countries fell under German occupation.

Perhaps Robin and I were still too young to understand just how close we had come to calamity that summer as we pursued our patriotic business of extinguishing the lives of cabbage white butterflies before they had a chance to devastate the vegetable garden. We also helped Thompson one night a week with the washing up, for which we got sixpence to buy a savings stamp, so that he could get off early to his Home Guard drill in the village hall.

The nights drew in and the summer faded. Mrs. Hickman and her minions in the kitchen salted the beans in large earthenware crocks and preserved the eggs in water-glass. The apple harvest was stored in the barn. The swallows massed on the telegraph wires to follow the sun and the skies clouded over into autumn. It was only a week later that we heard the first enemy aircraft throbbing high in formation on their steady menacing journey to London and the open cities beyond. Lady Lever began to talk about the 'German Bum-burrs,' her Canadian twang dividing it into two words of equal stress.

My mother's trips to Hampshire eventually dwindled to only three or four times a year. At first we went home ourselves during the holidays but once the 'bum-bing' started I used to go to spend some time with a childhood friend, Margaret whose family had moved to Sussex on the outbreak of war.

There were nights when the siren sounded close to us in Winchester and we would hear the distant cracking of gunfire and bombs bursting on Southampton and Portsmouth, but we were of an age when the unusual was exciting. It was fun getting up in the middle of the night when events became noisy and near at hand, traipsing downstairs with coats over our nightclothes to drink cups of tea with the whole household assembled awkwardly in the drawing room - emergency temporarily relaxing the barrier between servant and master. It did not happen often. More usually, after the siren had sounded I would lie in bed in the darkness and think about the war. Real life gave the impression of having stopped dead on the 3rd of September 1939, and the period which was passing - already cheating us of almost two years of childhood - was just an interlude until we could pick up the threads of normal existence once more. It also began to dawn on me that we had lived here in Hampshire almost longer than we had lived anywhere else.

We had soon found life here to be ordered and luxurious. Every effort was made for daily affairs to run as smoothly as possible to keep the shortages and deprivations to a minimum. Famous and distinguished people from the Levers' political and social life would often be entertained and somehow I was touched with guilt. I wanted to keep this house and its fairy-tale opulence secret from my schoolfellows in more frugal circumstances. So although it might have appeared we were suffering none of the inconvenience of war, even some of the fun, with few companions and a mother too preoccupied to pay us only the most sporadic attention, there was much lacking in this new life. Luckily I was able to gain some compensation in my happy school environment. I made a number of friends with whom I could relate quite naturally, none so much as Cicely, a local girl a little younger than myself. There was about her an ethereal waif-like appeal in her boyish undeveloped body reminiscent of the young Jane Eyre and surrounding her with a similar romantic aura. Yet it was her shrewdness, the large, intelligent olive green eyes that singled her out. She was the reverse of me - pale, lithe and blonde, sure in her opinions and forthright to the point of wounding. Although we were not alike, we were drawn together by common interests and similar emotional needs. Initially, it was a chance encounter which brought us together and sealed the knot of friendship.

"Do you believe in ghosts?" she asked as we found ourselves making for the same bus stop one rainy day after school, our hats set on the backs of our heads like haloes.

"Yes," I replied lightly.

"And fairies?"

"Yes - and giants," I responded eagerly.

"Now you are being ridiculous," she laughed scornfully and I was stung into silence.

Our fascination with the supernatural soon developed into a more tangible preoccupation with fortune-telling and horoscopes. She was a Sagittarian - 'fiery, mutable by virtue of Jupiter - aspiring in an Honourable way at high matters, doing glorious things, of sweet and affable conversation'! I was a Taurean. 'Shee signifies a quiet man, not given to quarrel or wrangling, oft entangled in love matters! Fixed, earthbound, governed by Venus!' Opposite ends of this ancient Zodiac, but we both knew in our hearts how well we complemented one another.

The next stage in our development was love, deep, passionate, romantic love. Love with all its attendant ecstasy and anguish was at the heart of my commitment. I felt a sense of vocation. Cicely and I read love stories, we hummed love songs, we marvelled at all that was happening around us in nature. Cicely and I were in love with each other. We were overwhelmingly in love with LOVE!

The facts of life were old hat. We knew the technicalities of sexual reproduction from biology lessons and a series of lectures given to the fourth- and fifth-formers by a lady doctor who was dressed from head to toe in white - white bandeau on her snowy hair down to the freshly-blancoed tennis shoes on her white stockinged feet. She was also armed with the most unlifelike charts, bearing little relation to men and women as far as I could see and she kept up this subterfuge by referring to the 'male body' the 'female body' and their 'union'. Nursing the secret belief that the fusion of body as well as soul was the masterstroke of

23

nature's romantic ingenuity, I had not been shocked into giggling conjecture about the King and Queen. In fact this aseptic paragon, who by her blanched appearance suggested a cold, clinical exercise, did clear up one or two fallacies for me. Up until now I had believed that every act of sexual union resulted in progeny. That this consummate act of love could be lusted after as an end in itself was yet beyond my comprehension. The female had no such feelings, the male apparently too much - no mention of love.

Meanwhile I looked forward to becoming a woman. I was pleased to be female. Long ago I had suffered childish envy that my body had not been embellished with the same interesting appendage as my brother's, but my changing shape was more than compensating for it now.

Unashamedly vain when alone, I liked to study my nakedness in the long mirror in the bathroom and took a secret pride in my development. Everything to do with being feminine, soft and pretty carried me forward in hopeful anticipation. Outwardly it appeared everyone was thinking in that direction too. Lady Lever was arranging for my hair to be trimmed and shampooed by her hairdresser "to encourage it into an easy, manageable style, my dear," and my mother was sending me pretty lace-trimmed underclothes to wear at weekends. At school everything had to be strictly business-like, black knickers and no petticoats.

With this new turn in self-awareness there came a growing sense of loss. For the first time I missed my father. My recollection of him was minimal, but over the years, from photographs and my mother's very graphic anecdotes, I had a picture of a loving and romantic figure - the prototype of perfection I would look for in the opposite sex. How dearly would I have loved this ideal of a father to have seen me take a pride in my approaching womanhood and help me overcome much of the raw torment of youth. Although love and romance were such absorbing - though still embryonic - emotions, doubts crept in too. As a child I had not suffered my deprivation consciously but now I felt the love of one parent was not enough. That, because of it, I must be noticeably different, half-developed, lacking in some essential which might make it hard for any man to love me. Fearful, even that I might not function properly as a woman.

Cicely and I, over the crest of our mutual infatuation, were always falling in and out of love meanwhile and with the most unlikely people. Our heroes were film-stars, artists, poets, whose pictures figured prominently in magazines, people utterly remote from our own existence on whom we could heap all responsibility for the helplessness of our condition. Robert Taylor, the King of the Belgians and Lord Lovat were just some who captured our hearts. And while they lasted, our love affairs were all-embracing, incorporating a great deal of day-dreaming and the most ravishing mental anguish.

Not surprisingly, it was not long before I lost my heart to one who was not so hopelessly inaccessible, and from a quarter I least expected. Lady Lever had seen to it from the beginning that we accompanied her to Church every Sunday morning. It was during one of these social and often emotionally-fraught morning services, bringing the whole village together that I became aware of a youth my age who fell somewhere within the bounds of my ideal. The chief choirboy, tall and blonde, he carried the cross at the head of the procession. My passion prompted me to Evensong when the evenings were light and I joined the Confirmation class. Later, I added early morning Communion to my list of reverent Sunday duties which made Lady Lever very satisfied with the way my spiritual education was shaping. At her instigation and the backing of the Rector, a Youth Service Squad was inaugurated under my leadership. The aim was to encourage the local boys and girls into giving some of their time to the war effort. We collected used magazines for the forces, gathered nettles for the extraction of chlorophyll and helped the old and infirm to cultivate their gardens. It was the perfect means of access to my choirboy. He was the first to join and on country walks, our hands protected by stout gauntlet gloves, our feet and ankles inflamed to the knees, we began to know each other. "He is absolutely angelic," I raved to Cicely. "His name is Tony - I am the Leader and he is the Deputy!"

On Thursday afternoons, our half-day off school, one of my classmates who lived on a farm invited a group of us home to play tennis when the weather was fine. We now arranged things so that carefully selected members of the Youth Squad came too, but very soon after it had become an established weekly practice we soon dispensed with the game of tennis and split up into pairs. There had been awkwardness and giggling to begin with, but after taking shelter in a barn during a shower things improved. Each week they got even better until secluded and intimate enough at last Tony had kissed me almost as if by accident. And with a pounding heart and burning cheeks, carried along on the momentum of my love, I had cycled the six miles back in record time my feet hardly seeming to touch the pedals. Long after the others, finding better things to fill their afternoons, stopped coming, we continued going and slowly, tentatively, our mutual love began to unfold. The totally innocent extrication of the physical from the metaphysical, the reconciliation of romantic love with human nature.

PART TWO

ROOM AT THE INN

'How can I meet you without the war, without the invasion of
Belgium?...
if Monsieur Gobeaux was not coming in England. If .....'

***

The last year had seen a dramatic change in the fortunes of my mother. In the early days of the guesthouse she had found little difficulty in letting her rooms. A few lines in the Telegraph advertising a comfortable room with breakfast had soon brought the result she hoped for. Many of her lodgers only came for short periods but she enjoyed the novelty and excitement of a constant change and variety of people around her. This life suited her well enough and with her money problem resolved for the time being, it compensated in no small way for the loss of her business and the separation from Robin and me. For several months she was able to reap real satisfaction from her residence in SW1 despite the war. But true to the pattern her life seemed destined to follow, the Duke of Westminster was not to have his illustrious tenant on his books for long. Her move out to the suburbs of London a year or so after our departure was precipitated by two factors: the prolonged aerial bombardment of the Capital and the other, she was often to declare, was no random stroke of fate.

During the heavy raids of the winter of 1940-41 my mother had many anxious moments, though when she wrote she always made them sound an adventure. The prospect of physical danger did not frighten her unduly neither did it appear to unnerve her that she might well emerge one morning to find her home a heap of rubble. The basements of the houses opposite had been converted into one large, subterranean air-raid shelter and that is where she resorted with the rest of the household when the worst was in progress. She was a courageous woman and the fact that many of her lodgers were not made of such strong fibre became an increasing irritation. As the weeks dragged on so she found herself continually readvertising the rooms, and as the raids persisted so the casual civilian or the odd military person looking for a bed-sit in town became harder to come-by. It was therefore not without some relief one gloomy afternoon, dark also with foreboding, for the nightly racket of bursting bombs and cracking gunfire was all too predictable, that she opened the door to a smartly-dressed stranger who had come in answer to her latest advertisement. He was quick to point out with charm and diplomacy that he was attached to the Belgian Embassy only a hundred yards or so up the road and was looking for accommodation for an elderly French-speaking Belgian refugee who knew no English whatever. My mother, game for anything, made up her mind there on the doorstep that she would be more than willing for the elderly foreigner to join her establishment.

My mother had picked up quite a bit of French from her yearly trips to the Fashion Houses of Paris. What is more, due to these business ventures and her own Italian connections, she delighted in telling the story of her great grandfather who had fought alongside Garibaldi in his Risorgimento - she had acquired a highly sentimental reverence for foreigners, none so much as the French and the Italians. The Latin temperament, according to my mother, was supreme! Sensitive, passionate, more acutely tuned in every way to the finer things of life.

"With a Frenchman or an Italian, you know where you are at once! You know if he likes a thing or hates it," she would declare with her customary worldly wisdom. "The French have style - and the Italians feeling. Why do you think we go to Paris for fashion? And you only have to look at a Botticelli to know it was painted by an Italian!" But for all her romanticism she was good with foreigners. They never intimidated her. So far it had only been the French to come her way with any regularity - I doubt whether she had ever set eyes on her own Italian kinsmen - but her welcome was always warm with none of the usual diffidence displayed by the average Englishman confounded by someone not speaking his language. Perhaps then with London in the ferment it was, giving refuge to all who could make their difficult journeys from the Continent - over-run in almost every direction by the Germans, it was the hand of fortune which had singled her out to welcome the elderly Belgian that dismal evening and, as soon as she shut the door on the envoy, she began to look forward to the new arrival. Somewhat to her surprise he came very soon after, complete with baggage, as if he too had some omen of the auspicious circumstances allowing their paths to converge. With much cordial greeting on both sides he came inside to take his place within the household which for a while revolved completely round him.

***

'If Monsieur Gobeaux was not coming in England, if your mother did not nurse him? If ...'

Monsieur Anatole Gobeaux was in his late fifties but looked much older. A prolonged and steady over-indulgence of good food and comfortable living had affected his health and faculties. Completely white-haired, he walked with a stick on two very shaky feet which appeared like two inflexible pegs below his very loose trousers that he wore braced high over his round, corpulent stomach and, like most ageing Continentals, he suffered frequently *des crises* of the liver. Throughout the four years he was to remain in this country he never attempted to learn any English save for two expressions: 'water closet' and 'thank you', obviously all he found necessary to get by. He stubbornly defended himself by insisting French had been good enough for him all his life and he was not going to embark on learning another language now at his age.

The fact that the new lodger could neither speak nor understand English isolated him completely. My mother needed to rely on her own slender accomplishment to make communication, and soon discovered it was in a decidedly rusty condition though she persevered quite unabashed. At first the exchange between the two of them was limited to the barest essentials, while the rest of the household remained predictably tongue-tied save for the cheery *"Bonjour"* with a certain bravado all round at the breakfast table. Nevertheless as Monsieur Gobeaux, unable to offer any details about himself or give any explanation of his business here, was left with an aura of mystery surrounding him, and was generally regarded with suspicion despite his constantly-repeated *"Il faut tuer les Boches,"* with the most blood-curdling gesticulations of how best to achieve it. Perhaps this was not so unreasonable since one of the first favours he asked of my mother was to order him a taxi, and to instruct the driver to put him down outside the War-Office. Could he be a spy? Stories abounded at this period in the war of Germans infiltrating the country in various guises. Notices declaring 'Walls Have Ears' and 'Careless Talk Costs Lives' began to crop up in appropriate places warning the public to be on the lookout for suspicious behaviour. No doubt enemy agents were infiltrating the country under the blanket guise of 'Refugees' but my mother's intuition was quick to deduce that this bewildered old man was none other than he purported to be.

Monsieur Gobeaux was ill at ease himself to begin with. As the only foreigner he found things most confusing. There were air-raids every night and often during the day - it was the height of the Blitz. All able-bodied men and women rushed to the shelters on the first panic wail of the siren and Monsieur Gobeaux, unfamiliar with the British system of warning, had yet to learn to distinguish the 'Alert' from the 'All Clear'. It was not unusual for my mother and the rest to meet him on the doorstep at the end of a raid, they on their way back from the shelters, while he was now on his slow and laboured journey across the road. He seemed forever to be going in the opposite direction. As my mother got to know him better she made a point of going to fetch him if he had not emerged from his room at the crucial moment. Using the situation to disassociate herself temperamentally from the phlegmatic English, my mother took Monsieur Gobeaux under her wing so that soon, reassured by her friendliness and her improving French, he began to confide in her. He told her that during the 1914-18 war he had worked for a Secret Organisation called 'La Dame Blanche' carrying messages on his bicycle over the border of occupied Belgium into France through the woods near his home. After the Armistice he had been acclaimed a hero. Then, when Belgium had been invaded recently the British Government, realising he was in mortal danger if he stayed behind, sent Captain John Orczy-Barstow (son of the famous Hungarian Baroness) to escort him over to England in true Pimpernel style. They arrived at about the same time as the evacuation from Dunkirk after experiencing a hazardous crossing of the North Sea, when their ship had been torpedoed and they had been in the sea clinging to wreckage. Eventually he reached London and the protection of his own exiled government, having to leave his wife and three grown-up daughters behind.

Developing his air of self-importance, he went on to say that since his arrival he was engaged on work of the utmost secrecy for the British Government. My mother was thrilled to be in the midst of such mystery and intrigue.

Other Belgians began to make their appearance in the house and it soon transpired that Monsieur Gobeaux had a profound love for his native-land and would talk about his home and family with tears in his eyes, thus showing himself to be the true Latin that ranked so highly with my mother. I think from that moment she extended her boundaries to incorporate Belgium in with France and Italy.

"A very artistic nation the Belgians - Van Eyck, Rubens - quite as good as the Italians - in their own way."

One evening just when my mother thought Monsieur Gobeaux had fathomed once and for all the subtle difference between the 'alert' and the 'all clear' he did not hobble down to the shelters with the others and she went in search. Half-way up the stairs began a trail of blood which led to his door. Shaking with fear she went inside and found him collapsed on the floor. The raid had hardly begun so it was unlikely his condition could be as a result of it. He was haemorrhaging profusely and the red patch on the carpet was growing bigger. She hurried outside to call a doctor who came and diagnosed a perforated stomach ulcer. Monsieur Gobeaux was terrified of going into hospital where he would be unable to understand and be misunderstood himself so my mother, once more on the spur of the moment, taking pity on this elderly foreigner now doing his utmost to resist being lifted on to a stretcher, offered to nurse him herself at home. He made a long, slow recovery. Part of the trouble was a delayed reaction to his escape from Belgium. All through some of the worst raids of the war, when he could not be moved, his dedicated nurse never left his bedside for longer than necessary.

It was spring when he was well again and his illness had welded a bond of trust and mutual friendship. He had also become very dependent on her for she was his sole interpreter of the English-speaking world. When he was able to resume his official business he would go off in the morning and if, during the course of the day, he needed to call in at a shop or pass on a message she would write everything down for him to hand over to whoever it concerned.

My mother began to suffer herself. The raids having petered out with the light evenings, she too found herself caught up by a delayed reaction. Several months of enemy bombardment and the resultant loss of sleep had affected her health to an extent that she feared that if the bombing was to resume with the same intensity she would be unable to cope. She had completely lost her nerve after being such a support to her neighbours. When she had thought nothing of going out during the height of a raid to man the stirrup pumps or bring in an injured victim with half London ablaze and shrapnel clattering down like hailstones. Now she was pale and jittery and had to be prescribed a tonic for her nerves. Monsieur Gobeaux was sympathetic and anxious to make some sort of adjustment. He took her a step further in his confidence and told her he was at the head of a section of men training for work of top-level security and in desperate danger should anyone discover their business. He suggested they moved from the centre of town but remained within easy travelling distance and if his plan met with War Office approval, and they could find a suitable house, the two of them could run a hostel for his little group. Like that, he would have them all under one roof where he would be in a better position of surveillance. She readily agreed, for she was desperate to leave Belgravia. It was also a way round her financial hurdle, for if Monsieur Gobeaux was true to his word she would have a ready-made set of lodgers without having to lift a trembling finger towards it.

Monsieur Gobeaux had seen this as a continuation of the Great War. Envisaging early in 1939 that war might break out again he mustered together the survivors of *La Dame Blanche* to be prepared for effectual resistance to the enemy once more should it prove necessary. He was of course considered too old for active service himself but in recognition of his valuable ground work he was put in charge of a small office. It was here that the small section of Belgians recruited for this specialised warfare could meet, to exchange ideas and air their grievances. He was a father figure, speaking to them in their language and generally offering encouragement, for the branch of the war department under whose command they came was staffed exclusively by British officers. The only qualification my mother needed for her part in such a top-security enterprise was to fill in a questionnaire. In due course she was visited by a British Captain and given the go-ahead to find a convenient house with the added assurance that so long as the emergency lasted, there would be a steady stream of young men to occupy the rooms. She and Monsieur Gobeaux soon found the very house, Edwardian and large, in the green suburb of Ealing Common.

***

"If I had not heard someone speaking about the job, if this … if that?"

My mother was ideally suited to this new role she was called on to play and I think, in the long run, it was to prove her salvation emotionally as well as financially. She had men again in her life, people to care for, who, because of the confidence she shared with them, looked towards her more as a friend than a landlady. Removed from danger and freed from financial anxiety, she soon regained her health and happiness. Normally she hated to be away from the hub of a busy, active life, and the air of secrecy surrounding the young men who now came to require her ministrations ignited just the right spark to set a bright flame to her adventurous spirit. She grew attached to her protégés and saw herself as the counterpart of Monsieur Gobeaux - a mother figure to cheer and comfort them while they were there. She called them her 'Boys' and they ranged in age from barely twenty to early middle age. Each one stayed in the house an average of three to four months and they came from all walks of life.

At this stage in the war, a few months after the Battle of Britain, patriotism was infectious amongst those who came from the Continent. There were partisans from every corner of Europe taking up active service alongside our own soldiers, sailors and airmen. The first year of the war when Britain had shown she could 'go it alone' had given a resurgence of hope to the occupied countries and, in answer to the call of Churchill to 'Set Europe Ablaze', able-bodied Europeans began to make their way here from under the noses of their oppressors, often at considerable peril -

men and women ready to avenge the monstrous assault of their homelands.

The Belgians with whom my mother was concerned were no exception. Belgium with its long history of invading armies had been a self-ruling country for little more than a hundred years. National pride was still in the honeymoon period. The group which came under the fatherly eye of Monsieur Gobeaux were all French-speaking though they didn't like being mistaken for Frenchmen. All volunteers, they had already embarked on their intensive training which they referred to as the 'Job' by the time they came, for which they travelled daily to a special school in Knightsbridge, a forty-minute journey on the Tube.

Pre-war Belgium with its *Code Napoléon* had been very much a man's country. In comparison to most Englishmen, the attitude of the Belgians towards women could be almost feudal. There were adjustments necessary. Though devoted to their families and charming to women in general, they expected to be waited on slavishly by wives and mothers. Some looked for this treatment from my mother to begin with. They were often irritated if she did not clean their shoes or press their trousers when ordered, but in a quickly-changing world where people were having to do more for themselves she, with her 'avant-garde' approach, soon showed them where to find the iron and the shoe polish, jokingly pointing out that she was playing her part towards the emancipation of the women they had left behind.

Ironically, this group when most men their age were in the forces was soon to arouse the curiosity of the neighbours, especially when it became so apparent they were foreign. No matter how they tried to fit themselves into the every day life of the district, their clothes gave them away. They wore berets and continental-style coats. The locals became suspicious and my mother, trusted with certain details but obviously precluded from the more confidential minutiae of the training, found it difficult to give a convincing explanation of their presence. She was soon reported to the police for keeping a house full of German spies!

At the other extreme, however, after this eye-catching household had been in the neighbourhood some weeks, this house full of interesting and often good-looking young men began to intrigue the young local women who were forever finding excuses for a closer look. My mother was sociable and liked people calling and if it kept her boys happy so much the better.

Robin and I had been back on several occasions never lasting more than a few days. The Levers, fearful for our safety, seemed to think we were the chief target of the Luftwaffe. We were, all the same, quite familiar with the new situation at home. Of course we did not understand the significance of this foreign group at the time, but we were quick to grasp the aura of secrecy surrounding it. It did not bother us. Surprisingly perhaps, we had no curiosity, no time to delve into the mystery of these Belgian men. They did not distract our mother on the short times we were at home. She was always overjoyed to see us, spoiling and affectionate and we, glad beyond imagination to be there, accepted everything as it was and left it at that.

PART THREE

CHRISTMAS IS COMING

'If this, if that, if one of the least things did not happen...'

The war had spread to every corner of the world. Russia had been invaded, battle was raging in North Africa and America had declared herself to be at war with Japan and Germany. I was now fifteen and felt with all the might of the great United States on our side the war could end soon. Life for Robin and me went on much the same in our genteel seclusion in Winchester. Once a month, one of the large food parcels which came regularly from Canada would be opened in honour of the Governor of Aden, the Bishop of Buffalo or the President of the Royal Academy; when we tasted cookies and candy and maple syrup and, I daresay, would have continued thus with little hardship to the end, so long as we kept regular hours, maintained a steady progress at school and did not stray too far from the village path. But in my new quest for love and romance I was becoming a little devious.

The nights were drawing in, the winter was getting cosy. Christmas was in the air and most people, a year wearier, a year more deprived - for whom 'Lending to Defend' and Digging for Victory' had taken on real meaning, looked forward to the year drawing to a close in the hope that a new one might bring an end to the conflict. There was excitement in making preparations. At school we had started to sing carols and to put up decorations in the classroom. Someone had hit on the bright idea of using the foil tops from our daily milk allowance to give the effect of tinsel mixed in with the various cut-outs, seed-pods and greenery we collected from the hedgerows. We worked with a will amongst the clutter in the Art room. We had been promised a dance but when we discovered no boys would be admitted, our ingenuity suffered a heartfelt lack of inspiration.

Our mother was coming at the weekend. We gleaned she had been sent for by our guardians and assumed it was to discuss conditions in London with a view to our going home for the Christmas holidays, or to review our clothes, which she did periodically due to our spurt of growth. I was debating with Cicely as we shaped the bottle-tops into bells whether to tell her about Tony. With my mother I was more open and at ease over the subject of boyfriends. She always intimated that she expected them, indeed, would be personally offended if they were not forthcoming. Any fraternisation with the opposite sex was frowned on at school. One of the rules forbade us to speak to a boy in school uniform, even our brothers!

Margaret, my friend with whom I often stayed in Sussex, was the youngest of four children. Her sister was married and her brothers were in the RAF. As a result she had grown up quicker than I. My mother knew that during my visits there I had gone to village dances and evening parties - though I never mentioned this to Lady Lever for under no circumstances, save those of immediate danger, was I allowed up later than nine o'clock, let alone out in the black-out. My mother had told me she welcomed my growing up and looked forward to the day I would be her companion; while Lady Lever, encouraging in all the outward aspects of growth and responsibility, regarded Robin and me as children. My mother had been out at work at fourteen, making the journey to the West End and back from the Elephant and Castle in all weathers, not always a peril-free undertaking for a young girl alone soon after the turn of the century.

***

'If one of the least things did not happen ...'

But there was no need to resort to letters to bring my story to life. I was there in that house, sweet-smelling of country air and fresh flowers, in that room, my private sanctum, with the pretty blue Chintz curtains with their newly sewn-in black linings which opened up a view of the downs and the sky, and the hollow wood that accommodated the rookery - known as the bower. To me it quickly became the 'lover's bower' since it was where I watched for Tony through the hedge and wrote about him in my diary in the Summer, when I would steal out after tea, during that hallowed hour when the Levers retired to change for dinner, hoping for just one glimpse of him as the flies and midges closed in. Sometimes not until the dew chilled my feet to the bone, or the evening mist descended to shut off the village for the night, did I concede it was too late and go indoors. But summer was over and it was nearly Christmas and all was not quite well. Had we been removed too far from the hurly-burly of the town, deprived too long of parental love?

I was awakened by the wind and the noise of the rain on the window panes. It was Thursday and it was pouring. When I drew back the curtains it did not look like stopping. I was immediately downcast. As I dressed, a defiant brightness beyond the beech trees, blown into confusion by the storm, raised my hopes only for them to be dashed seconds later by the emergence of dark clouds which made it seem like a return of night.

Sir Hardman was already sitting at the breakfast table as I crossed the hall. He was holding his gold half-hunter open in one hand while peering at the grandfather clock at the far side of him. Not yet aware of me, he screwed up his face in an ugly grimace of concentration as he tried to focus his eyes on both. "Blast," he muttered, while making a quick flustered movement to pocket his watch and, still appearing not to notice me, he hurried hunched-back over to the grandfather clock and with slow, calculated precision moved the large hand forward three minutes. I cleared my throat and hovered in the doorway. He turned and surveyed me.

"Good morning, Sir Hardman?" I greeted him.

"Oh - what can ail thee Marjorie Rae, alone and palely loitering? Come and sit down, I won't eat you," he said. I took my place at right angles to him as he worked his lips into a knowing grin over his even false teeth.

"I don't know what's good about the morning," he declared, and I felt guilty as if the weather was my fault.

"Rain before seven, fine before eleven - do you think?" I suggested hopefully.

"Pah! This rain's in for the day, I promise you," he said. "Red sky in the morning, shepherd's warning," he tossed back at me. "Too wet for - tennis, or whatever you play this time of year," he said, lowering his glasses over the bridge of his nose to stare at me. I cringed. "Actually - we play table-tennis when it's wet," I said to make sure he knew.

Breakfast was the one meal of the day not scheduled for a definite time. We came down about eight and served ourselves from the warming plate on the sideboard. Thompson hovered in the doorway to see if we were all assembled.

"Shall you wait for her Ladyship, Sir 'ardman or will you have coffee now?" Thompson proffered as he did with punctilious regularity each morning.

"I'll wait Thompson, I'm on the early side," he replied. "The weather may not be up to much but the news is better eh? What? Thompson? Russians seem to be holding Moscow!"

"Yes, very heartenin' Sir 'ardman?" agreed Thompson.

The grandfather clock struck eight and Sir Hardman spun round in his chair and watched it ring out every chime.

"Used to be a perfect timekeeper in Eaton Square, loses a couple of minutes a day here, darned nuisance - ah! Here's your brother." His expression softened, a boyish smile on his lips as he followed Robin to his chair. "And the schoolboy! Creeping like snail - not too unwilling I hope - eh? Your sister's beaten you this morning my boy - what's your family motto - 'Omnia Promptus' isn't it? Ha - that wasn't thought up with you in mind. Wait until you are the lover - sighing like furnace." He broke off to give a good imitation. "The ladies won't like to be kept waiting you know." He turned to me. "That's right, isn't it?" I felt myself blush. Robin and I suppressed a smile as our eyes met across the table.

Lady Lever, her hair newly frizzed, her face freshly floured, joined us and I felt more at ease. "What a morning!" she gasped brightly as she sat down. "And what plans have you for this afternoon on your half-day?" she asked, turning to me. I drew in a deep breath.

"I wondered," I began, "If I could go to the farm, the squad have arranged a ping-pong match," I said, trying to sound as if it mattered as little as going down to the pillar box. Lady Lever gave a long chuckle with her head back so that we could see the gold hooks on her teeth. "I don't suppose they thought it would be a day like this."

"No," I responded utterly crushed, "but - it might clear later." She ignored this as Thompson, full of his own importance, flounced into the room, setting the lustres ringing on the candelabras and placed the coffee beside his mistress.

"Sammy dear, can you suggest anything for the children this afternoon?" she said.

This was purely concessionary since Sir Hardman hardly ever made plans for us. Lady Lever poured milk for Robin and coffee for the three of us before sitting back to survey Robin and me sitting either side of her. "Nothing to interest my two young friends here?" she mused, her thoughts wandering and, suddenly coming to she smiled winningly at me. I took advantage.

"I've got some library books that need changing - I could go on the bus," I said. Lady Lever stared out of the window and said nothing.

Tony and I had an arrangement to meet in the public library when the weather was wet. I usually got permission for this. The rain streamed down the window panes relentlessly.

"I hope the weather clears by the weekend when your mother comes, it'll be nice if you can get out together and, Marjorie dear, before I forget, take the Chrysanthemums from this end of the greenhouse for your mother's room - I'm saving the white ones for the Church." Lady Lever instructed me while absent-mindedly sorting through the pile of letters Thompson had placed beside her.

"Yes," I replied. The dining-room went quiet as we finished eating. Only the relentless ticking of the grandfather clock reminded us that life had not stopped completely. The half-day was still unresolved and I searched for a way to re-introduce the subject without laying too much emphasis on it. I had to get things settled before I left for school.

"Well now," declared Lady Lever in that certain tone which heralded an unwelcome suggestion - as if trying to turn it into a pleasant surprise. My heart nearly stopped. "What about a trip to the cinema this afternoon? We could go in by car and you could change your library books on the way back - is that all right with you Sammy? And with you?" she enquired of me.

"Mmm," I murmured, too disappointed to say I thought it a good idea. I was keyed up to see Tony and now it meant waiting three more days until the Bible class on Sunday. I could have burst into tears.

"A visit to the movies on a day like this is worth a little petrol I think." Husband and wife regarded one another and nodded in complete accord. We had been to the cinema last Thursday arranged at the eleventh hour. I gazed over to the beech trees and made a forlorn appeal to the rooks to fly high when 'no rain is nigh'. The trees by the gates looked very woeful and the bower a dripping tangle of undergrowth.

I felt despondent for the rest of the morning and my brain worked hard on a means of escape for the following week. Even the activities of the Squad were beginning to tail off. There were no nettles to gather this time of year and we had a pile of magazines in store enough to divert several armies for the next fifty years. The cultivation side had never caught on due, most probably, to the real effort of work necessary. Strangely, Lady Lever was not encouraging new ideas for the youth of the village. What excuse would I have for getting out of the house in the snow? But my mother was coming at the weekend and with the thrill that accompanied this prospect I comforted myself with the thought that nothing was ever hopeless. I would revitalise the village youth by the New Year.

***

By Saturday the weather had cleared and we walked into town on either side of our mother to have tea at the Cadena in the High Street. "You children, you both look marvellous," she said, gloating pride reflected in her dark eyes as she sat surveying us across the table. "I can't get over how you've grown up. You look so well - lovely roses in your cheeks - sometimes I can't believe you're mine. Wouldn't Daddy have been proud of you?"

"When are we coming home?" we asked, more to the point. "Has Lady Lever arranged it with you?"

"No - not yet but I thought, as it's pretty calm in London now you might come home for a week this time, after all you're not babies anymore, are you?"

"That would be t'rrific," cried Robin.

"Have you thought what you want for Christmas?" she said in her most indulgent mood.

"We'll give you a list before you go back," we said, taking advantage.

"Mister Gobbo is looking forward to your coming home - I've such a nice lot of boys at the moment, two of them are officers – big tall men, the nicest boys I've ever had as a matter of fact."

We tucked into our tea. Somehow the thin triangles of bread, rationed to three each and spread so sparingly with margarine, tasted much more delicious in the company of our mother than the homemade scones and jam at Kingsworthy Court. I was filled with happiness as we listened to her chatting about home. Her busy life was very much the focus of her thoughts.

"One of them is so tall I call him Spider because of his long legs. They're full of fun - you'll love them."

"Did we see them before - in the summer?"

"No - these boys haven't been with me long, oh no," she said forcefully. "These boys are quite different - they are so well-mannered and polite - they're gentlemen. They won't let me carry the coal-bucket - one of them always jumps up to take it," she added. "The one I call Spider and his friend Bunny - they know a Count and he comes to the house sometimes, and my dear, he wears breeches and spurs!" She smiled triumphantly but her face soon clouded over. "They've had a shocking time. They were in a concentration camp in Spain! You want to hear what they think of the Spanish!" Then, pausing while we took this in, she shook her head with feeling and took a sip of tea. Intrigued, we began to question her.

"Why were they in a concentration camp?" I asked. Robin chipped in: "In Spain? I thought only the Germans had concentration camps. Were they tortured and starved and did they escape?" My mother chuckled.

"You've been reading too many comics my son, though in a way they have escaped, that is from occupied Belgium and right from under the noses of the Germans too," she added, doing her best to satisfy his lust for adventure.

"Well - how did they get to Spain?" Robin said.

"Walked there, all the way through France, hoping to get to Lisbon or Gibraltar and when they crossed into Spain they were caught and thrown in prison." She replied.

"Why?"

"Because the Spanish are a bit on the side of the Germans and tried to foil their escape, and do you know?" she said, turning to me, "One was engaged to a girl over here! And after coming all that way, going through all he did to find her, she told him it was over between them. Said he felt like turning round and going back again. A lovely tall man like that! She must have been mad. He was so sad when he first came."

"Why do you call one Bunny?" Robin asked.

"I don't know, the name suited him. He is rather like a big bunny rabbit." She laughed, then glancing to either side of her she confided "They prefer to have nicknames - one is called 'Roll' another 'Bear' and even old Gobbo likes to be known as *Dieudonné,* God given - the conceit of it! Can you imagine".

"Funny names. Don't you know their real names?" Robin asked.

"Oh, of course I do. The nicknames are for every day, more for strangers."

"Which one was engaged?" I asked.

"Spider - do you know he is six feet four! I measured him myself. He is a dear, so is Bunny. One day I met them coming out of the station and they fought over who should carry my bag, with all the rations in, and they challenged each other to a duel and said they would meet at dawn on Ealing Common. They make me die sometimes."

"Are they good-looking?" The names Spider and Bunny did not add up to my idea of the romantic.

"They're both fairish. Bunny's not so tall; Spider has a lovely straight nose - he's what I call a very fascinating man." She sighed. "I wish I was young. When he first came he was out every night, then one day he confided in me, told me all about his girl, said he had spent forty

49

pounds in one week just trying to forget. Since then we have got on like a house on fire." My mother gave another deep sigh of contentment, very pleased with the way her home affairs were shaping.

"It's a pity we can't have eclairs like the old days," she said, passing the plate of artificial-looking yellow cake which she turned contemptuously around to examine from every angle. "Made with egg-powder - ugh!" she proclaimed in disgust. "I don't suppose you remember tea at the Corner House in the old days?"

"I remember those eclairs," stressed Robin.

"Oh - I suppose those days have gone for ever. You always had to have a knicker-bocker glory when you were a little boy and it was nearly as big as you were." Robin sniggered at the mention of knicker. She gazed into the distance, a fleeting sadness in her eyes. I was fascinated by her description of the boys and eager to hear more.

"What's Bunny like?" I asked.

"Very sweet," she said, "- not quite so handsome perhaps, more of a joker. He keeps me in fits. One Sunday I was making a cake and they both came in the kitchen and said they would help. They put on aprons and kept taking the packets and things out of the cupboard and shaking them into the bowl. I can't tell you what went into that cake - salt, mustard, vinegar, pepper, mixed herbs. Worcester Sauce - everything they could lay their hands on, even a bit of soap powder!" I gasped. She burst out laughing. "Only the minutest trace of course."

"Gosh, what was it like?" we said.

"Not bad at all as a matter of fact, and when old Gobbo was eating a piece of it later those two devils kept praising it to him, saying it had a delicate flavour, and a beautiful blend of spices. Mister Gobbo kept nodding, saying, *"Oui, Oui,_c'est bon, c'est bon"* like he does and they were in stitches. Spider had to bend down and pretend he was tying up his shoelaces, he was laughing so much."

"Which one do you like best?" My mother settled back to give it some thought.

"It's hard to say, they are both nice," she replied slowly "But I think, if I was young, I'd go more for Spider, in fact I could fall for him. He's a soldier in the regular army *Officier de Carrière* they call them and in a crack regiment too." She took another sip of tea and looked up proudly in the air. "I don't know, I opened the door one day and there they stood, two great big men in uniform, I nearly died."

I was curious to hear about the rest if we were to live amongst them for a week. "Who else is there?" I asked.

"There's Mr. and Mrs. Peter, much older of course, not really one of the boys."

"How do you mean?" I said.

"I mean he's not - er - he doesn't do the same training as the others. Come to think of it I don't know what he does," she murmured. "Then there's Bear. His father has a big hotel in Belgium - he speaks quite good English, and there's Feather and Jefke."

"Nice are they?"

"Jefke sings and simply adores all those old Gigli records," she replied, ignoring my question. "The Belgians are very musical you know. You've heard of Cèsar Franck? He was Belgian."

"Is that all? No-one else?" I asked.

"There are some hangers-on who come and go from time to time."

"Nice?" I asked again.

"Not bad. They're all right." She studied my face and laughed. "You know what they say?"

"What?" I said.

"Curiosity killed the cat!"

"Well, I wanted to know and do please," I implored, "please persuade the Levers to let us come home for a week – please."

I mulled over the description she had given of her curious household as we finished the powdery cake, wondering whether I should be of the same opinion. I understood my mother well enough to know she was often taken in by superficial aspects of character. One only had to make a fuss of my mother, show her courtesy, or pay her a compliment and she was a friend for life. I also knew she was bound to favour the officers by virtue of their rank and the spurred and titled company they kept.

***

On Sunday morning Lady Lever made the excuse that, desiring a quiet talk with our mother "About the holidays and one or two other little matters", she would not be coming to church. My suspicions were immediately aroused. It was only for the gravest reasons she ever missed church and it would not take an hour to discuss the date of our return home which she could have done at any time, not necessarily in our absence. No. It was obvious she wanted me out of the way. I was not unaware of the recent change in attitude that had overtaken the Levers towards me, and of course I guessed the reason, although I had considered myself the essence of discretion in managing my meetings with Tony. Never once had I come in late; and in the better weather I always took my racquet along to the farm for it was genuinely our intention to start with a game of tennis, even if we only got as far as adjusting the net. I could not have told a bare-faced lie to save my life.

I spoke briefly to Angelic Anthony, as Cicely had begun to call him, after morning service but did not take advantage of my freedom to hang about, considering it wiser to hurry back to curtail any searching discussion between my mother and my fairy godmother. I hated to be at the centre of controversy. I decided finally not to breathe a word about Tony to my mother who could so innocently have blurted out over the dining table, 'I'm glad to hear Marjorie has made a conquest among the Choirboys!', erroneously convinced she and Lady Lever were on the same wavelength though, on the whole she suppressed her more forthright tendencies, which my mild-minded father so admired, when she came here and called it 'minding her P's and Q's'. There was nothing falsely genteel about my mother. Outspoken and direct, she took care to subdue this side of her nature for our sakes.

At lunch my mother gazed at me with new eyes, so to speak, and not at all in the disapproving fashion one might have expected. Several times I caught her looking at my bosom with a proud, satisfied expression as I came to realise, with mounting embarrassment, that sooner or later she would be unable to contain herself from drawing attention to this aspect of my development.

"I must say the children look wonderfully well, they do you both credit," she said at last "And Marjorie is really quite a young lady. As you say, she isn't a child any longer!"

My mouthful remained stubbornly hard to swallow in my haste to sit back with my arms folded across my body. Normally confident when praised, I was blushingly aware of three pairs of eyes burning through my clothes like X-rays, to say nothing of Thompson patiently waiting with his back to the sideboard.

"Marjorie is wearing a very pretty dress, the colour suits her." Remarked Lady Lever, the ultimate in tact. Sir Hardman appeared to be sternly mulling over the proceedings.

"I think as she is coming up to sixteen everyone had better give some thought to what she is going to do in the future," he tendered unequivocally.

My mother cleared her throat and I, conscious of Robin's startled expression, began to fidget with my napkin. My mother addressed me across the direction of her hosts.

"What would you like to be when you grow up, Darling?" she asked me.

The discussion of my future continued around me, both sides unwilling to offend or commit themselves too seriously. When finally we rose from the table Sir Hardman drew my mother to one side and I caught snatches of his words as I passed.

"Now don't forget - I know it's difficult, you're not here all the time, but I still think it's better for you to talk to her, you are her mother. I have told you what I would say."

I began to worry.

We sat drinking coffee, the atmosphere tense with contention and calm diplomacy. My mother did her best to keep up a façade of polite cheerfulness. She put her cup and saucer on the small table beside her and clasped her hands in her lap to admire her nails.

"Of course we drink nothing but coffee at home nowadays," she remarked casually.

"Oh?" replied Lady Lever hoping for her to expand.

"The Belgians are great coffee drinkers you know," she said.

"And so far you have found no difficulty in obtaining it?" enquired Sir Hardman who liked to think that rank and wealth brought advantages beyond the reach of most.

"No. I go to town once a week for the rations. I shop in Sloane Street, have done since my husband was alive, so I get good service. The Belgians are very particular where food is concerned, only the best is good enough for them," she announced proudly.

"They are very lucky then - do they realise there is a war on?" he retorted acidly.

"Oh, they are very brave men. If you knew what some of them have been through and the job they are doing you wouldn't begrudge it them Sir Hardman," she replied, springing to the defence of her boys.

"What job are they doing?" he responded.

"Well it's very hush-hush as a matter of fact. I don't know the details but I do know it is very important work. We have a Captain from the War Office down every so often to make sure things are all right, then there is an English Major in charge," she impressed on him.

"Sounds like some sort of reconnaissance to me or research if you say the War Office. Probably plotting the route for the second front with these continental chappies, that's why it's hush-hush," he countered sagely.

"Most probably," she replied, content for him to have the last word.

Lady Lever unfolded her long legs and got up as Thompson came in to collect the cups. "Well now," she began, "I have a few things to do upstairs," she continued diplomatically, a cue for Sir Hardman to make a similar move.

"Come on young man," he ordered genially, placing a hand on Robin's shoulder. "We'll take a tour of the garden before we all get too sleepy. Knows most of the birds. My right hand man don't you know?" he informed my mother, willing her to remain where she was.

"They're cross with me aren't they?" I said as soon as the door closed upon us. My mother came straight to the point.

"Lady Lever says you've got to the boy stage." A knowing expression flickered in her face, making one corner of her mouth twist into a little grin though she was trying her utmost to look stern. I felt ashamed, even in front of her.

"What else did she say?"

She shrugged. "She said, she realises it's inevitable, but Sir Hardman is a bit old-fashioned and doesn't approve."

"All the girls in my class have got boyfriends," I answered back churlishly.

"Boyfriends, yes" she said, stressing the S. "They're worried because you only seem interested in one particular boy."

"Do they know who he is?" I said in astonishment.

"They said his name is Tony and that he lives in the village," she replied.

I felt a thrill on hearing his name. "He's awfully nice," I confided.

"I daresay darling, but you must look at things from their point of view, after all you're not a child any longer. It's very worrying for them if you go bicycling miles out into the country alone with this boy. Perhaps they are a bit old-fashioned but I don't like the sound of it myself. What do you get up to in an old barn?"

Utterly flabbergasted, I swallowed hard. "Did they actually say an old barn? How do they know?"

"Of course they know. It's their business to know where you go; apparently the servants have seen you. Now look darling, the Levers are your guardians while you're here and I'm very grateful to them for having you to live in this lovely house. So dear, don't go worrying them, after all this Tony so-and-so isn't the only fish in the sea. Mix with a few more. When I was your age I was out with a different boy every night. I had one waiting up one end of the street and one the other, and when I'd decided which one I wanted to see I used to get my sister to go and make an excuse to the other that I had a headache or something and wouldn't be coming. Oh, I was a real devil at your age I can tell you, although I suppose I shouldn't," she continued, swept up in a sharp wave of reminiscence.

"But, he is the only one I know," I replied. "He is awfully sweet and we don't do anything really wrong," I pleaded, crossing my fingers in my lap.

"I should hope you don't," she exclaimed. "You remember your reputation, my girl and the Levers are doing their best for you. After all, when you are entrusted with someone else's children you have to be extra careful. Be sensible, or they will forbid you going out alone altogether. Sir Hardman has told me."

"All right," I acquiesced. "I'll only see him on Sundays or with the Squad," I assured her, knowing that this would be almost impossible as I think she did too for she suddenly sighed, still troubled.

"Oh dear, they said they are worried with the holidays coming, three weeks is a long time for you to be on the loose. I said I'd have you home for the whole time but they ..." I did not wait for her to finish the sentence.

"Three weeks at home!" I gasped. "Oh could we? Couldn't we possibly? Oh please, there's no bombing now. Do ask again, try and persuade them, it would be simply marvellous to come home, please - I'd promise anything." I could tell it didn't seem such an impossibility to her either.

"Yes" she murmured, reflecting, "Why not? There haven't been any raids for over a year. All right, I'll suggest it again, but don't bank on it. Yes, I think it would be a very good idea in the circumstances," she thought aloud, looking up and beyond me.

***

The approaching holiday and the trip to London were uppermost in our minds. Our mother had been clever. She had finally won over Lady Lever's approval for our going home by stressing that not only would I be removed from temptation but three weeks away from Tony would probably cause the friendship to fizzle out.

Christmas had a glory all its own. It had been the focal point of the year. The annual delight of rummaging in our stockings, later pillowcases, with our indulgent mother looking on, had been especially important when we had needed that tangible evidence of her devotion, and we had never been disappointed. She had a genius for knowing what pleased. Even her smile was broader than most mothers' but, still smarting in the depths of my consciousness was the pain from the setbacks for which none of us had expected. I knew that if I began to look forward with too much certainty to three weeks at home, the same emotion could turn at a moment's notice to one of bitter disappointment. Nevertheless it was difficult to contain our excitement.

Going home was a safety valve. In that state of half-child, half-woman, the no-man's land of growing up, I often found myself having to retreat into myself. My friends found it maddening, my mother described it as reserve and Lady Lever was beginning to hint at deceit. Despite the best intentions of our guardians, Kingsworthy Court had never become home and we referred to it always as 'the house'.

I was able to see Tony alone for a few minutes and for the last time after early Communion on the Sunday before our departure.

"Will you write to me in London?" I asked him.

"I won't promise," he replied, to my disappointment, though adding summarily, "You'd better give me your address in case I have a fit of writing letters."

His lack of enthusiasm cast me down at once. I wanted to be special, worth an effort, not part of some whimsical procedure meted to any and sundry. As I walked away in the chilly after-dawn perhaps, after all, not the time or place conducive to romance, I began to doubt if his feelings for me were as strong as mine for him. A small part of me wished I was not leaving.

I could detect a heaviness of heart as Lady Lever gave us our presents after lunch. In nearly two years it would be the longest period we had been away and there was no doubt we would be missed. Not once, since it had been agreed with our mother, had she mentioned the holiday, leaving her maid Cannon to act as go-between and supervise our packing. She came into the drawing room carrying two exciting-looking parcels wrapped in brown paper which she handed to us and we began to untie the knots in the thrifty fashion we had been taught by Sir Hardman. There was a brown leather handbag for me with my initials set into the flap and a writing-case for Robin which I sensed did not altogether meet with his approval.

"It's lovely, it really is, thank you so much," I said. If she had been my mother I would have rushed and thrown my arms around her neck and I know she wished I could have done so.

"I thought it would come in useful during the holidays and on our little excursions into town," she suggested.

There was not much to show it was Christmas in this house. Lady Lever did not display her cards along the mantelpiece as our mother did and there was no tree or holly. Either this elderly couple thought it not worth the effort since we were going or, more likely, had stoically decided to forego the trappings of Christmas altogether in wartime. I felt a pang of pity for them in this large unfestive house and a little ungenerous for wanting to leave.

Robin and I sat on the edge of the settee as we waited for the car to take us to the station, trying to appear relaxed and not too eager, but ready to spring up at the first hint of its approach. We had our eyes on the clock and Sir Hardman, watch in hand, had started his silent countdown. Then, precisely on zero hour, we heard the crunch of tyres on the gravel, the squeak of brakes and Robin and I had shot into the hall. A quick burst of unrelated staccato phrases issued alternately from us as our bags were placed in the car.

"I expect Thompson will miss us with the washing up," Robin began.

"Poor Thompson - it's a nice day that's one good thing," I replied.

"Do the trains stop at Waterloo?" he asked.

"Of course they do, silly," I said.

"Well I thought they might go on somewhere else."

"If they did," interjected Sir Hardman, "There would be a mighty fine accident!" We both giggled effusively.

"I wonder if they've cleared up all the bomb damage," I said.

"S'posing we had a raid while we're there."

"Course we wouldn't," I countered quickly.

"Perhaps the war will end over Christmas," suggested Robin, nearly losing control.

"Gosh, that'd be marvellous!"

"And we might never come back!"

"I hope you are not too pleased to be leaving," said Lady Lever, forlornly, "Your rooms will still be here just in case, and I'm sorry to disappoint you but I don't think there is much chance of the war ending during the next three weeks."

She drove with us to the station and as we went on the platform, she handed me the tickets to tuck responsibly away in my new bag. There was not long to wait before the train steamed into view and puffed to a halt in front of us. I turned to her and shouted, competing with the engine, hoping it might be some consolation.

"I hope you and Sir Hardman have a lovely Christmas and even if the war did end over the holidays, I would like to come back one day to see you."

The wind blew the white smoke from the funnel all over the platform, obscuring the goods van and muffling the sound of the porters busy with their trolleys moving parcels in and out of it. Lady Lever bent forward to kiss us and we boarded the train, impatient to be off. We waved excitedly from the window; out of her reach our smiles were broad. Lady Lever moved back from the carriage to stand aloof from the rest. Upright and stately she looked every inch the Lady she was in her immaculate tweed suit and velvet hat. She waved too, and I was proud to have her as our guardian. The whistle blew and cautiously we began to chug out of the station. We were on our way home at last and nothing but a serious accident could prevent us getting there.

With tremendous relief I sat down in the corner seat of the empty compartment, loosened my beige winter coat, arranged my skirt smoothly over my knees, and placed the new handbag squarely on my lap to admire the bright initials. Robin slumped down opposite.

"Bloody hell!" he cried out, throwing his cap to the ceiling and swung both feet up on the seat.

"Sh-sh," I rebuked him, faintly startled.

"Damn! Blast! Bugger!" he shouted defiantly and we both burst into peals of laughter until it literally hurt to take a breath. "I hope Mummy's got me that searchlight and batteries - cor what a present!" he said, adding quickly, eyeing my bag. "I s'pose you like yours."

"Yes, I do as a matter of fact, it's the best present they've given me."

"Looks as though she bought them at the same shop," he grumbled on. "I suppose I could swap it later, if anyone would have it. Hey, Marje, d'you think the war could end over Christmas? What d'you think would happen to us? Would we go back to our old schools? Would Nanny come back? S'pose Mummy'd have to get rid of those frogs for a start."

"Frogs are French and they're not French, they're Belgians."

"They're all the same to me. They speak French," he said. "Oh crumbs, I'd forgotten about them, they'll be there for

Christmas, unless the war ended tomorrow or the day after - and then."

"Well it won't end that quickly," I broke in. "Hitler and Churchill would have to sign a treaty or something - Armistices they call them, don't they. Don't swap it, it's awfully nice really. We're too old for a Nanny, at least I am, anyway she's married with a baby of her own. Let's pray terribly hard that the war will end over Christmas. Let's do it now, together. Come on, give me your hand and shut your eyes."

We held hands across the gap between the seats and prayed with our eyes tightly shut.

"Finished?" I asked.

"Yes - I don't suppose it'll work, worst luck." he said.

We had on our best clothes for going home and I lifted my legs unashamedly to admire the new nylon stockings which Lady Lever had presented me with that morning. 'Nylon, a new invention from the States, just as fine as silk but more hardwearing - they say it will never ladder - they make parachutes out of it because of its strength,' she had informed me. I was proud of being able to tie a bow so that it lay horizontally across my instep and my brown suede shoes looked very smart, laced up with wide Petersham ribbon on the ends of my svelte legs. I was glad too that I had managed to finish my green jumper for the holidays. Green was my favourite colour but my mother said it did nothing for me. She preferred me in strongish pink because, she said, it 'brought a nice reflected glow to my complexion'.

Having made this journey a number of times we were familiar with the local landmarks. From the window I looked for the bridge that passed on leaving the city, the line of terraced houses backing on to the Embankment. Then came the allotments, incorporating makeshift chicken runs, bringing in eggs to augment the rations, and the signal box, its name blotted out by a wide band of black paint. For a few hundred yards we were parallel with the old Roman road and I waited for the little white house in the hollow. As it came and went the train began to gather speed and soon the wooden spire of the Saxon church came into view, indicating we were already two miles on our journey.

There was sadness in leaving any place. The underlying possibility of not returning was well-rooted in our emotions. Suppose by some miracle our prayers were answered, would it mean back to school in the suburbs where my mother lived now? An abrupt end to my friendship with Tony and Cicely, the two people I loved best in the world. Such conjecture was futile; we were on our way home and no thought stayed long enough to become an anxiety. The countryside looked cold from inside the carriage. I remembered the lanes and copses best in summer, the hedgerows a tangle of dog-roses and honeysuckle, humming with the heat and wild bees, when dressed in my brief tennis dress, the sun warm on my bare arms and positively bursting with love, I used to cycle to those Thursday, evidently not-so-secret, rendezvous with Tony. I flushed belatedly for being found out. It seemed worse in winter retrospect. In the distance the chalk hills hardly appeared to move. Cicely was a valley person but I preferred the hills. Up there on top of the world we had found delicate bleached bones and pretty striped Roman snails amongst the stunted harebells quivering in the wind, while the skylark bubbled out his song forever.

Tony was uppermost in my thoughts as they wandered back over last summer. The bare trees and the dejected-looking cattle bunched together in the mud made it seem such a long time ago. Yet Tony, smelling pleasantly of sweat and clean cotton turning up to be recruited into the Squad, our first kiss in the hay as fresh on my lips as our last embrace in the copse on the way back last week, was the right culmination of my dreams. I did love Tony and to think of him when every mile was speeding us further apart brought tears to my eyes. I lay back on the starched antimacassar and puffs of heat blowing over my ankles lulled me into a doze.

I awoke appropriately when we stopped at Woking station. Two people came into the compartment and before long the wheels began turning and we had resumed our steady mechanical pace. "Christmas is coming, Christmas is coming," sang the engine again and again, with an occasional chorus of "Happy boys, happy girls". I looked at the newcomers. Settling himself opposite was an army officer, and as he unfolded his newspaper I was reminded of the two Belgian officers of whom my mother had spoken with such enthusiasm. The picture of home at Christmas presided over by our smiling mother flanked by her two courtly officers was beginning to take bright shape.

The train began to slow down. Soon the trees and fields gave way to factories, buildings, warehouses, all somehow more conspicuous since they had been cleverly camouflaged to look like the continuation of the countryside. The latecomers began to collect their belongings together. We were passing through the outer suburbs of London - endless backs of houses, sophisticated jungles of wire-netting, ramshackle chicken runs, lines of grim washing. I fastened my coat. Now we could see clearly the havoc wrought by the bombs in whole blocks razed to the ground. We slowed to a halt. A local train rattled past. The cold December light was failing as, almost silently, engine exhausted, we pulled under the dark-painted canopy of Waterloo station. Robin and I shifted into the corridor behind the others. The doors clattered open and we alighted from the carriage.

London looked very grey and as the crowds moved quickly to the exits we spotted our mother coming towards us. "Darlings!" she exclaimed as we fell against her. "My Darlings."

This station, the focus of so much coming and going, was extra busy with holiday travellers, by far the largest proportion being servicemen on leave. A party of carol-singers from the Salvation Army, determined the true meaning of Christmas should elude no-one, were huddled together under a lamp, singing, 'While Shepherds Watched Their Flocks by Night' to the accompaniment of a small brass band. I found myself clutching my mother's hand, my heart overflowing with childish love.

As soon as we were moderately free from the crowds she announced the news she was bursting to share with us. "We are going to have a simply marvellous Christmas - the Boys have arranged a party for Christmas Eve and everyone is to wear evening dress!" Beaming, she watched for our reaction but her words, coming as a surprise took time to sink in.

"Us too?" I said. Most ordinary people had given up dressing in the evenings in the cause of austerity. It was only those like our guardians trying to preserve the old order of things who still changed for Dinner at night.

"Of course, everyone. We want to forget the war for once."

"What on earth'll we wear?" I said, unable to remember the last time I'd seen my mother in evening dress.

"I'll have to wear my old blue chiffon, I suppose but you've got that pretty dress I made you for Margaret's party."

"That's rather childish and honestly I doubt if it'd fit anymore." I replied.

"Never mind - it's only for one night. I expect everyone will be in the same boat. We're having caterers in to do the food and each of the boys is bringing a girl along for the evening. Dinner'll be at nine o'clock in the big drawing room," she sprung on us when we settled into the Tube. "Spider and Bunny have chosen the wine!"

"Nine o'clock at night?" gasped Robin. Having fully expected some extra surprise once we got back, I felt nothing but delight. Dinner at night meant staying up late, joining the grown-ups, unheard of in Winchester. I felt myself to have grown at least six inches taller since arriving in London.

"Oh - and by the way!" she added to me, "They're going to take you out to lunch on Christmas Day. The boys have booked a table at the Hungaria. I showed them your photo and Bunny and Spider said they would like you to go with them." I glowed inwardly - things seemed to be getting even better.

"How old are they?" I asked. "Twenty-eight. Spider and Bunny are both twenty-eight."

"Twenty-eight!" I exclaimed. "Both of them!" I could not go out with men of twenty-eight, I told myself, only a day off middle-age and the fast run-down to senility. "It's rather old, isn't it?" I said, crushed with disappointment.

"Old?" questioned my mother. "That's not old - they're only babies."

On second thoughts, I consoled myself, it might be quite an experience to go to a restaurant in town. Something to boast about to the form. Not many would be able to equal going out with tall, handsome officers of twenty-eight. And the more I thought about it as the train bumped and whistled us on in its impatience to get us home, the more I grew to like it.

Outside Ealing Common station the newspaper placards advertised;

JAPANESE FORCES LAND ON HONG-KONG

The searchlights were active over the Common. War as a reality was brought home to us here. It was now quite dark and the three of us kept close as we began the short walk to the house.

PART FOUR

HOME SWEET HOME

In the street where my mother now lived the large Edwardian houses were built of brick and decorated pretentiously with stone mullions and marble pilasters. Nearly all double-fronted and detached, they were much of a muchness save for the odd, idiosyncratic addition of a domed conservatory or random steeple, giving a bizarre individuality here and there. At their fronts bordering the wide avenues of lime trees, where the square gardens had been neatly, if unimaginatively, set out, the iron railings had recently been wrenched off to make Spitfires, and on nearby Ealing Common, which used to accommodate a real country fair pre-war, there was now a searchlight and anti-aircraft battery.

Prior to the outbreak of war the neighbourhood had begun to run down. With the fashion for smaller families and the dearth of maids these outmoded dwellings, with their lofty rooms, were inconvenient by modern standards. Many had been left empty. Now, since the Blitz, they had taken on a new lease of life as W.V.S. depots, soup kitchens and hostels for the bombed-out. While the many opportunists like my mother, frightened from the centre of town, had transformed them into flats and boarding houses: just one or two had crumbled into a beautiful overgrown splendour.

Their front doors, set with stained glass in the style of Art Nouveau, had been boarded up as a blackout precaution and, as a protection from flying glass, most prudent householders had criss-crossed the rest of their windows with strips of brown sticky tape. Although giving an overall lifelessness, it neatly emphasised how each house was now a separate bastion, fortified against the darkness of both the winter and the war. As we walked on sometimes a front door would open far enough to reveal momentarily a hint of the cosiness within, then the murmur of leave-taking, the sound of the door closing, and all would be black again. Sometimes a new set of footsteps proceeded along the pavement with us, a dim beam from a hand-held torch swinging in rhythm. Complete strangers who we could not see clearly would often bid 'Good Evening' as they passed on their way.

There was excitement as well as sadness in the constant shifting of the population. 'All in it together' had made everyone friends. The war, as much as unleashing the worst in human nature, had undoubtedly brought out the very best. In this fraught and often charmed atmosphere one had the feeling anything might happen.

We were almost on home ground with its promised, if dodgy, security. From our safe, ordered, country shelter we were about to enter a new and different world - vital, equally rarefied, the occupants forced to mask their true purpose and maintain a pose of normality in keeping with the dull uniformity of their surroundings.

As soon as I came through the front door I was filled with a profound sense of well-being and a conviction, nourished by fairly regular doses of home-sickness that, once safely tucked under my mother's wing, nothing could touch me here at home. This particular home with its new smell of coffee was a novelty to be explored, thus adding an element of curiosity to the thrill of our return. Relieved to put down my case, I deposited it where I stood. My mother had no time to be pernickety over the minor details of housekeeping. 'There are far more exciting things in life than scrubbing and polishing - who ever heard of anyone winning glory for simply hanging out the washing or heaving up the coal scuttle?' Here there was no fuss, only a modicum of order and life was far more carefree. Once more welling up within me was the satisfying realisation that we would be away from Winchester for three whole weeks. I was positively tingling with contentment.

The drawing-room was the hub and the heart of the house. In this large square room with its high coved ceiling there was a hint of the past and grander days.The well-appointed architectural detail made the perfect setting for her collection of treasures. There was a Chinese carpet on the floor and a grand piano in one corner. Most of the occasional furniture was antique but pride of place had been accorded the magnificent, walnut-cased radiogram. Wishing to make some concession to modern living, she had been among the first of her friends to possess such a beauty deeming as vulgar the cocktail cabinets for which most of them had plumped. Everything here was conducive to relaxation. There were two settees, one on either side of the room, and a number of easy chairs arranged around the immense mock Regency iron fireplace - *piéce de résistance* of the industrial revolution - where the fire was always (coal rationing permitting) well-made up. The Belgians felt the cold and were continually chiding my mother that a great country like England, head of the British Empire, had evidently not heard of central heating which was, apparently, installed in every house in Belgium, no matter how humble. My mother had striven to maintain a domestic atmosphere of luxury and, considering her fluctuating fortunes, she had managed this well. A 'nice home' was high on her list of priorities and since she had not been there to enjoy its comfort for most of her working life, her success in accumulating the trappings for such lived-in and cosy surroundings was all the more remarkable. The furniture, ornaments and general bric-à-brac, all with their faint smell of mothballs - the residue of their all-too-frequent reposit in store - were the constant element in a continually changing background.

The room was quiet as we entered. Two large oriental lamps and the brightness of the fire gave a cheerful glow. Christmas was much in evidence in the cards and other seasonal knick-knacks displayed along the mantelpiece. Monsieur Gobeaux was already back from his *'bureau'* and had taken up his regular position plum in front of the fire. He always sat in the same high-back chair, his walking stick propped at the side, giving the impression of having completely taken over as *Chef de Maison*. It was the half hour of the day he enjoyed most, before the evening commotion began, alone, content and warm, free to indulge his thoughts and fantasies in the pictures constantly reforming in the flames. Sometimes my mother would ask him what he was thinking as he sat so peacefully, the bright flicker of the firelight reflected in his tired eyes. His reply was invariably the same - *'mes petites filles'* he would answer sadly. Although his two daughters were both married with children of their own, one could tell he saw them still as little girls playing before him in the hearth.

Robin and I approached cautiously, afraid to startle him, but he had heard us come in and turned to welcome us with outstretched arms. We each took one of his hands which were soft and warm and very white.

"Bonsoir mes enfants, ça va? ça va bien? bon, bon," he greeted us in his faint husky voice, not expecting any reply. He was quite used to being disregarded, but fresh from the Levers

and school we remembered our manners and took the plunge with our classroom French.

"Bonjour Monsieur Gobeaux," we chanted together. He then turned to our mother standing like a proud hen and made a few sympathetic remarks to the effect that she must be pleased to have us home.

"Ah oui, n'est-ce pas!" she assured him in no uncertain tone.

The formalities over, he sunk back into his former position, his hands clasped over his paunch, where he remained motionless until it was time to tune into his favourite wireless programme - the News in French which came on after the News in Gaelic broadcast daily by the BBC. It was intended primarily for those remaining under enemy occupation to give a true picture of the progress of the war and to raise morale. It was heralded by the tune of Lillibulero, and some rather chilling drumbeats of the letter V in Morse Code - the password to victory - echoed eerily on and off throughout, symbolically knocking on the secret hiding places of the oppressed urging them repeatedly, *'Chers Auditeurs ne quittez pas l'écoutes.'* The programme was also interrupted by mysterious announcements, such as; *'Jean et Paul aiment les pommes de terre'* and *'Roméo dit Bonjour à Juliétte'* bearing little relation to each other or to the war as far as I could make out. Yet these cryptic phrases seemed of particular interest to Monsieur Gobeaux who would sometimes draw the attention of my mother if she was nearby.

As the holiday progressed so we were to discover this obsession with *La Radio* was part of his nightly routine. The evening wore on before dinner. The boys came home and were duly presented to us. I found it satisfying to match my mother's graphic descriptions with each newcomer. They only made a brief appearance at this time, to announce their return and to pay respects to Monsieur Gobeaux who was regarded with affectionate esteem. At last it was the turn of the favourites, the moment for which I had been waiting. My mother met them both in the hall.

"Come and meet my children," I heard her say proudly as she came into the room followed by two tall men. Their height was all that gave a clue to their identity. Apart from an obvious rangy panache I had expected film-star good looks, dashing uniforms, effusive courtesy and uncontrollable high spirits. In these two, surely, would inhere those boyish elements to justify their collective nickname. Instead before us, their calm, mildly serious expressions masking perhaps an equal disillusion, were two adult men, older-looking than I had expected, both wearing dark lounge suits. My mother, typically, planted herself beside them ready to share in the impact she hoped we would make. Nothing gave her greater pleasure than to show us off. My eyes were drawn to the long spider legs.

"Don't be shy," she reprimanded us all. "Spider and Bunny - my son and daughter, Marjorie and Robin, the ones in the photos," she reminded the men. She watched, eager for their reaction. Both men broke into shy smiles as they offered their hands.

"How do you do, Mademoiselle?" they repeated one after the other in broken English before turning to Robin.

"Well, what do you think of my children? Of course they're a bit tired coming up from the country" she said, apologising for our reticence. "You're shy too!" she suddenly accused the men. "Shy of my children" she exclaimed in disbelief.

"Of course" spoke the one she called Bunny. "Madame," he began, "You say - cheeldren, I - expect - *de petits enfants,*" he stressed, lowering his hand to the level of his knees.

"But it not so - your cheeldren is — are," he corrected himself, "One young lady - and one - very beeg - gentleman, not cheeldren." He bowed to us with a smile.

"They are still my children and will be for the rest of their lives," she chuckled. "And these two are my favourites and they know it," she added, giving each man a pat on the bottom at which they broke into disarming grins. "Yes - here they are my two little Darlings," she continued proudly, carried along by their response. "And these are the two who are going to take you out on Christmas Day," she reminded me.

I just about recovered myself to reply in my best country fashion. "How nice."

Both favourites were brown-haired and dressed in almost identical navy pin-striped suits though in other respects they were not alike. It was not difficult to distinguish the professional soldier; very slim and straight, he was the tallest man I had ever met. He wore a pair of dark-framed glasses which suggested studiousness and intelligence, and I noticed his nose but it left me unmoved. He was clean-shaven and fairer skinned than his friend whose small moustache, heavy five o'clock shadow, dark shirt and tie put me in mind of an American gangster. But there the likeness ended for as their desire to make friends soon dispelled all reserve; I noticed that both men seemed to have gentle dispositions.

The evening meal was the highlight of the day. It was the one occasion when everyone came together after the day's work to relax and, since there was often a guest at table, it was on the whole a lively, if not frivolous, time. My mother took care with the cooking. It was the only means left for her to exercise her creative skills. With so many ration books and only one meal a day to prepare she was able to keep the menu ample and reasonably varied, and with the food-conscious Belgians to give a spur to her ingenuity she often excelled in her culinary efforts. Monsieur Gobeaux, bon viveur, also took an interest in the cooking and liked to know in advance what to expect. He was not above taking over the stove himself, a big apron tied around his very ample middle. He taught my mother to cook mussels, a Belgian speciality, and horsemeat so that it tasted like the finest fillet steak. As the British go to war to fight for 'King and Country' so the Belgians go to *'Defendre le Bifteck'* and at certain times it would appear that the sole inspiration for his patriotism was to act on the words of his own 'National saying' quite literally.

At dinner that first evening we met the rest of the household as they took their places around the large oval table in the dining room. At first it was a little overwhelming to be among so many men who found their places easily. It was Robin and I who felt like strangers, foreigners in our own home! In this very English setting with the Hepplewhite furniture and the Staffordshire figures along the mantelpiece, spoken English sounded incongruous. The Belgians had taken over. Their accents, the French language, even the *consommé* now being carried in, were far more in keeping with the spirit of this new *ménage.* Monsieur Gobeaux sat at the head of the table nearest the door. He liked to make a quick getaway once the meal was finished, before anyone could usurp his favourite chair.

All eyes were on Robin and me. Everyone looked happy for our mother who was herself brimming with delight. Straightaway she began to ladle the soup from a big tureen on the sideboard. Monsieur Gobeaux, a napkin tucked into his top waistcoat buttonhole, was served first. He began to eat at once, sucking the soup noisily from his spoon which he had been holding ready. Robin and I, always with a strong sense of the other's presence at such moments, dared not let our eyes meet across the table. At this point Mr. and Mrs Peter made their entrance. My mother, busy with the soup, swept her free arm in our direction letting her actions, for once, speak louder than words. Mrs. Peter erupted into a girlish laugh.

"Ah your cheeldren!" she exclaimed, smiling at us. We smiled back. "They are sweet - that is nice, you are happy madame?"

"What do you think?" replied my mother a bit too curtly I thought. Mrs. Peter stayed to help pass round the plates while her husband, bidding a general 'Good Evening' proceeded to his place with an air of self-importance. The room went quiet and he, conscious of the attention, wrung his hands over the table before laying them palms downwards on his knife and fork. He looked down to admire his nails and fussily adjusted the gold ring on his left hand. Mrs. Peter was noticeably younger than her husband and her presence prompted a fair degree of masculine interest. The tone of conversation brightened when she came close to pass the soup and I perceived the men looking at her legs and figure as she turned away. Her job completed, she went to her own place beside her husband and next to Spider. Not until everyone was busy with their soup did I begin to feel at ease yet I was glad to be here, to take a part in this extraordinary assembly, and hoped it would not be long before we fitted in, no more the focus of curiosity and our mother's swamping attention.

As the meal progressed it was easy to see why my mother was so happy with this group, for there was a steady flow of wise-cracking. Most of the jokes being in French passed over my head but I noticed that she was kept amused throughout. When she was ready to take the plates into the kitchen Bunny rose up to open the door and as she passed in front of him he untied the strings on her apron so that it fell off in the hall.

"Oh!" she shrieked, "Who did that? - you are a devil!" and quickly popping her head round the door she exclaimed with an expressive wink, *"Il faut pendre le fou dehors!"* Everyone laughed and Bear, the hotel-keeper's son who was sitting next to me, turned to say it was a result of a joke they had had earlier in the week. Bear had a friendly manner and spoke English well. He struck me as being detached from the others, for he often commented to me on their high spirits.

"They are like children," he said, "They plan a party for Christmas - they are exciting themselves - and they all behave a little foolishly," he added with a shrug.

With Bear seemingly bringing me into things I began to feel less out of place and wondered why my mother had not made more of him. He was reasonably nice-looking with a fashionable Clark Gable moustache. Sitting the other side of me was a very quiet member of the gathering. He made no contribution to the repartee darting here and there across the table. Sometimes he laughed, but his was a jumpy interest. Most of the time he appeared preoccupied with his hands. They were never still. I noticed with fascination as he rolled crumbs of bread into tiny balls which he constantly rearranged on the cloth as if puzzling out some perplexing calculation. Occasionally, he would pop one in his mouth as if that element at least had been resolved. Next to him sat another quiet boy with gingerish hair and a very pink complexion. I soon realised why these two fairly unremarkable personalities had been at the end of my mother's list and, I suspected, it was not just coincidence that they were also the farthest removed from her at the table.

My first impressions were usually very decided. Not shrewd like Cicely, I made up my mind especially with regard to the opposite sex, quickly and extravagantly. Apart from the stars who glistened and were to shine even brighter as time went on, there were those who were never to remain more than shadowy figures in the wings.

If this was like some play in which as yet I had no role then surely Mr and Mrs Peter had star quality. Both good-looking they made a glamorous couple. Being of Dutch extraction it was as difficult for Mrs Peter to converse in French as it was in English yet she chattered away in either language her incompetence and slight lisp adding to her attraction. Her name was Dinah and the boys, evidently fond of her, called her Mrs Dinah and they teased her unmercifully. She appeared to revel in her position of the only young woman in their midst. I noticed from time to time she put her hand on the arm of her tall neighbour as it rested on the table. However, she had her husband at her side, enough to keep any would-be libertine in check. Discreetly made-up and fashionably dressed, there was about her an air of propriety which did not go with trying to attract attention. If her behaviour sometimes belied her actions it seemed to spring from an abundance of good nature and affection and a desire to have some of it reflected back on herself. The more we smiled at each other across the table, the more out of place she seemed, with a sadness in her wide eyes in contrast to her bubbling personality.

Mr Peter was dark and suavely handsome with regular features and the slim athletic build of a much younger man. He spoke English with a faultless accent and it was not difficult to see he considered himself a cut above the rest. He also seemed to derive pleasure from seeing his wife teased by the men, and may even have encouraged it.

The officers sat together next to my mother. They were in good spirits. Most of the humour centred on this end of the table. Spider handled Mrs Peter with chivalry and I wondered if they might be secretly in love until I remembered the engagement my mother had mentioned in the tea-shop. Much to my embarrassment he caught my eye and, raising his eyebrows, the light flashing sparkles in his glasses, he pursed his lips ready to speak. He reminded me of a Pierrot.

"Mademoiselle - you are happy to be in this house with these funny Belgian boys?" he asked, and before I had time to reply Mrs Peter nudged him.

"*Et moi,*" she reminded him peevishly.

"And one funny, young lady," he added, fixing me with a steady gaze. Mrs Peter let out a petulant groan. "Please," he excused himself and began again. "Excuse me, of course, we have one very beautiful, funny young lady," he said. He had spoken slowly making sure of his words but my mother heard him.

"What about me?" she cried out. Bunny came to the rescue. Holding up two fingers he spoke in even more hesitant English. "Two, beautiful ladies, *N'est-ce pas?*"

"That's more like it," responded my mother. "Never bite the hand that feeds you." Everyone chuckled though it was doubtful whether they had understood apart from Peter.

"Mrs Rae," he began in his surprisingly English manner, "You have your own remedy for the unfaithful ones *"pendre l'infidel dehors"*. The table rocked with laughter and Mr Peter, smiling at me, addressed the company.

"You must realise there are three ladies present in the house now." No remark could have been more calculated to topple my slowly developing self-confidence. I closed my eyes to the resulting looks and concentrated on finishing my dinner.

It struck me that here was a group of people, brought together through war, laughing, joking, and yet there was the feeling that in normal times no two of them, the officers apart, would ever have found a common meeting point, let alone the basis for such a close relationship as now.

***

"Mr Peter is a nice man, he likes Art. He and I get on well, do you like him?" My mother enquired of me in the kitchen where I had followed her when the meal was finished as a chance to escape.

"He looks older than his wife," I replied.

"He is, a good twenty years I should think. She's only twenty-one."

"Golly! He speaks very good English," I told her.

"Shall I tell you something," she said, "Keep it to yourself because he told me this in confidence. His father is Lord Dawson of Penn, so he says."

"Isn't he Belgian?"

"Half-Belgian I suppose. Said his mother was his father's mistress. Whether it's true or not, who knows."

"What is a mistress exactly?" I asked.

She clicked her tongue against the roof of her mouth and snorted. "I suppose I shouldn't be talking about such things but I shouldn't be surprised if it is true, that he's half-English I mean, seems to know the inside of most of the big private houses, and some of my old customers even".

"He does look rather superior."

"Oh - he's quite a snob, talks about the elite and the lower orders and only deigns to have anything to do with old Gobbo and Spider and Bunny. The boys are supposed to call him Captain and they won't - Spider says he's as much right to be called Captain as his little finger. Old Gobbo can't stick him."

"Why not?" I asked.

"To tell the truth, I think he's jealous. Peter likes speaking English and the old boy can't bear it when we get too engrossed and he can't understand what we're saying. Glad to be home, Darling?"

"Gosh, yes."

"We'll look at the dresses in the morning."

"Do I really have to go out on Christmas Day?" I asked.

"Don't you like the boys?"

"They're all right but I don't know them. I'd much rather stay with you. Couldn't you make an excuse? I'd feel awfully awkward, really I would. They're all much older than I'd imagined," I implored her.

"They wouldn't let you feel awkward I know. Anyway, Spider may not be here for Christmas after all, he told me. He may be going up North. I shall be sad if he does. I want them all here for the party."

The first significant observation I made after being home a few hours was how my mother's new life had exposed another façet of her character. With her eyebrows arched high in a perpetual expression of childish wonder, her dark eyes wide open as if wanting to take in the whole world at a glance, her forthrightness and modern outlook, unusual in a woman her age, impressed the boys. She was a good sport, never afraid to call a spade a spade. In direct contrast to her manifest ebullience she was always soberly dressed. In fact, anyone coming upon her for the first time might have found it hard to place her in her previous role of a fashionable dressmaker. She wore comfortable suits she had made herself which were invariably navy blue. The only relief in her colour scheme were the subtle shades of pink, paler blue and ecru she chose for her blouses and twinsets. When urged to wear brighter colours she said that, with her dark hair and complexion, she would be mistaken for a gypsy. Now that we had arrived her excitement was gathering momentum.

Dinner finished, the day's work was over for my mother and she liked to relax with whoever was home for the evening. With the boys around her she enjoyed teaching them English as well as having the opportunity for polishing up her French. Her progress had been considerable and she was now able to converse moderately fluently with all-comers. I was full of admiration for her pluck and hard work as much as I came to be continually surprised at her changing attitudes and frequent lack of tact.

After dinner we settled in the drawing room with only half the *ménage* present. Some of the boys had lingered in the dining room, chatting and smoking. One or two had gone out altogether - the greedy ones no doubt to have another meal! Monsieur Gobeaux did not take much part in the social proceedings yet his chair remained in the middle of the room so that people addressing one another on opposite sides of the room had constantly to move their heads to talk around him. My mother brought in a tray of coffee which she set down with aplomb on a table in front of her as she eased herself into the settee beside the Peters. I found myself sitting somewhat nervously between Bear and Spider opposite.

I was tired after the eventful day and content to watch and listen to the others. The whole mood seemed one of peace. Bear had the Christmas edition of Punch on his lap while Spider unearthed a pipe from his pocket which he took time and perseverance to light up before sitting back to gaze into the fire. Tobacco smoke and the smell of used matches wafted into the air radiating contentment. Only Bunny looked somewhat ill at ease, perched on a chair by the door. He evidently did not intend to stay and appeared to be working out his best manoeuvre to get away. He knew it would be tricky. After shifting awkwardly on his seat, he stared pointedly at his watch and brought his empty cup back to my mother, a wistful expression in his eyes.

"Madame," he began full of apology. "Excuse me Madame, I must go out. I prefer to remain in here, of course with you and your charming children, but ..."

His words tailed off and my mother did not make it easy for him. He pointed his finger at his watch again and raised his eyebrows to convey that wherever he was going he was already late. My mother spoke for him, smiling sardonically.

"You have an appointment - ah?" He knew he was trapped. The man beside me with the pipe giggled.

"Yes Madame," he pleaded, aware that his persuasive charm had been rendered ineffective by the arrival of Robin and me. "Oh Bunny," she whined like a spoilt child, "You're not going to leave me tonight, when my children are here?" He shot a sidelong glance at his friend, mumbled something in French and deciding quickly any further hesitation would be fruitless, clicked his heels together, bowed to me, bowed to my mother and smartly retreated from the room. My mother watched open-mouthed but once he had gone her expression underwent a rapid change and she broke into a girlish laugh. "He's a scream," she said, shaking her head and giving me a knowing wink. "We understand one another," she added. Both men beside me laughed and the one with the pipe clenched between smiling teeth caught her eye so that she gave him an affectionate chuck on the chin. "Laugh at me, would you?" she taunted, and leaning over dealt a similar blow to Bear. Although I sensed less of a feeling of affection in the second attack, I was glad she had allotted them equal treatment.

"Well - what do you think of my children?" she suddenly enquired. Someone muttered something complimentary and I felt Mrs. Peter examining me from my shoes to my hair. "What did you say? Do you think my daughter's like me?" she said and answered the question herself. "No, she's not, is she? Better-looking than me". There was an awkwardness, perhaps a sensitivity as if the men would like to have flattered me but wished to save me embarrassment.

"Have you got a Christmas tree?" I asked to change the subject. It would be Christmas in two days time and nothing much had been done in preparation. The boys fortunately had booked the caterers: it was their party and where food was concerned they acted impeccably. My mother had been glad to assign this responsibility to Bear with his experience of the hotel business.

A Christmas tree and some holly and mistletoe had been delivered and were waiting to be dealt with. Christmas meant much to my mother, as much as it did to us. She was like a child, too in her anticipation. Perhaps it was because her life had been subject to so much change she had a need to keep up traditions to give it balance. "There's a lot to do," she moaned, "The tree, the holly and mistletoe to put up."

"Leave that to us Madame," suggested Bear. "Every year we make the decorations in the hotel."

"That's good," she replied and began to apportion duties. "Bear's going to decorate the room, you do the tree?" she instructed me. "And what about you? What'll you do?" she enquired of Spider.

"He is necessary if we have to put something high on the walls," chipped in Bear with a smile.

"And I will help also," lisped Mrs. Peter excitedly.

"And I will tell you if it was all worth it," added her husband raising his head condescendingly from the illustrated London News.

That settled my mother, who looked round for more inspiration. "Where is everybody tonight?" she asked with a frown. "Where is Roll?"

"Piano!" chorused the two either side of me in a tone of resignation. This answer, though satisfying her, mystified me and I shot a glance at the firmly closed piano in the corner.

"Not this piano," laughed Bear, noticing my puzzlement. "They have the 'Piano' in the dining-room for the practise of Morse Code."

"Oh - I see" I said though I had no perception of what he meant. Spider enlightened me.

"Piano is di-da-di, di, di, di, da, da, da," he recited while tapping his fingers rhythmically along his thigh. I was distracted by the length of his legs and agreed how aptly my mother had chosen his nick-name. "Roll is doing Piano all the time - I think he is full of anxieties," he said with a shrug.

"Poor devil," sympathised my mother. "He hasn't much longer, *n'est-ce pas* Monsieur Gobeaux?" she said rousing the chef. *"Roll partira bientôt n'est ce pas?"*

"Oui, oui - commencement janvier," he answered huskily. *"Mais ça depend! Vous savez,"* he called out as an afterthought.

"It is not good that he is so *inquiété* he thinks everybody is against him, you know? It is not good - it is dangerous," Spider continued.

"Let's hope he has a good rest over Christmas - the party should do him good," said my mother.

I wasn't curious as to why there was a Morse Transmitter in the dining-room. Many Groups learnt Morse Code. The Girl Guides, the OTC at Robin's school. I had the alphabet in my Schoolgirl's Diary. What I was to notice, however, was how all the boys had this obsessive interest in the 'Piano' which manifested itself in the habit they had of tapping their fingers on any surface at every opportunity. It was reminiscent of a string player practising vibrato, training their fingers to move almost involuntarily. No doubt it was equally a mark of dedication as it was a symptom of underlying tension.

***

The evening dresses were hanging in the large wardrobe that used to be in my mother's showroom. I sorted through the old models - the tucked chiffon, the beaded satin, the sleek velvet, for my own dress. It was made of pink taffeta, my first long dress, and I had only worn it two or three times. There was still a newness in the material and a novelty in the full skirt with the pretty ruching at the hem. I took it gingerly off the hanger to try on. Although it was tight in the bodice, it was otherwise wearable. I had not grown much in height during the last two years. I swirled vainly about the room manipulating the skirt so that it rustled.

"Spider's definitely not going away, at least not until the New Year. He's made up his mind - he says he likes my children and is looking forward to Christmas now you're home and, he says, he's going to buy the game of Monopoly to play over the holidays. Isn't he sweet? I think you've cheered him up," my mother informed me all in one breath as she came into the bedroom and started straight away to fuss with my frock. "Well, there's nothing wrong with that, it's a pretty dress, it suits you - in fact, it suits you better now you've got a figure than it did when I made it." I hunched myself round-shouldered, wondering if Spider's decision meant the dinner in town was also a definite fixture but decided against asking, reminding her of it hoping it would all come to nothing in the end.

"This dress smells horrible, all fusty and ancient from being in the cupboard and it's torn here," I said.

"That's nothing, just a stitch come undone, leave it out. I'll see to it later."

"You don't think it's too childish? My hair's awful, it needs washing again," I said, scraping it back from my face. "Certainly looks awful like that. We could buy some flowers to dress it up a bit." I gave another self-critical turn in front of the looking-glass.

"Where's your dress?" I asked her, beginning to sort afresh through the cupboard.

"There's plenty of time for that later. Come on if we're going up to town. We've got a lot to do. It's the party tomorrow you know," she called out, already along the landing.

Even though it was wartime, there were crowds in the West End. The shops had made a good Christmas display despite having to board up most of their plate glass windows as a precaution against flying glass. Inside there was the same frantic rush as shoppers, weighed down with carrier bags, darted here and there to make their purchases, and in Harrod's there was as much activity as in peacetime.

Robin and I, liberated from the country, were two excited youngsters swept up in the full magic of the city once more. There were the usual monumental displays in the food halls, lines of turkeys, guinea fowl, game; pyramids of fruit and flowers, mostly English apples it was true but they had been polished until they shone, rosily reflecting the coloured lights amongst the evergreen. The smells were marvellous - perfume, cigars, freshly baked confectionary and chrysanthemums. My mother, buoyed up by our company, raced with unusual energy in and out of the various departments, up and down in the lifts while we traipsed behind, flagging noticeably. My mother was so happy with the Belgians that she had stinted nothing in preparation for the festivities. Even though it was a time of shortage many items were not yet as scarce as they were to become. It was still possible to buy luxuries at a price or a little underhanded persuasion! For many of the boys who had experienced the deprivation of living under German Occupation, it must have looked as if there was no war at all here.

Once home, I soon lost track of Robin. He and I had been inseparable in Winchester, but had no such dire emotional need of one another here. With his pals, likewise in London for the holidays, he pursued his interest with his model paraphernalia of the war, while I tended to keep near my mother, wrapping presents, cooking, relishing every menial and mundane task for which I had no opportunity with the Levers. We had dutifully written to inform them of our safe arrival and, once the letters were posted, tended to put Kingsworthy Court and all it stood for to the back of our minds.

The forty-eight hours since our arrival were passing in one mad rush as we caught up with lost time and delayed opportunity. The house seemed enormous, crowded with people coming and going at all times and in contrast to the stillness and leisurely tempo of life in the country. I met the boys on the landing, coming out of the bathroom and up and down the stairs. It was a nice, convivial atmosphere to have at Christmas, even if it was taking me a few days to feel at home. I liked the way the boys stood back to let me pass, their manner of shaking hands every time we met and I liked being addressed as Mademoiselle. At the same time as their impeccable courtesy, like most young men, egged on by the next, they were high-spirited and lusty, cracking private jokes and constantly ragging each other over what was obviously their main leisure activity - the pursuit of young female company. At rare moments I caught them looking at my legs and figure which left me in the uncertain predicament of not knowing whether to feel flattered or offended.

My mind, like my mother's, was soon dominated by the party; the splendour of everyone in evening dress, the boys, their girlfriends and the feast. I also anticipated a somewhat lonely time with no companions my own age. I thought of Tony and how marvellous it would be if by some miracle he could be transported to London for the evening. He would see me in my glamorous dress and we could be quite openly friends here. Perhaps we could even steal away from the excitement for a few romantic minutes alone. I wondered if he would be moved to write and whether I should I write to him. Then back came the gnawing fear of having to go out with these foreign men on Christmas Day.

My horoscope in the Daily Mail predicted I should receive a long-awaited letter, that the disappointment of another would turn to my advantage and the prospect of romance augured well. It made a good start to the day. The Christmas tree was standing in a tub by the French windows. On the floor beside it lay a box containing the lights and decorations which had been carefully preserved for as long as I could remember. My mother was in her most business-like mood. Still in her apron, a stub of a cigarette in her mouth on which she continually blew in an effort to keep the smoke out of her eyes and lungs, she dragged in a branch of holly across the carpet. I began to unwrap the ornaments for the tree from the grubby tissue paper. In the shape of bells, spheres and fabulous birds they brought back reflections of Christmases past. The room was full. Some of the boys were standing up watching our preparations with fascination, angling for some little task to make them part of the activity. After a while two disappeared altogether and my mother, preoccupied with her branch of holly, deposited it beside the only one who looked ready to do nothing, hoping to rouse him into some kind of action. He winced as the prickles penetrated his trousers and pushed it away. "Never mind Jefke, it will be your turn tomorrow," she taunted him good humouredly as he got up and slunk over to the radiogram to delve in the box of records. "I'm putting you in charge of the music."

Still puffing though with more agitation on the cigarette which she did not realise had gone out, she stood in the middle of the room with her hands on her hips. She then went out of the room. Monsieur Gobeaux sat immutable in his favourite chair, only showing a glimmer of life when he heard the tinkle of glasses as my mother reappeared with some wine on a tray.

"For God's sake let's have a drink while we're doing this, after all it's nearly Christmas!" she exclaimed, beginning to pour the wine. Roll drained his glass quickly and, after contemplating its emptiness a few seconds, left the room. "Give it a rest tonight," my mother called after him. He reappeared to make some polite excuse in French. *"Mais demain,"* she remonstrated, "Will be Christmas, the party! Your girl will be here. I'm closing the dining room for the night. At Christmas you must forget yourself my boy." He stood patiently listening and, offering no further excuse, backed out of the door closing it behind him. She gave up and sighed, "Poor chap," mumbling to herself.

Mrs Peter came over to help with the tree. Between us we carefully threaded the fairy lights over the branches. Miraculously they lit up as soon as I plugged them in. My helper stood marvelling at the glittering spectacle like a bedazzled child. "They are pretty!" she exclaimed and we both stood back to admire our handiwork. The pale blue eyes of the young Belgian woman sparkled with the reflection of the lights. They also picked out the gold strands in her curly blonde hair which was like a halo around her head reminiscent of a Botticelli angel.

"It's so nice," she bubbled delightedly as she picked up the silver star from the floor.

"Oh, that goes at the top of the tree," I said and she went to fetch a chair. My mother was having one of her many rests and watched our efforts with smiling satisfaction as she sipped from her glass. Suddenly the door burst open, giving everyone a start, and the officers had returned, carrying armfuls of evergreen they had gathered from the garden.

"Happy - days - are - here again," they sang lustily as they deposited their load on the carpet. My mother was delighted to see them back and Mrs Peter, poised shoeless on the chair, giggled drawing attention to herself.

"Mrs Dinah, what are you doing?" exclaimed Spider walking over to us.

"I put this up here," she indicated with a little upward stretch of her body as she reached forward to secure the star. Then taking hold of his hand which he offered she jumped down at his feet. He turned to me.

"Mademoiselle - you make all the things very beautiful," he remarked and, flattered by his praise, I felt a glow of achievement.

The wine and the return of her favourites had put new life into my mother. "Have a drink," she invited them. "Help yourself, *servez-vous?*" she said, indicating the wine with a flourish.

"But – certainly," responded Bunny, dropping everything and made for the tray. Mrs Peter ran ahead to help and reached it first. Bunny placed his hands around her waist, "Mrs Dinah," he breathed sensuously in her ear and guided her out of his way. He stood a minute in contemplation then, picking up one of the bottles, he weighed it in his hand a moment. Then slowly, his head inclined backwards, he began to pour the contents to the back of his throat without it touching his lips. We all marvelled at his skill.

"Bravo! Bravo!" applauded my mother, clapping her hands. Spider all set for a little playful rivalry, moved over and nudged his friend out the way. Smiling confidently, he took hold of another bottle and setting his head at just the right angle, he proceeded to pour the wine at an even greater distance from his mouth until a thin stream of red liquid was trickling past his lips. Bunny patted his shoulder so that the wine ran from the corners of his mouth as he laughed, swallowing hard and spluttering.

"*Mayala,*" Bunny cried for it was a trick they had picked up in Spain as well as some of the dubious expressions too.

"Marvellous!" exclaimed my mother, "You must have a steady hand."

"We have had much practise," Spider enlightened her with just a hint of sarcasm clouding his triumphant expression, as he went in search of a cloth to wipe up the wine he had spilt.

"Come here I'll do it," urged my mother, taking over from him. "It takes a woman to do a job properly."

"Madame - woman must remember - she is coming from the useless rib of the man," reacted Bunny poker-faced. It was very noticeable how these two friends had the knack of keeping my mother constantly amused. Their warm personalities, their boyish tricks and a certain shared charisma made them always the centre of attention. I found I was beginning to miss them too when they were not around.

All this time Bear had been quietly and diligently weaving the bunches of evergreen into a long festoon to swathe around the picture rail. He also looked well-practised. His colleagues helped fix it in position and we all admired the effect. The room was beginning to look very festive and my mother, noticeably moved, stood silently surveying our efforts. She tapped Monsieur Gobeaux on the shoulder to draw his attention. *"Ah oui, c'est beau, oui c'est beau,"* he acknowledged. "You've done a wonderful job," she said, a faint catch clipping her sentence. The determination with which the boys had set about the preparations had triggered off some private thought to touch her inside.

For most of them it would be their first Christmas in freedom since the invasion of their country. For some it might be their last, indeed, for all of us. Allied victory still lay a long way ahead. But she was quick to realise we must all make the most of this one and, with a swift composing flick over her face with both hands, she picked up the Mistletoe.

"We mustn't forget this," she stressed, handing it to Spider. "This is most important, it'd better go up in the middle".

"What is that?" he chuckled, taking hold of the loop of string. "For what is that?" he insisted.

"Mistletoe, don't ask me the French for it. In England we kiss under the Mistletoe at Christmas - it's a good excuse to have a little flutter with who you fancy," she said with a nudge.

"So!" exclaimed Bunny and playfully swept her up in his arms as the Mistletoe was positioned above them.

"Merry Christmas, you dear boys," she said quite overcome, drawing Spider to her.

"Come on Dinah, you can forget you are married for once, anyway your husband's not here for the moment. Christmas only comes but once a year. Come on Bear, Jefke, let's all indulge in a little seasonal good will." The boys kissed Mrs Peter and the excitement brought a flush to her cheeks.

"Monsieur Gobeaux - et vous?" she cried out.

"Et Mademoiselle?" someone called to me. "Is it not Christmas for you also?" I looked at my mother who beckoned me over. Still finding communication difficult, I accepted the invitation as a gesture of friendship. They were including me as one of the company. We stood in a tight little group under the Mistletoe. All the men seemed to be kissing us in turn and to my surprise, due probably to the glass of wine I had taken, I found myself joining in quite readily. Monsieur Gobeaux shuffled over to where we were gathered without

comment though his eyes gleamed brightly as he snorted mild disapproval between knowing smiles. *"Bonne nuit tout le monde - amusez - vous bien, moi je vais me coucher,"* he said as he hobbled out of the room.

The kissing changed its nature from cheeks to lips, from a token peck to a light embrace. The Boys devised a game whereby they blindfolded Mrs Peter and me so that we should guess who was kissing us. I enjoyed being accorded the same treatment as Mrs Peter. She was able to distinguish them accurately but when it came to my turn, although I knew that two had moustaches, I found it difficult - I wasn't even sure of their names. They were determined I should pick them out. They cleared their throats and whispered audibly to throw out clues until, one of them unable to contain himself, declared loudly:

"It is better - the moustache, *ne c'est ce pas Mademoiselle? Ce qui_donne du piquant, de l'intéret,"* he added, rubbing his prized whiskers against my cheeks. I tore off the blindfold and pointed at Bunny.

"It was you," I cried out, my cheeks on fire.

***

Most of the furniture in the drawing room needed to be re-arranged for the caterer and the large trestle table on which they were going to serve the banquet. My mother and I, alone in the house, stood estimating what needed to be done. The wireless was tuned into the carols from King's College Chapel and outside the daylight was fading as the shops, traffic and general bustle in the Parade would also be slowing down. It was good to be indoors, warm and comfortable, looking forward to the evening before us when all is dead outside and can be forgotten.

My mother liked to change things round. She made the excuse that it gave the furniture an airing and dispersed the wear and tear but I believe that secretly she liked to take stock of her possessions, to place a value on her treasures and to revel in their high quality and craftsmanship. With a duster in one hand and a tin of Min cream in the other, she polished the stretchers of the chairs, the backs of the cabinets, and all the little nooks and crannies that never saw the light of day from one move round to the next. Working with her was always an ordeal, taking twice as long as one could have done it alone, but we had time.

"Half the fun of a party is the preparation beforehand," she impressed on me and she certainly went about it in a very thorough manner. Our aim was to clear a space in the centre of the room by pushing the chairs and settees against the walls and removing any small extraneous items from the room.

"It'll do for dancing afterwards," she said, resting on the arm of an easy chair, panting from exertion. "They're a nice lot, do you like them better?"

"Mm - they are quite nice," I replied, my cheeks still burning from the events the previous evening and they flushed even hotter when I considered how easily I had been drawn into the game under the Mistletoe. The pious voice now reading the lesson on the wireless gave me the feeling that Christmas at home this year was going to be rather wicked.

"I think we should have some good fun tonight when all the girls are here" pronounced my mother as she resumed pushing and heaving.

"Who's coming?" I asked.

"God knows - I only know Bunny's girl and her friend who's coming with Spider." Momentarily distracted, she glanced around making a mental note of what needed doing. "All I know is that they've all raked up someone to bring along as they've all paid for two. There will be twenty-six of us altogether sitting down for dinner. At least it was twenty-six at the last count. Here, give me a hand with this." Between us we swung one of the settees up against the French windows. "Phew! Mind the Christmas tree" she warned.

"Do you like Bunny's girlfriend?" I asked.

"Eve — yes, she's rather a nice girl as a matter of fact. Been here several times - speaks good French, s'got lovely legs."

"Are they in love?" I asked. "Will they get married?"

"No!" stated my mother emphatically. "He's married already."

I was stunned. I turned to her. "Where's his wife?" I exclaimed.

My mother shrugged as if the question hadn't occurred to her before. "I don't know - suppose she stayed behind - perhaps they didn't get on." Just when I was beginning to know them, to sort them out as individuals - the kissing the other evening having broken the ice - back came cause for disillusion. A married man with a girlfriend did not fit in with my scheme of things.

"Are any of the others married? Is Bear married?"

"No, Bear's sort of engaged to an English girl, has been since before the war, can't make his mind up whether he wants to marry her or not. He's asked her tonight - doesn't think she'll come. I think she's keeping him on a string if you ask me. He will be on his own in the end."

"He speaks good English. I think I like him the best," I said.

"I notice they are all speaking English since you've arrived and they're all on their best behaviour too." My mother shot me an old-fashioned glance over the top of her glasses, which rippled an unaccountable wave through my body.

"Do you usually only speak French?"

"Most of the time, though Spider and Bear like speaking English and sometimes we have an English evening when I won't let them speak a word of French. Old Gobbo doesn't like that at all - he calls it treachery, funny old thing. He's so pig-headed wouldn't you think he'd try and learn a bit of English? Oh! He's proud and cocky enough when he says - water closet! Don't you like the officers?"

I thought for a moment. "If they're officers, why don't they wear uniforms?"

"They will tonight, they've promised. They both look very handsome in uniform. The girls next door couldn't leave them alone when they first came, especially the younger one - she's a nice little thing. I encouraged Spider to take her out but he wasn't interested, perhaps she was too nice".

"Too nice - how do you mean?" I asked.

"Well - he wanted taking out of himself, he was in a bad state when he came, I told you, he needed more of a girl to amuse him, that's what I mean, he needed amusing". She stuck at that.

"He doesn't look very sad to me" I said.

"He's better now, he's got over things a bit - and the party - I'm amazed how that's made a difference - they're all looking forward to it you know. It was a good suggestion of mine... I daresay we're in for a few shocks tonight" she began in her wordly way.

"In what way?"

"Well - I don't know where the boys have picked up their girls - it's best to keep an open mind, after all it's only for one night."

***

Promptly at six-thirty the caterers arrived and took over the kitchen. None of the boys had been in the house since morning. It seemed a long day to me already and I was glad to sit down for a cup of tea with my mother and Monsieur Gobeaux. The cooks, in their white starched aprons, enclosed themselves behind the glass-panelled door of the kitchen. Marie, the girl who lived in to help with the housework, began to put the finishing touches in the drawing room and my mother, satisfied that all was under control, suggested we went upstairs to get changed.

I brought my things along to her room so that we could talk. In those early days I wished to be close to my mother the whole time. With Robin and me on our own she was quite different from the image she presented to the world, despite her obvious preoccupation with her new life. I loved the gradual unfolding of all those titbits of gossip she gleaned regarding her new associates.

Soon we heard evidence of the boys coming home for there was a lot of bumping and laughter as they came upstairs. My mother, pleased with their sounds, exclaimed between chuckles.

"Listen to them! I expect they called in at the Granville on their way back."

My mother began to search in the wardrobe for the chiffon evening dress she had made about five years previously. I think she would rather have continued in the jumper and skirt she had been wearing all day but she wanted everyone to dress up so felt duty bound to make the effort herself. She took the dress from the hanger cautiously, loath to touch it almost, gave it a vigorous shake and pulled a face. It smelt ancient and was creased. It did not appear to worry her unduly, yet she had taken care with my frock, now arranged pressed and perfect, over the back of a chair. Pent up with excitement, which showed in her trembling lips and hands, she pulled the tired garment over her head and eased it down her body. She had grown fat since the war, one of the reasons she took such little interest in her clothes now. Unable to manage the fastenings, she left it undone while she combed her hair.

I quickly slipped on my dress. The crisp taffeta was cold against my skin and I began to shiver too. My mother came over to arrange the skirt in her very professional manner and there was a loud burst of laughter in the next room. Her tongue clicked happily against the roof of her mouth.

"Listen to them," she chortled, "They sound happy that's one good thing. Poor old Roll - let's hope he forgets himself for once." She gasped in her tight dress as she tried to get her parting straight. "Don't you love Spider and his way of looking at you with those eyes of his? They make me curl up inside. I think he's so fascinating," she pronounced girlishly.

"I don't know that I like the name Spider much," I said. "Makes him sound like a gangster or something. I don't think it suits him, apart from his legs."

"It suits him very well," she said mysteriously.

"He was engaged, you said?"

"Yes, poor chap, he was."

"What happened - why did it break up?"

"Oh darling" she smiled pityingly, "She just didn't love him I suppose, that's life." She shrugged. "I still think she was a fool. Don't they say unlucky in love, lucky in war, or is it the other way round? He's a Cavalry Officer you know, very swish, very well thought of."

I was conscious that the tightness of my dress, although flattening my bosom, also drew attention to it which did not altogether displease me. I drew in a deep breath and pulled out the bodice in two points, hoping to encourage the material to give a little.

"Don't you mean, all's fair in love and war?" I suggested as a long afterthought, and set about vigorously brushing my hair which had been set locally that morning - a last minute decision - before fixing the semi-circlet of white flowers we had bought, over the curls at the back, just as I had seen Ann Rutherford do in an Andy Hardy film; Ann Rutherford and Deanna Durbin were my role models. "I think Mrs Peter or whatever her name is, is rather keen on the officers," I said, voicing my observations of the last couple of days.

"That's pretty obvious," replied my mother.

"Doesn't her husband mind?"

"Doesn't seem to - I think he's proud of her," she said, then turning round and seeing me almost ready, she exclaimed "You look lovely! Put a bit of powder on your nose."

I liked having her approval when it came to using make-up and went over to the dressing table and helped myself to the swan's down puff with alacrity. I also applied her bright Louis Phillipe lipstick to my lips before wiping it all off on a piece of cotton wool. I pressed them together and smoothed on an extra trace of colour with my finger.

"Do they fancy her?" I said, stroking some mascara guiltily on my lashes.

"Who?" she replied, preoccupied with her own reflection in the mirror.

"The officers - do they like Mrs Peter?"

She came and edged me away from the table. "She's an attractive woman, they all like her but she's married isn't she?" She gave herself a very false smile in the glass and examined the reflection of her teeth. "I don't know, there's something odd about those two," she muttered, carelessly upending an almost empty bottle of Arpège on the front of her dress. "I can't make up my mind about her. Spider thinks he's a fraud."

"What do you mean?" I asked.

"I don't know exactly," she added, nodding her head abstractedly and pinning on her diamond brooch – her trade mark - "It's almost as if she, or he…" she muttered, shaking her head.

"Why are they here?" I asked her.

"I really don't know."

I began to shiver more markedly from nervousness as much as the cold. We could hear the boys going in and out of the bathroom, excited and noisy, doors banging, voices raised amidst a good deal of horseplay. Then all at once we heard someone singing a familiar aria with all the requisite expression and pathos.

"That's Jefke," she said gleefully, stopping to listen. "He's got a lovely voice - Verdi isn't it, or Puccini?" she hummed the melody too and broke into song for an instant.

"I thought he would have been one of your favourites as he likes music," I suggested.

"I like him all right but he can be a moody chap. He's got an artistic temperament I suppose."

"Isn't that what you rather admire?"

"It's all right, difficult to live with. I suppose I've got too much of one myself," she said, patting her hair.

"And Bear, do you like him?"

"Bear's all right, there's not much about Bear." She rubbed some pink cream into her face. "They're all good fun together. I've never had a group that got on so well before."

Distracted once more by her image and not entirely satisfied by what she saw, my mother turned sideways and appeared to try and set her head on her neck at a more becoming angle. She took a deep breath and pulled in her stomach.

"Here, do me up," she begged, sidling towards me. "Let's hope the dinner'll be worth eating after all this." I fastened her hooks and eyes with difficulty. It took the whole of five minutes to coax the sides of the dress together. Every now and then we heard the front door close, then all at once the house went quiet. We were ready. Suddenly, I felt shy of going downstairs amongst so many strangers.

"Mummy, do I look all right? Is this dress really wearable, not too childish, is it too tight? Have I got too much make-up on?" I implored, hovering in front of the mirror to make last-minute adjustments.

"Go on, you look lovely, you know you do - it's me who should feel worried. Look at me in this old thing. I feel like a parcel tied up in the middle." She started laughing and we heard stitches splitting. "God, I'd better go down before the whole damn thing falls apart," she said, making a bold rush forward. She stopped in the doorway on her way out and turned, her eyes full of loving pride. Just what I needed to give me the confidence to follow her down. I ran and put my arms around her neck and kissed her.

"You look nice too, I like you wearing pretty clothes," I said, and just as spontaneously I was overcome with excitement. This was Christmas Eve at last, the highlight of the holiday, the evening my mother and her boys had been planning for weeks. I was ready to join in all the fun of the party.

PART FIVE

IT CAME UPON A MIDNIGHT CLEAR

Despite my mother's lack of organisation and her dislike of housework, she could put on a marvellous show, fit for a king. The large trestle table with its freshly laundered covering, still clinging to the square folds into which it had been pressed, looked set for a multitude. Pushed back from the fire it appeared to fill the whole room. The man who came in to clean the silver had worked with extra assiduity that afternoon. He had also made up the fire so that it would need little attention during the evening, its cheerful glow reflected in the shine on the nearby furniture. Every light was switched on and their sparkle danced in the mirrors and darted like quicksilver in and out of the crystal drops of the sconces and the cut glass on the table. The glittering tree in the corner and the festoons of evergreen gave just the right Christmas touch. The atmosphere was taut with expectancy.

Monsieur Gobeaux had been ready a long time and was impatient for the party to begin. In his usual chair, his face red from the fire, he could not rouse himself to move back. Sweat began to break out in tiny drops on his brow and periodically he took out his handkerchief to mop them away. Captain and Madame Peter, both in evening dress, were talking to him, their backs to the fire.

All three looked up as I sidled into the room where, surprised to find so few people, I made for Monsieur Gobeaux's outstretched, clammy hand. He congratulated me on my appearance and directed me to a nearby chair. Mrs Peter, looking radiant in anticipation of the fun to come, purred out compliments while fingering the material of my dress. With quick, plucking movements she also began to fuss with my hair. She then threw her arms around my neck and started kissing me on both cheeks.

"Three times in Belgium," she asserted pulling me back and I banged my nose in the confusion. Wafts of expensive perfume emanated from the front of her dress, down which I had managed to see in the closeness of the embrace, that she was wearing nothing underneath. Any underclothes would certainly have spoilt the sleek outline for she had on a close-fitting frock cut well below the waist at the back. The dullness of the crepe silk enhanced the softness and the whiteness of her skin. I was sure she would appear even more attractive to the men dressed in this revealing fashion. I ran my finger down my nose and brushed away the tears which had gathered in the corner of one eye. The slight shock of her dress and the irritation of the blow were welling up into a feeling of precocious rivalry. I looked down on my prim bosom, of which I was so proud, constricted by the tight bodice, and sat down feeling just as female as Mrs Peter. Her husband, looking even more aloof than usual in his immaculate dinner jacket and black tie, was the only man to appear in formal evening dress. He shook my hand and I sensed something odd about this couple, nearly always together, yet she seemed happier in the company of the younger men.

Almost unnoticed, one or two of the boys had come in with some shy girls and they soon retreated to the far side of the table. Bear and my mother arrived together and she hovered in the doorway a moment to acknowledge the resulting flutter of excitement as if she expected it. Mrs Peter laughed girlishly.

"You look nice Madame!" Mrs Peter exclaimed.

With so many eyes looking her over my mother was overcome with embarrassment, which was unusual and she compensated for it by lifting her skirt just above her ankles and breaking into a comic dance step.

"Well," she said. "Once again our horns we blow." Mrs Peter clapped her hands.

"Ah, the hostess," proclaimed Peter in his smooth, polished fashion. "We have been waiting for you," and Mrs Peter began to lavish her with the same exuberance as she had me.

Reeling from the wafts of perfume and the cleavage, my mother levered herself upright. "My God - you don't leave much to the imagination do you?" she remarked, casting a further critical eye over the dress. "You'll have to watch your wife tonight - I can tell by the look in her eye she is up to something," she addressed Peter with a wink who then turned to his wife and smiled with only one side of his mouth. I was glad to see Bear and that he was unaccompanied. As I hoped, he came across and sat beside me.

"Now what are you all going to drink?" demanded the hostess, rubbing her hands together in a business-like fashion. "Come on Bear, give me a hand - you're good at this, the party's begun you know. *"Monsieur Gobeaux, que buvez-vous?"* Still in the same breath she enlightened everyone. "Spider and Bunny have gone to meet their girls at the station."

My mother was in her element as she passed round the glasses, sticking her little finger in the air. It was still a manifestation of her initial stage-fright. She was uncomfortable in the tight dress and was trying consciously or unconsciously, to divert attention towards a feature of which she was proud. She was aware she had beautiful hands. They were small and supple and her nicely shaped nails were well-cared for - her one vanity being to have them professionally manicured and lacquered a bright, shiny red. I loved my mother's gentle hands, no practical task involving the most intricate or exacting detail ever beyond their capabilities. She also used her hands expressively in conversation, another vestige of her Latin origins she was pleased to point out. Her gestures became infectious and the guests, pleasantly roused, posed their fingers in imitation. Flattered by the attention, she played along with the audience. "My legs aren't bad either!" she said, kicking up her skirt with her heels at the back while setting her full lips into an affected rosebud.

I sipped my sherry which made my shoulders ache. My mother had Bear pouring the drinks and I watched the company gradually assemble. Most of the boys were entitled to uniform of some description. Many had been in the forces before volunteering for this special work. Even if it was only battledress they had smartened it up, especially to wear open-neck with collar and tie. Those without wore their best clothes like Monsieur Gobeaux. Some of the girls were pretty and appropriately dressed for the occasion and one or two were unexpected as my mother had warned. Not only were they all unknown but a couple of strange men turned up too. It encouraged pretentious behaviour which suited perfectly the continental manners and the mood of the moment.

It became noisier and jollier as second glasses of aperitif were passed round. The atmosphere thick with cigarette smoke and the affluent whiff of cigars was also heady with scent. 'Californian Poppy' and 'Evening in Paris' rivalled Worth and Lanvin. The room was hot and the company relaxed. The wine loosened tongues and everyone was chatting, sometimes in English, sometimes in French and sometimes both together and above the din I could often hear my mother - loud, excited and managing. Only the officers had yet to come. Bear, his duties over, was back at my side and I was glad.

It was almost on the point of nine o'clock and the waiters in short white jackets and black bows at their necks were busy on the scene. The smells they introduced were mouthwatering. Dinner was just about to be announced when the door opened quietly and Bunny walked in with his girlfriend Eve in front of him. "Hello Mrs Rae," she greeted my mother with surprising calm considering she was the focus of such gawping interest. "Is it too early to wish you all a happy Christmas?" The company as one raised their glasses. "Happy Christmas, *Joyeux Noël!*" was the unanimous cry but my mother's eyes were beyond the newcomers and on the tall figure behind them who had come in alone. She looked up at him anxiously and darted her gaze back to Eve for an explanation.

"Oh there's been a silly mix-up I'm afraid, Dora isn't coming," she said, looking towards Spider to make his own excuse. My mother was unable to contain her disappointment. Apart from wanting a good crowd she wished her favourite more than anyone to have a girl for the evening, to have his mind deflected from his lost love. Her expression changed radically. She appeared to have been gripped by an attack of acute pain.

"Oh-oh-oh!" she groaned, loud and long, overcome by the sherry and devoid of any tact. "What a sh-a-me!" she lamented. "Poor old Spider - never mind, I'll be your girl tonight," she said, rapidly regaining her spirits to offset any dampening effect. All eyes were on the forlorn yet dignified figure, but with the repose of most distinctive men, used to being noticed without the need to attract attention, he smiled and promptly went over and kissed her hand.

"This is my pleasure," he said playfully as he swept her a bow.

Aside from this moment the arrival of these three had been impressive. Here were the real soldiers in their uniforms and what a difference it made! Unmistakably officers - lieutenants - their only distinguishing mark the regimental colours on their collars - they stood out from the rest but with no standoffishness. And like all foreign troops now on the side of the Allies they had the name of their own country embroidered in red at the top of their sleeves. Stirred by some of the same feeling as my mother on opening the door on these two shining characters, I was relieved they had come at last. My mother fluttered round, giving them drinks.

"Get this down," she urged gaily. "You'll feel better after that."

I watched Spider with new interest for his bonhomie in handling my mother and because he seemed quite unperturbed by this latest rebuff. He was completely different from my first impression - spirited, youthful and handsome. And without the habit of many tall men, of slightly bowing their shoulders to bring them more in line with the average, he carried himself as if proud of his height with no military stiffness. If anything, he appeared even taller dressed as a soldier and the bright overhead light shining on his hair showed it up as being quite fair. Was it imagination, or did I catch a glimpse of glamorous Mrs Peter edging her way over in his direction and the Mistletoe? With everyone here at last and Bear at my side to keep me from feeling left out, I began to thrill to the evening ahead.

Without any warning my mother suddenly darted from the room with such a thrust forward that hardly anyone noticed until an icy draught blew in through the open door. I went after her, fearing the worst, that her dress had finally split at the seams. But it was soon evident that she had shot through the front door too, flinging it wide. I hovered in the freezing hall wondering whether to go in search, when she was back again.

"I've just been next door to invite the younger girl round to partner Spider - but she's out. I've left a message for her to come later," she said breathing deeply to recover her wind.

Dinner was announced. The disorder that ensued as everyone tried to find a place next to their respective partner soon resolved itself. The harsh overhead lights were switched off and we all admired the centre-piece of holly and candles which had been lit up to take their place. The table glowed temptingly making it seem smaller and all of us closer together. Spider offered me the empty chair beside him but I refused on the excuse of wishing to be next to Robin. Bear was on my other side.

"There's an empty chair next to you," I said to make conversation.

"I have invited a girl to come for the party - but I was not seeing her since a very long time," Bear replied, "since the beginning of the war" he added.

"She is not coming?" I asked.

"I think it is not possible - it is too late," he said giving a cursory glance at his watch.

"It is coincidence, but she also has the name – Marjorie."

"Really - it isn't all that common either. My mother said you are engaged, that you hope to marry her - perhaps? No?" I ventured cautiously. He inhaled deeply and coughed into his chest, knocking his mouth nervously with his fist.

"It is possible - but I am not sure if I will recognise her today and until I see her again - I am not sure of marriage - you understand?" he said in a jokey manner. Turning from me, he smoothed his moustache down on either side of his top lip. Unsure how to follow on, I waited.

"Do you write to each other?" I began again cautiously. "Do you and your - friend send each other letters?"

"Yes, we shall meet again very soon - I am sure of it, perhaps at the New Year. I cannot forget her," he confided shyly.

"That is nice, then maybe I shall see her before I go back."

We continued our slow and stilted conversation as we ate our soup and gradually I found myself coming to share his idiom of broken English. It seemed to come naturally after a few days at home.

"It is nice soup, you like it?" I said.

"Yes, very nice soup, how you say it - in English?"

"I think it is called giblet soup, in French you call it?".

He cocked his head on one side and shrugged his shoulders in the very disconcerting manner of foreigners, appearing to be either nonplussed or faintly suspicious.

"I know it not, this soup, I cannot recognise it - I think we do not have this soup in Belgium," he chuckled.

"We only have it at Christmas, you do not have Christmas in Belgium?"

"Oh yes," he assured me. "We have Christmas but not like you in this country - just the family - not a lot of celebration. In Belgium we have a party for the New Year - you know."

I had soon discovered when talking to foreigners that it came instinctively to exaggerate one's facial expression. Every word was meticulously pronounced, questions were always sparing and to the point. Sometimes it was difficult to keep track of an argument but then one had a built-in excuse. Abstract thought, wit and irony alas, were often sadly lost. The occasion was certainly not proving as lonely as I had imagined.

"Tomorrow you will have another party?" I suggested and Bear looked puzzled. The lunch in town had not once been referred to since the first evening and it was bothering me.

"Tomorrow" he repeated. "Where is it - in this house?"

"No - you are going to have Christmas dinner again in a restaurant, aren't you?"

"Ah," he granted. "Yes - and you will come also?"

"Well, I'm not sure - will the boys take their girlfriends?" If some girls were going perhaps I might not feel so out of place.

"Surely - but not me I have no girlfriend here."

"And me, I have no boyfriend," I said, feeling rather forward.

"OK," he said, giving a decisive nod, "We shall go together?"

"That would be nice," I responded, wondering how that would fit in with any pre-existing arrangement.

The feast went on for a long time. People seemed generally slow and too engrossed in one another to want to hurry things. They were lighting cigarettes in between courses and some couples had their arms around each other and were brazenly flirting. I was aware of my mother only when the Christmas pudding was set down in front of her. Having made it herself, she had also expressed the wish to serve it herself.

"It's made with real eggs," she declared proudly, "None of that *oeuf-poudre* or whatever you call it," she added, taking delight in showing off the English custom of first setting it flaming with brandy.

***

It was obvious that my mother had eaten and drunk too much. She rose from the table nearly at midnight and had to be helped to an armchair. The waiters came in to clear the table with such deftness and speed that it hardly seemed worth their time and trouble to have set it up in the first place. This stage of the party left a feeling of anti-climax as I surveyed most of the company slumped back too. Finally, after removing the table from the room, we were left with the large open space my mother and I had striven for that afternoon.

With the coffee the lights went on again, revealing and too bright. Some couples cowered together to avoid exposure. Robin and I exchanged a few amusing observations. Others left the room ostensibly to freshen up. The rest recovered slowly. "Who's-in-charge-of-the-music?" my mother called out, her words slurred together. No-one moved and she looked languidly around for her *Chef de musique*. "Ah, there you are, come on Jefke, you're in charge of the music - don't forget. The night is young, we want to dance, bring on the dancing girls," she ordered tipsily. Jefke sat tight a little obstinately until, judging for himself that enough people had regained the necessary energy, he moved towards the radiogram. After some discordant oscillations and whistles which, with the coffee, had a markedly astringent effect, he tuned into Victor Sylvester and his Dance band. The perfect tempo lifted everyone on to their feet. My mother got Monsieur Gobeaux out of his chair and they managed about two rounds of the floor, to everyone's amusement, before flopping back even more helpless than before. The dashing officer and the glamorous lady circled the room also attracting attention for they made a handsome couple. The khaki uniform was the perfect foil for the sleek black dress. Upholding one pale arm, his left hand on the small of her naked back, he sometimes offered her further support by placing both his arms around her when, for an instant, her head flopped on to his chest. But it was soon apparent that this was not the tender embrace it appeared for Mrs Peter was swaying uncontrollably and her partner was having difficulty keeping her on her feet.

I wanted to dance. My trips to Sussex had given me a taste for it. I studied the few recumbent males to judge my chances and came to the conclusion they were slim indeed. Bear was still busy, and with so many attractive females around, no-one would want to dance with a fifteen-year-old save out of politeness; and the dinner, the wine and the new intoxication of the music had put paid to all courtesies for this night. It was only too obvious that each one was out for himself from now on.

There had been a new influx of party guests soon after the table was cleared. Both girls had arrived from next door with some other neighbours getting wind of events. The new arrivals were out to be picked up and our men looked them over with impertinence and audacity. Some even changed partners. The dancing and the flirtation continued with accomplished abandon until all wireless programmes closed down. This left such a misplaced silence that Jefke moved quickly in search of some suitable records to take their place. The first he chose was a Rumba. It came as a shock, causing most people to fool around. Bear came in and we almost fell into each other's arms, not to Rumba properly but to perform an easy step that rocked from side to side. It needed little effort. We were much of a size and as the records were changed so we kept going. Several times we tried the more formal steps but always reverted to our own uncomplicated movement. It did not matter as many couples, unable to recognise the tempo, kept going as best as they could.

The night wore on, we rested. Spider came over and sat beside me; then suddenly, Mrs Peter collapsed in the middle of the floor. She soon came round and her husband and some others coaxed her upstairs. My mother, relishing the emergency to regain some of her own self-importance, followed them up with a glass of water. The dancing resumed to the hum of enquiring chatter when she was back, still clutching her glass of water.

Shaking her head in a mixture of bewilderment and disbelief she informed us.

"I don't know what's going on up there, two or three in with her and she completely naked on the bed! Captain Peter pushed me out of the door."

Someone put on a Strauss waltz and the couples still going welcomed the change of mood and moved in closer, cheek to cheek. It had its effect on my mother too. Decidedly maudlin under its influence - doubtless her private thoughts having caught up with her once more - she made towards Bunny. Ruefully she interrupted his dance with Eve. "God bless you my boy," she said, reaching to kiss his cheek. He put one arm around her shoulder and drew her into the partnership. The three of them circled precariously round until she caught sight of Spider in the chair next to mine. She came over to him. "God bless you my boy," she began a second time, her expression saddening as she bent to kiss him. "Let's hope - next Christmas it will be your own mother kissing you - in your own home." Tears welled in her eyes as she stroked his face with a motherly caress.

"God bless you dear - you are such brave men. God bless you Spider." Touched by her concern, he got up and gently guided her into his seat where she slumped back against the cushions. With one elbow resting on the arm of the chair to support her head she began to weep. He pulled a handkerchief from his pocket and placed it in her hand, at the same time trying to comfort her as one might an unhappy child. Soon she had fallen into a little doze. He saw that I had noticed and smiled, a brief, understanding smile which made me pleasantly self-aware, and I smiled back without embarrassment.

With the first unmistakable bars of the Blue Danube striking up, Spider invited me to dance. I rose up eagerly for I considered the waltz an easy step. He placed his hand under my elbow and steered me towards an empty space on the floor. Suddenly daunted as I took my place opposite the tallest man I had ever known, I stood on tiptoe as we joined the other revolving couples, my arms and legs stretched to capacity. We made an awkward beginning. Not wishing to appear too inept, I concentrated hard, following the steps stiffly and repeating to myself - one, two three, one two three as we started off. We seemed to have a fairly steady rhythm evolving between us when my partner toppled all my gathering self-confidence by declaring, "Mademoiselle Marjorie- this evening you are very beautiful."

Beautiful was an adjective he had used several times during the last couple of days to describe different effects. I had noticed that many of the boys once they learnt a new English word often tended to over-use it, its meaning not always exact. For these reasons his compliment did not make quite the impact it might have done although it shook me enough to lose count so that I had to improvise a hurried back-step to synchronise my feet with his.

"Everyone looks nice tonight," I remarked, shooting a wary glance up at his face only to find him watching me intently which brought a warmth to my cheeks.

"Yes," he agreed, "But - not every one is — beautiful," he persisted. Thrown completely off balance I stumbled against him but once more I was able to retrieve my self in order to continue. I had never sorted out the most gracious way of acknowledging a compliment. In any case it was difficult to know whether he was praising me as a child or flattering me as a young woman. Unused to such gallantry at the best of times, I pretended not to have heard him the second time, whereupon he tried again as if I had misunderstood.

"You are beautiful - with the flowers - and the beautiful dress." The shift of emphasis was more acceptable and I glowed within.

"My mother made my dress," I said. As we turned the corner once more I caught sight of the other capricious couples and, remembering my partner's facetiousness towards Mrs Peter the first evening at dinner, I flushed as it occurred to me that what he was after now was a similar caper with the daughter of the house. No match for such games I missed the steps and stopped.

"May we begin again?" I suggested. "Of course," he agreed and allowed me, with some amusement, to position myself in the best way for starting off again with my left foot. When I was ready I looked up and our eyes met for a second which sparked off a new sensation in the pit of my stomach. On the next bar I slid my foot back into the waltz and hoped he realised I was only fifteen.

"Are you happy?" he enquired solicitously after another turn of the room.

"Yes, thank you," I replied and, hoping to forestall any more personal remarks, decided to remind him of his vague responsibility to another even though she had not turned up as arranged. "I'm sorry your girlfriend couldn't come," I said pleasantly, and he dismissed it with a shrug.

"It is nothing - I am responsible, she is not my girlfriend," he said. Slightly disconcerted I nevertheless endeavoured to keep the one, two, three going in my head each time I was about to falter. He continued, "I forgot to telephone her to - *fixer de façon definitive* the engagement - you understand? and I think she is angry against me but it is not important".

"Didn't you want her to come?"

"Ye-s," he replied as if he cared neither way. "I have seen her -er, perhaps on three occasions. It is ok I have made my peace with her," he assured me. "She is - just a girl, a friend - that is all. You understand? of no importance," he stressed with a chuckle. Very confused, I decided it might be better not to try and talk. I needed all my wits about me to avoid tripping over his long feet. One, two, three repeated itself rhythmically in my head as we continued in silence until, with more concentrated effort, he got the feel of manoeuvering a partner of only five foot two. Soon there was firm directing contact and I began to move easily. He had the waltz under his control and I had found my second wind.

We circled the floor with renewed confidence. Our pace quickened into an old fashioned waltz more in keeping with the music. This was fun; my skirt billowed around me. We seemed to be dancing at a faster rate than anyone else and as we flashed past those sitting down, I was overcome by a strong temptation to show off, with a more exaggerated turn of my head, a more energetic twist to my body. The Blue Danube came to an end and we rested, panting and smiling, eager to continue.

With tireless energy the party revolved around us. The gramophone throbbed out waltzes, quicksteps - the same ones over again. Shoulder straps had to be secured, hairstyles became unhitched and periodically the dancers refreshed themselves with the remains of the wine or whatever was left. This was like no party I had ever known either in reality or my wildest dreams. My partner was holding me firmly now so that I could move freely with no danger of stumbling. It was marvellous, romantic! I had never danced like this before and each step, as it became more involuntary, more deliberate and impeccably placed, allowed me to express my joy with the whole of my body. Effortless, light as air, we spiralled and cornered, precisely timed. Finally, the music crescendoed into a fast gallop and as we whirled back into the room from the Vienna Woods my partner spun me round lifting me off my feet before we stopped.

"Phew!" I cried out, breathless, though radiant with excitement. "Oh, I must sit down, oh, oh," I sighed loudly, "I am so tired." I am not sure whether Spider took my hand or whether he had never let it go but the next moment he was leading me by the hand towards an armchair on its own in the corner.

"Once upon a time - I - dance with a young girl and we fall on the floor - after the waltz. It was in a very big chamber with much important people," he recounted with an expansive gesture of his free arm. Glad of an excuse to release my feelings, I burst out laughing as I pictured the formidable creature beside me in a heap on the floor with some luckless, enviable female. We exchanged another swift glance and broke into a new fit of giggles. Tears streamed down my cheeks but once we reached the chair I recovered rapidly as, without any ado, he sat down and guided me on to his lap. From sheer exhaustion I relaxed over his knees.

"So you like to dance?" he remarked, teasingly running his index finger down the length of my profile. My fatigue disappeared instantly, his action having sent a marked but not unpleasant shiver through my body.

"Yes, I do," I said, abruptly turning from him.

"As well as - to kiss?" he teased gently with a little half-turn of his head. In my confusion at being reminded of the kissing game my hair brushed his face. I blushed and sat upright. He stroked my cheek.

"You are warm," he said.

"Yes, what's the time?" I asked urgently. He released his arm from around me to consult his watch which was loose on his wrist so that the face had fallen to the inside. He crooked his elbow and held his head steady to focus his eyes. In repose his expression was kind, serene and proud, and behind the glasses he wore all the time, there were two big, solemn brown eyes. His thin, well-defined nose - in profile, was large and faintly Roman. Yes, I told myself, it was a nice, straight nose.

"It is towards four hours," he announced after placing the watch to his ear to check it was still going.

"Gracious," I exclaimed.

"Yes," he said, glancing sideways and smiling, "it is already tomorrow."

His smile was generous, displaying good, even teeth.

"I ought to go to bed," I said, searching out my mother who was still in the same chair, dead to the world, and made a move towards getting up.

"Are you - *Mademoiselle_Cendrillon?*" he enquired wistfully, coaxing me back against him and my spine tingled as his arm slid around my waist.

There was not much evidence of the party breaking up and, encouraged by his reference to the fairytale, I rested my head on his shoulder, my fatigue having returned at the discovery of the time.

"You know the story of Cinderella?" I asked. "You have it in Belgium?"

"But - of course!"

"Do you really?"

"She was a little girl with very small feet." At that moment my left foot disconcertingly raised itself in its silver shoe. "Just like this one" he nodded, pursing his lips in approval. I was vexed with my wayward foot and covered it modestly with my skirt. We remained some while without speaking, then he made one or two more complimentary references to my appearance which I was now beginning to enjoy. He spoke carefully, having to pause often to search for the correct English words which he pronounced with the French intonation and he raised his voice questioningly at the end of each sentence as if wanting constant re-assurance that I understood what he said. I was soon beguiled by his accent. It reminded me of Charles Boyer.

"Do you like the name Spider?" I asked.

"It is your mother who has given to me this name."

"I know, but it isn't very nice," I said crinkling up my nose.

"No?" he asked in surprise.

"I - don't think so. What is your real name?"

"Jean - perhaps you prefer that one?"

"It's nicer than Spider. May I call you Jean?"

"If you wish," he replied but fearful of sounding impertinent I added quickly.

"Jean what?" He obviously didn't understand.

"What is that - Jean what?" he asked as if he had been dealt a rather pleasant blow.

"I mean," I said, trying to extricate myself, "What is your other name - like - um - *Monsieur Quelque Chose?*" The French suddenly offered itself as I realised he might not understand the word surname. His eyes twinkled.

"So you know French?" he declared in surprise. I felt myself blush again.

"I have got four names but not one of them is *Quelque* or *Chose*," he teased, affecting a serious expression and very slowly his mouth widened into a smile as I became aware of his arm tightening very slightly around my body. I felt very much a little girl and of only about six years old.

"You know this - er - Monsieur *Quelque Chose*," he repeated. "What is that in English?" he enquired as if it might be veiled in some obscure Anglicism.

"Oh - it just means - something, nothing really but I meant what is your last name like mine is Rae?" I tried again. He digested this slowly while regarding me over the top of his glasses which had slipped down his nose. His features were very mobile, especially his eyes which seemed to light up from within when he was animated. Before they looked solemn, now they had a soft, mischievous expression. He also raised his eyebrows as he spoke in a mixture of surprise and enquiry, pushing up furrows across his high, broad and rounded forehead; and around the turned up corners of his mouth were fine hairline creases - the legacy of a laughing nature.

I was still uncertain how he was regarding me. At times he seemed to be assuming the role of a small boy as a complement. He was nevertheless very much a man and, as my eyes strayed to the uniform, the gold stars, the white flashes on his collar - the cachet of his crack cavalry regiment - I knew the response aroused in me was not one of pure and simple childishness. I observed his free arm resting on the chair which at times he moved to push his glasses more firmly on his nose, to smooth out a wrinkle in my dress or to tap his fingers absent-mindedly along the arm of the chair. His arms, like his legs, were long and as I inadvertently fingered the shiny brass buttons on his cuff, I noticed - surprisingly in the middle of winter - the remains of a suntan on his wrist. In between the middle fingers of his long lean hand there was the slight staining of nicotine.

Do you know - I have got the most important letters in the world with my name and *prénom?*" he began again. "I am very proud to have the letters J.C. with my name."

"Do you mean initials that J.C. are your initials? Why are they important?"

"J.C. are the een-eesh-shalls," he tried to imitate me. "Of *Jésus Christ, Jules César* and - the most important Jean Cornez!" he joked proudly.

"Ah!" I exclaimed, sounding like my mother, "Cornez is your surname!"

We were both amused by this artless exchange and broke into a new, though more restrained, fit of laughing. As we continued sitting together, comfortably talking only when moved and smiling a lot, I was conscious of him continually watching me. Sensing, vainly perhaps, that he was a little admiring, a little fascinated, and whereas normally I would have been helpless with embarrassment to be sitting in such a compromising position with a comparative stranger, I was surprised at the ease I felt at this moment. Pleasantly tired within the security of his encompassing arm, I gradually relaxed so that my brow came to rest against his cheek.

All the lights had been switched off long ago so that it was only the soft glow of the Christmas tree which dispelled the darkness, but there was still music and some couples, slower and more intimately united, were still circling the room. Almost unbelievably the doorbell rang and my mother began to stir. It rang again more insistently followed by a loud knock. Now was my chance to escape but I had lost all desire. The knock had jerked my mother from oblivion and she shot automatically from her chair immediately wide awake. She moved shakily into the hall where there was a commotion.

"Of course, yes bring him in," I heard her. Feeling the rush of cold air keenly after her sleep she retreated backwards into the drawing room shivering and yawning, followed by a very subdued Bear dishevelled, equally cold, escorted by two helmeted policemen. She turned to the constables and offered them drinks, her sleep of the last couple of hours having completely upset her sense of time and occasion. They readily accepted, looking prepared to prolong their business if necessary.

"What did you say - where did you find him?" she asked as if this sort of thing happened every day. Bear, a little shamefaced, gingerly made for the nearest empty chair, shook himself like a wet dog and sat down. He closed his eyes and lay back, his head uneasily supported on one side. One of the policemen took it upon himself to be chief spokesman.

"It was like this, Mam," he began. "We saw him going down the road not exactly walking in a straight line, if you get my meaning." My mother, who only appeared to be half-listening, handed them each a glass of whisky. The men looked dazzled. "Thank you Mam, cheers! Happy Christmas everyone," they chorused.

"Going down the road?" queried my mother, attempting to pull herself together. "At this time of night?" The other constable cleared his throat and uncovered his wristwatch.

"Uhm - morning would be a better word. It's ten minutes to five on Christmas morning - I see you are having a party!" he exclaimed, his eyes roving round the room.

"Yes, a Christmas party," she said.

There were just one or two who were completely oblivious to this interruption. My mother was pretty much herself again and the chief, self-assured and cocky, continued his narrative. "As I was saying - when this - er - gentleman spotted us, he turned round and walked into your rear entrance. Naturally, it was our business, like I mean, we were not to know he lived here, if you'll pardon my saying so." He cast a glance at the prone figure of Bear to reassure himself he could talk freely. "To say the least he was behaving in a most suspicious manner - a little worse for drink if I may make so bold Mam." My mother followed the story showing progressively more interest. She chuckled nervously.

"Why was he outside? He should have been in here with the others." The constable was saving his punchline.

"It was like this, Mam - when we came up to him in the yard to discover his intent so to speak, he took off the lid of one of the dustbins and proceeded to climb in!"

"Inside the dustbin?" gasped my mother. "Yes Mam." At that moment Bear lurched forward from the chair looking alarmingly pale and retraced his steps from the room. My mother followed him anxiously, just in time to see him grab the bannisters for support as he attempted to climb the stairs. He turned and waved cheerily. *"Il faut pendre le fou dehors - il faut pendre – le..."* his words tailed off.

She came back. "Poor old Bear. I suppose he had a drop too much. It's rotten, he was hoping his old flame would turn up tonight, but what the devil was he doing up the road? I thought my daughter was keeping him company." At that very moment her eyes alighted on me and her expression changed to one of total disbelief. "Oh," she let out, "You're there - still up at this time of night!"

The policemen continued, "We had a tussle with him, I can tell you. He was determined to get in this 'ere dustbin, said no-one wanted him like, that he was the fool who would have to be put - away or such like." His words fell on my mother's almost deaf ears. She looked to be having difficulty in believing her eyes too.

"Poor devil - I see - the only one without a girl," she remarked slowly.

"A foreign gentleman, isn't he?"

"Yes. Belgian. They're all Belgians here," she informed him proudly, gazing on our armchair.

"Wouldn't have thought you would've had any trouble with this lot," she added with new reservation.

"You'll have to excuse us, Madam. We have to be so careful these days, what with spies and enemy agents, and this house has a reputation," he added pointedly.

"Spies! Enemy agents! Don't make me laugh!" she chuckled.

"Anyone acting like he was is bound to arouse suspicion - then when he said he lived here we had to make quite sure." But my mother was not listening. This intrusion had nevertheless started to break up the party. Most of the guests were preparing to leave and, finally, having seen the policemen out, my mother came straight over to where I was cosily reposing on the lap of her favourite. She stood by rubbing her arms and smiling. The room was getting cold. Just one or two, their arms entwined, remained and it was difficult to distinguish them in the gloom.

"Come on Darling," she coaxed. "I thought you had gone up ages ago with Robin and Mr. Gobbo. I don't know what people will think letting you stay up all night! It's Christmas Day!" Her tongue clicked mild reproof against the roof of her mouth.

"It is already Christmas since a long time - since five hours" my partner asserted, gently easing me up on my feet. He stood up too. All friendly and comfortable, connection between myself and this exciting stranger was severed. I was cold also, and unbelievably tired. My mother stretched out her hand to me.

"Come on darling, it's much too late for you to be up. It's been a very special occasion," she said guiltily. I took one hesitant step away to separate myself even further from my companion for the best part of the night and started to shiver. I turned back to look up in his face.

"Happy Christmas J.C." I said sleepily.

"Happy Christmas *Mam'selle Cendrillon*" he echoed and stooped to kiss my cheek. I closed my eyes and swayed. My mother took over. She put her arm around me and led me into the hall. I leant against her as we attempted to climb the stairs, whereupon Jean Cornez came to my assistance. He lifted me up in his arms like a child and carried me right up to the top.

I unpinned the crushed flowers from my hair, stepped out of my party dress, now pressed into long creases by the warmth and proximity of our two bodies - the trappings of the night which had made me beautiful - and, after the longest day of my life, fell into the sweetest and deepest sleep as soon as my head was on the pillow.

***

I was crawling out of the sea - a vast ocean - touched by the sky on all sides and, as the water shallowed, I could see pebbles glistening. Dragged from my fingers by the tide, ebbing and flowing as if to music, I straightened myself upright to walk up the beach and the heat of the sun warmed my naked body so that the moisture evaporated, leaving my skin glowing and golden. The stones had disappeared and each step I took along the fine, silvery sand needed less effort until I was bounding along six feet high in the air. Tireless with no sense of gravity! Newborn but with none of the helplessness of infancy! Warmed through to the marrow of my bones by some indescribable force for good! I awoke, my bedroom full of daylight, my very vivid dream deceiving me into believing that Spring had come all of a sudden and my intuition telling me that life would never be the same again. Overnight I had undergone a transformation and today was like no Christmas Day I had ever known before. My mother seemed aware of the change and was standing in my room surveying me as if I was suddenly a stranger to her too. She was regarding me with a concentration that could only be described as mystified pride. For a moment I was rapturously happy, eager to get up.

"It's nearly one o'clock, she said, handing me an envelope which had come in the post. "Dinner won't be until about three."

"Aren't I going out?" I asked her anxiously. "What shall I wear?" She sat down on the bed and spoke comfortingly.

"Spider gave me strict instructions not to wake you. Anyway, you didn't really want to go - did you?" I lay back on the pillow, not sufficiently alert to feel much reaction but I knew it was not relief.

"Did you tell him that? Have they gone?"

"I didn't say anything. They were late getting up and in their usual rush. The table was booked for one o'clock."

I stuck my finger under a loose part of the envelope and opened the long awaited letter in its guise of a Christmas card with a certain happy anticipation. The very brief message was nothing like I had built up in my expectation.

Hope you are having a good time in London. Happy Xmas. Yours T.

Tears pricked the backs of my eyes and as I dressed all I could think of was writing to Cicely to share with her the fact of spending practically all night on the lap of a Belgian Cavalry Officer! Relishing the fact that she would find it hard to believe, as I did myself today, though some little string deep inside me tensed when I remembered his eyes and his smile, for me alone.

Downstairs the house was painfully quiet. Every Belgian save Monsieur Gobeaux had forsaken it, as if it was their intention that the Patronne should have her home to herself and family on Christmas Day. I made for the drawing room in which the cold light of day bestowed a decided disenchantment where there had indeed been a touch of magic last night. A pall of tobacco smoke hung low. Californian Poppy alone lingered with the stench of sour wine to permeate the fibres of the furnishings. The curtains had not been drawn apart with the usual meticulousness. A match had only just been put to the fire and the profuse smoke from the damp wood and sooty coal added to the general rankness that stressed so depressingly the morning after. It was chilly in this large room and I hugged myself while taking stock of the disorder. No-one had been in to tidy up. The chair on which I and my attentive dancing partner had spent most of the small hours was exactly as we had left it, still with the indentations in the cushions made by the combined weight of our two bodies. My skin tightened as I sat down, placing one arm along the arm of the chair exactly as he had done.

It was difficult to believe so many people had been dancing here less than twelve hours before. With the house so silent and deserted I began to feel keenly my exclusion from the lunch engagement. I wondered why it had been their decision to go without me in the end. Were they disappointed with me? Was he disappointed? This mattered now, yet he had been so friendly, so gentle and attentive, or was it just the affectionate concern one might have for a child? What about Bear - and my arrangement with him? Was no-one taking me seriously, just humouring me at the moment? I felt miserable and rejected like the smeary wine glasses lying around, nostalgic for the party which was so evidently over.

My mother came in to see to the fire.

"Wasn't it marvellous last night?" she said. "I think they all enjoyed themselves. The dinner wasn't bad either - considering. You did look sweet, sitting on Spider's lap."

"Do you think he liked me?" I responded on impulse.

"He couldn't take his eyes off you, I know, I watched him." Her reply was more gratifying than I expected, though she was prone to read too much into things. Anyway she had been asleep for most of the time, so what could she really know? But I clung to her words, hoping that she might have been quite a penetrating observer in the little she had seen.

"I expect they went off early, especially - to go without me," I remarked trying not to be concerned.

"It wasn't all that early, no - I think Spider realises you are nice little girl and that your place is with me on Christmas Day - not up in town with a lot of men and their fancy women. He's a nice man and you did look lovely, even though you are my own daughter, so fresh and wholesome compared with some of the beauties we had in here last night. No - I think you touched something in Spider and he wanted to look after you. They're a bit sentimental - after all it is Christmas. I daresay you and Robin remind them of their own homes and families."

The records were still lying where Jefke had sorted through them on the floor. I made a start at tidying up until I caught sight of myself in one of the mirrors where I lingered to gaze at my reflection. The part of me that was already a woman recognised that, to most people, I was still a child and could not expect to be treated as anything else. I pulled my green jumper down over my skirt in disgust to give a more flattening effect. And yet, I was almost positive that my dancing partner had intended stirring something within me and knew that I was aware of it even if, today, he vested it with no further importance in his eagerness to go off with his friends. I realised in some exciting way he was connected with my dream, as if he had been there to see me naked. The prospect of eventually confronting him again caused me to go hot and cold. Half of me was relieved he had gone out.

My mother gave the fire a good poke and tipped the contents of the ashtrays onto it. She began to plump the cushions.

"It was rather a good party - I suppose," I understated.

"It's the best party I've ever known. The dancing did the carpet good, gave it a damn good beating," she said, straightening the hearthrug. "I should put on your pink corduroy later. Christmas Day is worth more than a jumper and skirt."

"It was practically dawn when we went to bed," I sighed with a certain satisfaction.

"When did the rest finally go?"

"There weren't many left when we went up - who was still here?" my mother asked.

"It was difficult to tell. They were sitting around making love," I replied innocently.

"What!" she exclaimed. "I hope not! Not as far gone as that surely!"

"How do you mean? The lights were out, you couldn't tell who was who."

She broke into a knowing chuckle. "You'd better not say that in front of the boys - it means something else to them."

"What does?"

She cleared her throat uneasily. "Making love." She said.

"What does it mean to them?"

"Use your imagination, Ducky. Something far stronger than kissing - some of them are pretty hot stuff you know." A new prickling of excitement surged through me. Until this moment making love had meant only kissing, cuddling, any display of apparent affection no matter how innocuous or arbitrary. Fred Astaire and Ginger Rogers talked of making love in their films.

"Did Bear go too?" I asked.

"Yes, as far as I know," she replied. "I nearly died seeing him come in between those two policemen - he looked just like something they had picked off the rubbish dump." She threw back her head and laughed "And in a way they had, hadn't they? I felt a bit sorry for the poor chap. Christmas and the only one without a girl, although there were enough to go round in the end, even without you." Warmth filtered into my cheeks.

"I didn't think Spider would be on his own - what happened?"

"Dora apparently didn't come because he had forgotten to ring her - so he said - to make the engagement – hmm," she smirked. "I've a feeling he didn't want her here - and as for the little thing from next door, she never got a look in after all!"

"What's she like - Dora?"

"Never seen her."

"Is he keen on her?"

"Not as far as I know - though I daresay she wishes he was. Weren't they nice policemen?"

During lunch my mother relived every moment of the party to compare details with Monsieur Gobeaux.

"You should have seen me dancing with Mr Gobbo," she informed my uncle who had come for the day. "*N'est-ce pas Monsieur Gobeaux? Nous avons dancé ensemble hier soir?*" While he, delighted to be the sole centre of attention, laughed too, his cloudy grey eyes glistening almost rakishly.

"What about the Peters?" I asked, "Did they go also, with the others?"

"No - she's upstairs, properly under the weather today. Captain Peter's gone off on his own - in a bit of a huff I think."

"Because of her?"

"Mr Gobbo thinks it's more to do with Bunny and Spider - taking the rise out of him or something." Hearing his name, Monsieur Gobeaux interrupted, asking for an explanation. My mother swiftly translated what she had said and he responded. They both shrugged and exchanged a grimace of perplexity. "He said," she interpreted, "It's all very childish but apparently they didn't introduce Peter as Captain to some people they met yesterday and this morning he refused to shake hands with them." She shook her head pityingly. "Spider thinks he's a fraud."

I was somehow relieved that Mrs Peter had not gone too as I pictured the boys sitting around their table in the Hungaria. Even though I had not the slightest idea of what the place was like my imagination was vivid. I heard Gypsy music, I sensed gaiety, girls - laughing, flirting. Not Mrs Dinah, but perhaps Dora with whom he had made his peace.

***

I must have fallen into a deep sleep on the settee beside the fire. When I awoke the lights were on, the blackout curtains drawn and I was immediately aware of someone standing over me. I rubbed my eyes and it was a few sleepy

144

seconds before I came alive to the tall, uniformed Lieutenant smiling down on me and something like a small electric shock convulsed my stomach.

"Happy Christmas - one more time," he greeted me as he shook my hand.

"Oh! Happy Christmas," I responded, taken too much by surprise to feel awkward or shy. I combed my fingers through my hair and smoothed down my clothes in what I hoped was one composing action. Still in his outdoor clothes he produced a long flat box and offered it to me with both hands.

"This is a present for you, for you and your brother," he specified with smiling eyes. I was excited as he placed the box squarely on my lap.

"Thank you - it's very kind of you," I replied, eagerly unwrapping the game of Monopoly my mother had mentioned. "Thank you very much."

"You know this one?" he asked quizzically.

"Yes, though I have only played it once, it's a good game - goes on for a long time."
"It is necessary that - you will teach it to me - yes?"

"Yes, I will," I readily agreed.

He pulled up the long stool before the fire and sat astride it directly facing me, first separating his trench coat at the vent down the back to bring round to cover his knees. His face was flushed from the effect of coming in to a warm room from the cold and his collar was turned up at the neck. I imagined he would look much the same astride a horse. He was not wearing breeches or spurs but looked very dashing nonetheless. We were alone in the room.

"How are you today, Mam'selle Marjorie?"

"Very well thank you," I said politely, from habit. He removed the box from my knees and placed it on the floor before fixing me with his whole concentration. I retreated back against the cushions. "I was very tired but I've had a sleep and now I feel better," I offered quickly.

"*Pauvre Petite Mam'selle Cinderella,*" he commiserated and patted my knee. "It is too late, that night for you!" I watched his arms resting on his thighs as he played with his cap and found it unbelievable that last night they had been around me.

"Did you have a nice lunch?" I asked.

"So-so, not so good as the dinner in here the last evening," he replied, placing his cap on the stool behind him.

"Was it a nice restaurant?"

He raised his eyebrows. "Yes - *comme-çi comme ça* you know."

"Did all the boys go with you?" I could not bring myself to ask about Dora today, not even as the nameless entity she had been last night.

"Yes, many of them - and I am happy that you were sleeping," he declared, massaging his hands together. "I - I cannot sleep much - this night," he added with some sort of implication.

"Is it cold outside?"

"Oh yes," he replied with conviction, reaching across to touch my cheek.

"Ooh - it's freezing," I gasped, hunching myself to disguise the very pleasant shiver that shot through me.

"You are very warm," he said and turned to hold up both hands to the fire. He sat relaxed, watching the glowing coals before picking out some lumps from the scuttle to pile on top. He wiped his fingers on the hearthrug afterwards. A contented smile flickered on the corners of his mouth.

"Are you alone - or did some others come back too?"

He turned to me slowly, mischief sparkling through his glasses. "Did you hope it will be your friend - *Monsieur Quelque chose?*" I looked away quickly, positively tingling with enchantment.

Jean, a very pure name I thought, and much nicer than Spider; I made up my mind to think of him always as Jean - it helped to prolong the magic and to establish, in my mind, a relationship that was special. He stretched out his long legs until they touched the settee on which I was sitting, trapping me inside them. He covered his knees with his hands and, tapping his fingers reflectively, allowed his eyes to stray upwards over my body to my face where they rested, seeming to flirt with my shy glances. After a few seconds he moistened his lips, pointed them into a satisfied pout and rose from the stool. "I go to put my overcoat upstairs," he said.

My mother made some tea and carried it into the drawing room. "Just you is it?" she remarked, addressing Spider as he came back into the room and sat beside me on the settee. He smelt pleasantly of soap. He had also brushed his hair smoothly in place with either oil or water. Today he looked so much younger and I noticed, when his back was turned, that his ears stuck out at the sides of his head, giving him a pronounced boyish look from behind. The fire was beginning to burn brightly and he picked up the rules of the new game to study before reading them aloud, mispronouncing some of the words on purpose I suspected to give us an excuse to laugh.

"Well, what did you think of it?" my mother enquired, pouring tea for the three of us. It was easy to see she was still in a state of elation after the previous night and Spider was pleased to play along with her.

"The dinner at the restaurant or the party, the last evening?" he teased, eyeing me obliquely.

"Oh, the party of course," she stressed.

He took time licking his lips before declaring: *"un succéss fou!"*

"You've said it - and we all know what happened to the *fou!* Poor old Bear - never for the life of me did I think he would take it literally." She laughed and Spider laughed too.

"I think everyone is - enjoying himself very much - and some people too much," he declared, blinking collusively at me.

My mother reacted predictably. "Do you mean me?" she challenged him haughtily, her smile soon breaking through.

"I did not say that," he said and placing his finger against his lips to stifle his giggles, he glanced my way and winked.

"I don't think I misbehaved myself," responded my mother, thoroughly enjoying the attention if a little wary of his implication.

"No Madame - you were very nice, very gentle - you were kissing all the boys and you were saying - 'God bless you!'" he said.

"I was?" she gasped, having no recollection of it herself. "No Spider - tell me the truth, was I really kissing everybody?" she asked him almost proudly.

"Your mother was very nice," he said leaning towards me for corroboration and he placed his hand over mine and gave it a squeeze. I could only smile and nod in silent conspiracy. Nor did his action escape my mother's notice though she pretended it had, neither did her assumption of indifference disguise her secret pleasure.

"Do you know?" she spoke out. "I can't remember that at all - I can remember Dinah fainting and someone taking her upstairs. I can even remember dancing with old Gobbo. Was I as far gone as all that? Doing things I don't remember. What did I do Spider, tell me again?"

"You were under the Mistletoe with somebody." The custom of kissing under the Mistletoe had captured his imagination. "Perhaps it was Monsieur Gobeaux - I am not sure. The light was not good." He knew he could make such a flagrant assertion for there was never a hint of impropriety between the two *chefs de ménage*. Good friends, certainly, at times quite mischievously equivocal in their connivance of something more, when she would call him Anatole and he would respond with Letitzia; but on the one hand my mother would have been horrified to think they were taken seriously and on the other, Monsieur Gobeaux hardly had the energy to conduct his daily affairs, let alone the capacity for philandering. Spider observed her with fascination and, goaded by her expression of horror so transparently masking her delight, continued, "And you were saying to this man - darling, dear I am not sure —"

"What to old Gobbo?" she interjected. "Oh stop it - you naughty boy," But when she saw him nearly doubled over she guessed the joke and remarked with relief. "Now I know you are only pulling my leg," and she collapsed into a fit of laughter bringing tears to her eyes which caused her to relapse into a bout of coughing. "Oh dear, it's a good thing you tell me these things to my face and don't make them up behind my back - at least I hope you don't," she added, taking off her pince-nez which she placed in her lap while laying back to wipe her eyes. "Oh dear," she sighed, polishing her glasses on the hem of her skirt, before clipping them back on her nose. "Spider, you are a devil!" she cried, fluttering her eyelids to adjust her vision, and to me she said: "He's a devil - I'm warning you."

Since he had squeezed my hand, a sign I took to mean he was going to continue from where we had left things last night, my involvement with my dancing partner surged from the amorphousness of dreams to his substantial presence at my side, his arm relaxed against mine, and my eyes were drawn once more to the accoutrements of his uniform, the stars on his collar, the pockets, cuffs and lapels, all cut slightly differently from his English counterpart's. And I noticed with some indescribable feminine contentment that his shirt was made of soft material, like Vyella, that looked comfortable around his neck.

Bunny arrived back from the Hungaria with Bear, flushed and inebriated, and on discovering his friend ahead of him, seemed at once surprised and vexed.

"Qu'est-ce qui se passe ici - hein?" he asked, casting a bleary glance around him. The two friends had a spirited exchange in French, almost verging on a skirmish for Bunny, in his wrath, raised both fists in an attempt to spar with Spider before relegating him to the position of a small boy having to answer for his behaviour.

"Tu t'amuse bien?" Bunny derided, tapping his foot. I was alarmed but my mother was smiling and winked at us as Bunny turned to list to her in halting English each item of contention.

"Madame," he began calmly, pointing to Spider "This man is my friend, you think so? He is coming to the restaurant - you understand? It is comfortable, the food is good."

He paused to revise his opinion. "Not so good - *ça va* - there is beautiful music."

I could imagine Gypsy violins.

"I find some *gentilles amies* for him," – Dora, I wondered? *"Et enfin!* When he sees my back - he is going." He shrugged disarmingly and, with a mystified expression, pointed accusingly with his thumb at Spider.

"Poor Bunny," my mother humoured him simpishly, "You did your best," and he edged up to her and placed an arm around her shoulder, pretending to seek solace. He stared contentiously at his fellow officer.

"Enfant gaté, enfant mal élevé!" he taunted. "I am too good as a friend for him," he sulked with an expression that made me shudder. After a moment he was quieter and surveyed both Spider and I with a puzzled frown which rapidly softened. He leant towards me and whispered, "Mam'selle Marjorie you must excuse me - of course," he began and shook his head. "Of course Mam'selle - he is coming back to you," he suggested kindly.

My mother was excited at having her favourites together. She was also warming to Bear since the episode in the dustbin. Spurred on by their form, more to cause a stir than a reprimand, she suddenly coughed loudly to draw their attention.

"Hum, hum my daughter says - you were all making love down here last night!"

I was absolutely stunned, utterly unable to understand why she should make such an accusation after her pronounced warning to me. The men seemed to take it philosophically and Bunny took in a deep breath which he released in a repressed whistle as he surveyed the ceiling.

"Mayala!" he exclaimed.

"Which people were making love?" Spider enquired, his glasses two black circles of amazement. I broke out into a rash of goose pimples.

"I only meant kissing," I said, trying to pass it over. "I told her making love is something quite different, *n'est-ce-pas?*" she said and nudged Bunny. The men were not embarrassed. They cleared their throats in an understanding fashion and, much to my increasing horror, she continued her interpretations.

"You see in French to make love is something quite different - in English it is more indefinite, it can mean anything from a mild kiss to - well, you know what," she sniffed.

"Oh Mummy!" I said, "don't keep on about it."

"My darling, the French have such a lovely way of putting things - to make love," she sighed. "Just imagine the coarse ugly expressions the English use to describe the same thing." The boys remained silent then Bunny spoke out in his customary inscrutable manner so it was hard to tell whether he was serious.

"Sometimes the two are going together, kissing first - and after? C'est la vie - it is the life, no?"

"He means - one thing leads to the other," she said frowning over the top of her glasses. "You should know," she added accusingly.

I shivered at the prospect of what she might be tempted to say next. Spider took hold of my hand and clasped it firmly.

"I think you understand this very – well," he said as if to put an end to the matter and I was convinced that an empathy existed between us.

Jean Cornez   Marjorie

My Mother, Monsieur Gobeaux (bottom right) and members of
the Belgian Resistance

PART SIX

THE TWELVE DAYS OF CHRISTMAS

Many wartime winters were hard and this one was no exception. On waking in the mornings my bedroom was icy, all the more keenly felt after the central heating we had become accustomed to in Winchester. The condensation from my sleeping breath was frozen into a layer of rime on the window-panes, beautifully etched into starry leaf patterns that scraped away under my fingernails. Outside, the garden appeared remote like the fairy-tale kingdom of the Snow Queen, indistinct, veiled in a cold grey mist: the trees festooned in thick hoarfrost. The light faded early in the afternoons and sometimes the lamps were alight all day. Home with the fire banked brightly with logs, to eke out the coal, was a cosy place to be and the drawing room, particularly the fireside, was the pivot around which our existence was to spin dizzily during the next few days. No-one ventured out unless they had to and then it was chiefly the boys in a quick dash to the Underground en route for the more artificial, and often spurious, warmth of the city.

Christmas came close to the weekend making an extra long holiday and during the day, much to mine and my brother's delight, Spider did not share his compatriot's enthusiasm for getting out and about. To everyone's surprise he stayed close to the family. We taught him to play monopoly and he in turn, with much laughter, showed us card tricks and amusing games with pencil and paper. Sometimes these sessions, under the watchful and contented gaze of our mother, lasted so long that she was often prompted to draw the attention of Monsieur Gobeaux to the trio happily engrossed around the card table set-up especially. He would look up and nod benevolently, intimating that Spider, not so far removed from childhood himself, was benefiting from our companionship, forgetting himself and his tribulations at last.

The evenings, however, never lost their enchantment. When the boys came back, and Eve was there again with Bunny, the girls from next door would be invited in and there would be more dancing to the wireless and gramophone. Whenever there were one or two girls present it was a good enough excuse to push back the furniture and switch on the radiogram. It prolonged the festivities and came as a welcome break from the exacting work in which the boys were daily immersed, although at this moment the 'Job' could not have been further from anyone's mind, most of all mine, ignorant of the whole business. 'Sand in my shoes', 'I don't want to set the world on fire' and 'Blue Moon' trilled and reverberated from the 'Home and Forces' programme until it was time for the old stand-bys to take over. And after the first flush of intoxication had worn off I found to my ever-intensifying delight that I was dancing with the same partner the whole of the time.

Mrs Peter, looking pale and ethereal, emerged from her room and ventured downstairs on the day after Boxing Day. She was dressed in a black jersey and skirt which, with the single row of pearls at her neck, heightened her fragility. Her lank blonde hair fell naturally on her shoulders. She could easily have been taken for another schoolgirl. Her entry into the room was welcomed by a hail of cheers and the boys began to tease her for the over-indulgence which had caused her ignominious retirement from the party, and she lisped and giggled out protestations accusing each man in turn of having mixed her drinks. She revelled in the new gaiety in the evenings. I thought she looked defenceless and beautiful, sensing in the re-emergence of this highly popular figure a threat to the dream which was rapidly becoming reality.

I need not have worried, for nothing changed. With the company as a whole my tall partner played hard-to-get, while literally dancing attendance on me with tirelessness and solicitude. I was being swept off my feet with every change of tempo. At the same time the difference in height never made for an easy partnership. Spider was competent in leading me through the various steps but it was only in the waltz that we ever achieved any degree of accomplishment. With my hand clasped in his, my body gently embraced as we moved closely in rhythm around the room, my imagination ran riot. I could see him holding many girls in his arms to have become so adept and self-assured in his manipulation of me. Nothing escaped my scrutiny from the gold threads in his hair, picking up the light, down over his uniform to his shoes. My eyes lingered on his face with the well-defined muscles at the corner of his jaw, and more particularly, since it was on their level, the long neck and the prominent Adam's apple above the knot in his woollen tie. Bewitched by his accent, I liked to watch his lips as he spoke, faltering slightly when he stumbled over the difficult Anglo-Saxon aspirates or outlined the open throaty vowels as he groped for the unfamiliar words. But it was even more thrilling when he made the occasional remark in French for then his native words flowed confidently, crisp and precise. It was exciting too to feel his leg against mine or when he pressed me close as we progressed around the room. His attentions were never furtive. He seemed happy in my company and pleased to show it, and when we sat together I welcomed it as a gesture of affection when he placed his arm around me or held my hand. The music, the rhythm of the dance, had been a perfect foil for my girlish reserve, allowing me to express my joy naturally so that, I hoped, some of my own embryonic charms might gradually unfold for him. But as the relationship developed, so a more disquieting element presented itself.

It was not difficult for anyone to see that some kind of mutual attraction was blossoming between the tallest man and the youngest girl and if my mother was only able to keep half her customary vigilance it could not have escaped her notice either. Hourly as I grew more at ease, more poised, ever more enchanted that someone of his own free will should wish to court my friendship, so the foundation of my pride and happiness in becoming more public also appeared to become more precarious.

Mrs Peter came and sat beside me during a break in the dancing.

"You are a pretty little girl," she said. Her compliment was unexpected and I modestly shook my head. "You must be careful," she added and I looked at her. She turned away and played with the gold ring on her left hand. "It is late - you are tired?" she asked.

"Not really," I replied.

"Sometimes you look like a young lady," she said, and I felt myself somewhat dubiously complimented a second time. I smiled at Mrs Peter in an appeal for her not to be too severe. "But I know you are at school," she said.

"I hate looking too childish," I confessed.

"But you must not be growing up too much, too fast!" she protested.

"I suppose not," I said coolly.

"You are not tired?" she began again and I fancied detecting an expression of sadness in the clear Flemish eyes and the blonde hair fluffed into curls since the morning. She seemed to be having difficulty. "Not tired - after all the dancing?"

"A bit," I said. "I like dancing."

"But - people will have a bad idea," she said.

I found her remark baffling. What bad idea would people have? Unless the monopoly of one partner was brazen - or selfish? Then was not my partner equally to blame. I hung my head as if she had seen beyond the childish innocence to some underlying streak of hitherto unrecognised wantonness. She began to probe cautiously.

"You like to dance with - Spider?"

"Yes," I replied, determined to give nothing away.

"You look funny," she said, and raising both hands she slowly lifted one higher while pointedly lowering the other. I did not reply, conceding with secret pride the truth in her observation. "What about the other boys? They are nice - you do not like to dance with them?"

"Sometimes."

"You prefer - Spider?"

"I suppose I do."

"He is a big man, you are a little girl, you must be careful. He thinks you are not a little girl."

"He can see I am small," I replied in some confusion believing her to be still referring to my height.

I chewed over this cryptic conversation. If I was behaving badly then, of course, Spider was responsible - unless, there was something behind his attentions I had not seen. The vision of a web somewhere threatened. After all men were still an unknown quantity. Boys my age who sidled admiring glances I could deal with but a man was different - and a Continental at that - with their reputation of being 'hot stuff' as my mother had so graphically put it, was frightening. Yet there was nothing that had given me any anxious moment until now. Although my Spider has so far treated me only with kindness I had enough discrimination to realise that he was not thinking of me as a child purely and simply. One would not hold a child quite in the way he was holding me, close, intimately enough to send exquisite shivers the length of my body. I wondered if the habit he had of moistening his lips and pursing them together was a lascivious gesture as if licking his lips in anticipation of his prey. But despite these misgivings, I was moving unremittingly towards the tormenting, yet rapturous, condition of helpless infatuation. Craving that the object of my romantic fantasy must feel exactly the same intensity of commitment, and being almost sure he did; yet the tantalising want of complete certainty only heightened the excitement and aggravated the anguish. I had been under the spell before but this time it was more compelling both by its unexpectedness and the absolute lack of contrivance necessary to sustain it. The fact that we both lived in the same house meant we were separated only at night which gave my feelings little time to subside before we were together again and which, in spite of the doubts, was never long enough to put a break on their ever-gathering intensity.

The most remarkable thing was that my mother had never expressed disapproval. Such a stickler for decorum, as far as her children were concerned, she would have been the first to warn me of the pitfalls in the association if she had considered it at all suspect. Yet while watching us together, the secret, almost informed expression on her face showed she was not oblivious of developments either. And the fact of not having schemed towards their beginning probably gave her all the more satisfaction.

***

"You like him - don't you?" she challenged me on the Sunday after Christmas Day. It was Marie's day off and I was helping with the washing up.

"Who?" I asked. I could not have admitted my feelings to anyone.

"Go on, you know very well who I mean," she replied, adding with a chuckle, "The only one you ever dance with."

"I-I'm not sure," I lied.

"You don't have to pretend to me - it's written all over your face and his. Oh, go on with you - do I have to spell everything out? You know very well what's happening. Only this morning I overhead him say to Bunny - *"Je suis fou de cette petite fille!"*

162

"What does that mean?"

"It means literally - he's crazy on you." A warm, pleasurable feeling welled in the pit of my stomach though I did wonder over the significance of his remark.

"He is too old," I despaired with a sigh.

The kettle began to boil and my mother made the coffee in the way Monsieur Gobeaux had taught her on his arrival, which was to pour boiling water on to the coffee grounds contained in a woollen bag hanging inside the pot. The bag had been knitted like a sock and had felted up with use so that it took a long time for the water to filter through. The boys teased my mother that if she had used an old worn sock it would make it taste even better! While waiting for this lengthy procedure to be completed I saw Tony's letter on the dresser where I had cast it aside on Christmas Day. I read it through, trying to decipher some hidden message and decided to write back. Although it was nothing like I had hoped for, I would be going back to him after the holiday. This was only a passing transgression.

Instead of going to have coffee with the rest I took my writing things along to the dining room and settled myself before the remains of the fire where I would be alone and warm. I wrote to Cicely first, the only one on whom I could unburden a little of my euphoria. I gave her more than a hint of the marvellous time I was having, describing in some detail the new house full of the most intriguing foreigners, and I told her about the party. I even dared single out one for special mention, but only by his nickname, thus keeping the relationship quite impersonal and, therefore, I hoped, credible.

I was glad of time by myself and soon back into the flow of writing, I began my letter to Tony. Remembering my previous passion for the blonde boy, I began my letter in affectionate terms. I almost began to look forward to the afternoons on the farm when the spring came. Yet as I sat there, channelling my sentiments into words which I knew in my heart were nothing more to do with him, the door of the dining room quietly opened and there was the one responsible. The one I was having the greatest difficulty in separating from my thoughts, with his head already inside the room, was peering across at me.

"You are in here!" he remarked in surprise and came right on in, closing the door behind him. He walked over to where I was sitting and I became nervous.

The whole house was enveloped in its usual after Sunday dinner lethargy. All who were in were firmly enclosed behind the door of the drawing room the other side of the hall. I had never been so isolated, so completely alone with this man before, and I remembered the dissembled warning of Mrs Peter. It flashed through my mind that he may well have the wrong idea. I had shown I was easily persuaded. He had gained my confidence and now he had come to carry his plan a stage further. I looked from the closed door to his face. I did not know how to interpret his expression. His eyes mesmerised me and his lips were forming into their enigmatic pout. He could have been smiling to himself in triumph. I sat motionless and my mother's phrases bombarded me from the air: 'the girl from next door was too nice', 'some of them are pretty hot stuff'. What should I do?

"Mar-jor-ie," he spoke out, giving each syllable equal stress. It was the first time he had used my Christian name alone. My heart pounded in my rib-cage. If only I could swoon - but that might be even more dangerous! I closed my writing case with a loud snap, a conscious appeal for help and stood up, feeling less trapped. I took a step back from him.

"Stay one minute," he begged, widening his eyes and placing one finger against his lips which seemed to indicate he meant truly one minute and his purpose in searching me out was quite harmless. He appeared so tall and omnipotent as well as strangely vulnerable standing before me that I was touched by his insistence of needing something - from me! He placed his hands on my arms and looked into my eyes with a directness that was both artless and appealing.

"You know," he said smiling, rooting me where I stood and losing no time, for I believe he sensed my agitation in the rigidity of my arms under his grasp, he uttered softly and with an air of mild disbelief that I had not already guessed it for myself, "I love you." These highly sublime words which I believe I had been waiting to hear since the day I was born nevertheless came as a profound shock. All the nerves in my body went numb before the most acute prickling sensation sparked them back to life. I looked down and the pattern on the carpet appeared to writhe and come towards me as I searched for some appropriate response.

"I have been so happy with you the last days," he continued, and he lowered his head to gaze up into my face.

"Do my words make you angry? No," he both asked and answered. I nodded and smiled wanly. *"Chérie?"* he spoke tenderly, straightening himself up and taking my face in his hands, he directed it towards him. "I like that you smile at me," he said, stretching my cheeks with his thumbs to encourage me to smile again. "I love also your eyes - and - your *timidité*, the way you are a little afraid of me but, I hope - you will soon lose that silly fear - I do not wish to be an ogre for you! You are afraid now?" I could only nod my head and attempt another meek smile for him.

Still clasping me near, he stroked the hair from my brow and stood with heavy eyelids contemplating my eyes, my nose and my mouth. Here his gaze settled. I regarded his face too, his eyes and his lips, serious, tremulous and then as they parted slightly they came forward on to mine. I closed my eyes and swayed and my head, seeming to have detached itself from my body, floated away into the air. *"Je t'aime,"* he said again, as if by saying it in French he could put more feeling into his declaration. With one hand keeping me close, he removed his glasses with the other before kissing me again, drawing me to him in his arms. I went utterly limp in giving myself up to him, frail and pliable, and if at that moment he had carried me off for whatever evil purpose he might have been plotting I would have been powerless to stop him.

He let me slip from his grasp like a tiny animal he had held captive and now wished to reassure himself he had not harmed or frightened in the process.

"Are you happy?" he enquired as he took my hand and led me from the dining room.

"Yes," I replied, knowing that never in my life before had I been so unexpectedly and so overwhelmingly happy.

***

During the five days of festivities practically everyone had put the war out of mind though no-one could completely escape its priorities. There was the everlasting blackout needing regular and meticulous application and there were the interminable French broadcasts to be nightly endured. But as it was superimposed by the excitement and glamour of Christmas, so we all came down to earth as it encroached with all its urgency on the routine of this unusual household.

The Christmas holiday was over. The girls went home and the boys returned to school. Ironically the uniforms were put away and the soldiers were dressed again in civilian clothes. Everything appeared to have returned to normal. Spider became Jean.

For me, however, the situation was far from regular. A man twelve years older had declared his love for me! Jean, a stranger, a foreigner, about whom I knew nothing save that he had recently suffered, physically and emotionally, and was now in training for some highly-secret work, monopolised my brain twenty-four hours a day. He was the chief character of my daydreams and the Prince of night, unveiling the sweetest facets of my sub-conscious. In the ordinary way I would have half-expected the enchantment of Christmas to have proved itself a five-day wonder, but when I discovered the attentions of my new admirer had not dried up with the holiday, that he had not laid aside his love with his uniform, I found it almost unbelievable and moved about as if under some kind of spell.

***

Two or three days later an event took place ousting any lingering lethargy attaching to the holiday. Roll departed for good or, as my mother whispered to me, he had 'left on a mission'. Since Christmas, showing marked signs of stress when he emerged for meals, he had been almost continually closeted with 'the piano' in the dining room. With most of the Boys on the eve of departure there was little change in either their demeanour or their daily routine. Just as on any morning of the week, they would bid good-bye to my mother; perhaps there would be a shade more warmth in the handshake, an *'Adieu'* rather than *'au revoir'* plus a vague promise to see her again one day and they were gone just as if they intended returning at the end of the day. Since another boy usually came immediately to fill the vacant bed it was a few days before it registered that one of their number had gone.

At certain times, Monsieur Gobeaux, knowing one of his charges was about to leave, became keyed up and extra-attentive to the cryptic announcements of the BBC which were indeed secret messages. Though how they worked or why they should be relevant to our establishment I had no clue. On this occasion, the phrase to alert him had prompted him to draw the attention of my mother, and pointing his walking stick at the drawn curtains it seemed to suggest some unknown quantity presiding outside on whom rested the last word. Although zero hour might well be at hand for the whole operation to be successfully accomplished, everything depended on the whim of this mysterious, nocturnal force. This was my first intimation that the work going on here could be on an international scale for the sky beyond the window-panes suggested a vast and boundless enterprise. The evening before Roll left, his compatriots took him out for a farewell celebration, perhaps hoping to relax him a little. It was a manifest example of their marvellous *esprit de corps*. The next day Pierre arrived to begin his term of trial under the watchful, if somewhat lax, eye of Monsieur Gobeaux.

I had always known that the purpose of the Belgians in our house was secret but now my curiosity was aroused and I wondered if my mother was really held in the strict confidence she liked to make out. By the way she spoke so arbitrarily of British Intelligence, the Secret Service, MI5 or was it 6, and all seemingly in the same breath, convinced me only of her own muddled grasp of the exercise. So although my appetite for a little private detective work had been whetted, it was not my chief preoccupation. Alone with my mother as we pursued our womanly roles of clearing up after Christmas, I was able to assess the whole unreal situation. I found myself dwelling more and more on the broken engagement. Even now my feelings for Jean were by no means free from underlying doubt.

"Tell me about the girl he was going to marry," I urged my mother.

"I don't know much about her - except that she was Scottish and lived in Brussels before the war."

"Did he love her very much - do you think?"

"Yes - he wouldn't have been so sad," she said this with a certain amount of feeling, perhaps seeing again as when he first arrived.

"Do you think he still does?"

She smiled knowingly. "I know he wouldn't say anything he didn't mean and he told me he was getting over it."

"When did he say that?" I asked in some relief.

"Oh, once," she replied mysteriously.

"When? Before or after I came home?" I suggested.

"Don't worry, I know what's going on between you. He's told me that too." She blurted out, "He's a changed man since you've been here - you've no need to worry."

"What did he say - when did he tell you?"
She composed herself to reveal her secret which she seemed to think would come as a surprise to me. "I feel a bit mean telling you, because he asked me not to say anything yet, but everyone knows." She comforted herself. "It's obvious - just seeing the two of you together."

"What did he say?" I repeated.

"He told me - he fell under your spell from the first moment he set eyes on you, before that even - from your photograph and he asked me whether I had any objections."

Having taken my mother into his confidence, it would seem that his intentions towards me were unlikely to be other than honourable unless he was a very devious character indeed. A warm feeling of reassurance flooded over me. "Why doesn't he want you to tell me?"

"Because he wants to wait and see how you feel about him - he doesn't want me to sway you."

"When did he tell you?"

"Ooh - it must've been Christmas Day, or Boxing Day perhaps."

"What did you say?"

"What could I say? You both looked so happy. I was pleased for him and pleased for you. I knew how you felt! It was decent of him to ask me and I said I didn't mind. How could I mind?"

"Weren't you surprised?"

"Not really. I have lived too long to be surprised by anything. Actually, I was delighted. It was as if he was telling me he had fallen in love with me myself." She raised her head and smiled with the satisfaction of someone at least ten years younger.

"Oh well, I wonder if he really means it," I suggested to draw her further.

"My dear, darling daughter - if you can't see it, I'm sorry for you. Anyway you are just as smitten as he is." There was a taut pause while I nursed deliciously to myself what had taken place in the dining room. That at least remained private; we had been quite alone.

"How can you love someone very much and then stop loving them to love someone else?" I asked as I thought of Tony.

"I wouldn't say it's been all that sudden. He's had a few months to get over it. You're a funny little girl, he's crazy on you and you're crazy on him and you're worried. There are some who'd give anything to be in your shoes."

"You don't think I'm too young?' I asked. "Mrs Peter thinks I am."

"What's it to do with her? She's a married woman, why should she worry? You know what I think? She's jealous - anyway he isn't the first is he? You've already had one boyfriend," she pointed out defiantly.

"But he's the same age as me. Isn't Spider too old?"

"He doesn't think so. Your father was ten years older than me."

"You don't think it's all a bit disgraceful?"

"Disgraceful!" she exclaimed. "What's disgraceful about it? I am your mother and very properly he has been perfectly honest and open. He is a dear, sweet boy and I love him." Another moment of silence passed before I spoke again.

"What didn't she like about him?"

"I know - that's puzzled me, I expect the truth was she'd met someone else. She was young, hadn't seen him for a couple of years - well." She shrugged. "It's a good job she had."

"I wish I'd never met him," I lied. "It's going to be awful when I go back."

Things came to a head around the New Year. The rocky sympathy between Monsieur Gobeaux and Peter, foundering a long time underground, finally cracked on the surface, the latter appearing to win some sort of dubious revenge. The two senior men were arguing together in the drawing room with raised voices. Monsieur Gobeaux came into the hall to call my mother in. *"Dîtes Madame! Dîtes Madame!"*

After a short interval she and Peter left the room to resume their argument in the kitchen, in English. I hovered in the hall to listen.

"I don't care what you both think - I trust him," declared my mother. "He has told me he is in love and it's unlikely he would take advantage of the girl he loves in her own home in front of her own mother!"

"Love, Mrs Rae, you speak of love - it is wartime, surely you, as a woman of the world, can appreciate the state of mind of a young man in wartime. He is doing a dangerous job, not knowing if in six months time he will be dead. Your daughter is an agreeable child, infatuated with an officer who dances with her, flirts with her. Oh Mrs Rae - you know yourself the sort of girls who come here - it is too easy for him."

"I beg your pardon," responded my mother, taking great offence. "The girls next door are perfectly respectable. This is an innocent little flirtation, if you like, that I don't suppose will come to anything - but let's suffer it in the open while it burns itself out. It can do no harm to anyone. You are taking things too seriously; after all she will soon be going back to school."

There was a hollow laugh from Peter. "I've met young men like him before - arrogant and conceited, cannot even address a superior officer with courtesy - and selfish! In six months he will not even remember your daughter's name," he said over his shoulder as he left the room.

"And it's your wife who's put you up to saying all this because-" retorted my mother bitingly but her sentence was abruptly cut off as she closed the door on him.

The situation having at last penetrated his narrow world of *le bureau, l'estomac* and *les nouvelles* Monsieur Gobeaux was angry that the affair had been developing under his nose, obviously annoyed with himself for not having seen its beginnings to 'nip it in the bud' and irritated beyond reason that it had needed Peter to bring it to his notice. The idea that one of his own countrymen, especially one who having won his way into the intimate family circle, should give him cause for reproach, annoyed him even more.

He did not know any of the boys well enough or for long enough to form an opinion of their moral integrity. And even if he had, with his markedly old-fashioned outlook, a love-affair between a man and a schoolgirl with the best will in the world went very much against his better judgement. Frequently suspicious of everything going on around him - believing people took advantage of his age and his inability to speak English, Monsieur Gobeaux thought it time we all came back to reality. Heedful of the welfare of Mrs Rae and her children, as much as his boys and anything threatening their harmonious co-existence, he acted spontaneously, breathlessly and officiously. First, seeing it his duty to offer me a caution through my mother, he set down the hard facts as they appeared to him. Secondly, he arranged to have a private talk with Jean, to whom he referred to as *un type flagrant egoïste* as soon as he came in. *"C'est la guerre!"* he exploded with passion, and laying back with both hands folded over his heart, he lingered like this for several seconds. Finally, he closed his eyes and allowed his head to fall forward on to his chest as if he had that moment been dealt the finishing stroke.

"He was white with rage, his hands were shaking - I thought he was going to have another haemorrhage at any minute," my mother reported to me after catching a glimpse of Jean being ushered into Monsieur Gobeaux's room for his dressing down. "I was quite alarmed. I told him I wasn't worried - that Jean had laid his cards on the table from the beginning but he wouldn't listen. *Honi soit qui mal y pense!* I told him."

Normally shy of my mother sharing my emotional life, I was glad of her support now and heartened, too that Jean was taking things responsibly enough to keep her informed. That most of the storm was passing over him, leaving him unrepentant protected me from the aftermath of Monsieur Gobeaux's wrath. Later Jean told me what had passed between them.

"He said you are a very young girl, of good family, and that I must not be flirting with you," he recounted, furrows across his brow. I thought he was telling me that he must comply with this instruction. He caressed my cheek. "He does not know me - he thinks I want - only to play with you, to be not - very serious and that is bad for you," he added, but I could tell by the candour in his eyes, the sincerity of his smile, that whatever existed between us could not be ended thus easily. Yet I was also pleased to think there was someone interested in my well-being, making a protest on my behalf. It was reassuring.

"What did you say?"

"The truth. I say to him that I am serious - that I love you," he said taking hold of my hand and looking into my eyes. "Monsieur Gobeaux is a kind old gentleman, he thinks of you and your mother - and he wishes that - no upsetting things will arrive." Never tired of hearing him declare his love for me, I did not consider anything beyond it. *"Chérie,"* he comforted, "You must not worry, it is something only between you and me - and perhaps your mother, a little," he conceded with a smile and kissing me. "Nobody can know how we feel and there will be - no upsetting things," he said, and placing an arm around my shoulder he lifted his glasses to study me at close range. "You are happy?"

"Yes," I nodded.

"That is important - and me, I am very happy," He replied.

***

The boys had the weekends to themselves. There was no school on Saturday and Sunday and they usually spent their free time away from the house, in dance halls, clubs, cinemas and the like. While the more serious amongst them took the opportunity of seeing what they could of London while they had the chance, even though most historic buildings were boarded over as an air-raid precaution and all moveable treasures had been packed off to the safety of the provinces. Jean said he would be at home. He had bought a camera and wanted to take some photographs. I looked forward with delight to the second weekend of the holiday.

I found him alone in the drawing room when I came downstairs, lying full length on the floor on his stomach, his face set in a grimace of concentration, his glasses by his side.

To see his long, slim body stretched out in such an unfamiliar position gave me a mild pleasurable shock. He was wearing becoming, casual clothes - white linen trousers, a khaki pullover and a pair of rope-soled espadrilles on his bare feet. I watched him a moment, puzzling to myself what he was doing and my stomach screwed itself into an exquisite knot of awe. From that moment all my misgivings resolved themselves. I was quite safe, there was no black Spider's web, no dubious schemes and my feelings crystallised into the realisation that never in my life had I felt so intensely about anyone.

"Bonjour," I said.

"Bonjour Chérie," he replied, beckoning me over. "Come, I lose a part of my camera and my eyes are not good enough to find it." I knelt on the floor beside him and soon spotted the small black roller eluding him under the settee. As I reached for it he gently pulled me down into his arms. "I must say thank you to your beautiful eyes," he said kissing each one and my newly discovered passion prompted me to put my arms around his neck and draw him to me so that we kissed again on the lips longer than before. "Who has taught you to kiss like that? I adore you," he whispered and I could not answer for it had been my own instinctive reaction to coming upon my love so unexpectedly. For one daring moment we lay on the floor in each other's arms.
"You have a boyfriend?" he asked cautiously as we sat up, quickly arranging ourselves to look less discreditable should anyone come in the room.

"Well, yes, I did have," I owned.

"And you were loving him?"

"I - I thought I did."

"And now - you are not sure?" he said, kissing me long and tenderly once more. "I ask myself - what is arriving to change your mind?" A knowing smile flickered on his lips.

"I think I know that reason - am I correct?" he asked.

"I don't know what you think," I said.

"That both of us - we did not know we would meet each other, that something has happened which we did not believe was possible?"

"Perhaps," I conceded.

"And your boyfriend, what age has he?"

"The same as me."

"And he loves you?"

"He said he did - once."

"Of course he did, he could not help himself. And he has taught you to kiss? Poor little boyfriend. You know - I am sorry for him - but he was clever, I think you were a good student," he added, enveloping me in his arms again before picking up the film and its wrappings to put on the table.

"Am I too young?" I confronted him.

"Am I too old?" he shrugged. "What does it matter, the age? We are old - or, young enough to feel - in love - the age is of no importance," and looking at me askance pretending not to know he asked, "What age have you?"

"I'm nearly sixteen," I told him, feeling more like a six-year-old with him towering beside me.

"You have already fifteen years?" he teased and I frowned, feigning offence. "Come," he offered impulsively. "I will take you out of this house - away from all the eyes watching us - where will you like to go? Perhaps to the cinema? We shall see your mother."

"That would be lovely - let's look in the paper." I rushed to fetch *the Daily Mail* and, like two children, we spread it on the floor and squatted over it on all fours.

Having agreed on what to see - 'Suspicion' with Cary Grant and Joan Fonteyn he said, "I must go to put on some better clothes because - I cannot go out like this," he indicated, plucking at his pullover. "How you say it - looking like a - vagabond?"

"A tramp," I corrected him with a chuckle. For anyone less like a tramp was hard to envisage. Although not dressed suitably for going out on a winter's day, he was clean, upright and quite startlingly attractive in such informal clothes, more so than his pin-stripe suit. "Will you wear your uniform?" I ventured plaintively, and he seized on my request as if it was the crux of the matter.

"Aha! So you prefer the uniform?" he said, pressing his finger on the tip of my nose. "Surely, if you wish that."

As we had not yet been out of the house together, the excursion promised to be doubly exciting and as we went down the road together, warmly wrapped against the weather, I was impressed all over again by his stature and his rank and I fancied myself walking alongside such a dashing figure, for quite a few turned for a second look. In having him so completely to myself, the daylight and fresh air seemed to add another dimension to our relationship. He did not walk like my preconceived idea of a soldier. There was no rigid military bearing, rather did he amble along, his short sight and his longish strides giving more an impression of an endearing absent-mindedness. While we were in the side streets, he placed his arm protectively around my shoulder but when we turned into the busy Parade we had to draw apart as he was often saluting or being saluted. It was less cosy but I was still warmed by pride and a feeling of importance.

Once inside the Tube train I was astonished to discover that he knew most of the Ministry of Information Jingles by heart. That 'Billy Brown of London Town' was his favourite and that he could recite all his little admonitory slogans word perfect - 'Coughs and Sneezes spread diseases, Trap the germs in your handkerchief' and 'I trust you'll pardon my correction - that stuff is there for your protection' à propos the netting on the carriage windows which travellers loved to try and peel off.

The people on the seat opposite, as charmed as I was smiled which encouraged the exhibitionist streak in his nature, so that he began to reel off the adverts too with only the most cursory glance to refresh his memory. 'Seven minds with but a single thought a Bravington ring and the girl is caught!'

***

The end of the holiday was looming closer. In just over a week I would have to return to Winchester, to school, to a different world and it was hard for me to reconcile these two contrasting environments. On the one hand, the wisely-ordered existence in the country where time hung heavily upon us and I was in bed each night by half-past nine, and on the other the relaxed and charmed touch of madness of this homecoming with every evening a party. I liked it best when there were other girls around, for then I had Jean to myself and we could lose ourselves in the company.

He had begun to talk to me a little about himself and his life. He told me he had been engaged to a girl called Anita who came from Scotland and it had made him very sad when he discovered she didn't love him. He had also spoken about his home in Brussels, his mother who was a widow, and lived with her sister and the different places in which he had been stationed as an officer in the Belgian Army. He especially liked living in Spa in the Ardennes where he had a house. He had also touched on his imprisonment in the Spanish Concentration camp of Miranda de Ebro. He had not yet mentioned anything about his work or going away but I knew he was here for a limited period and would depart like the others before him. Like my mother I had not considered any future in our relationship, nor had I not considered it. I had just not thought about it. I was just living dizzily from day to day. The prospect of going back to the Levers, leaving him behind in London, was beginning to sadden me. Rather half-heartedly I cheered myself with the thought that Tony would be there waiting for my return. He had written again to say he would. Then a sudden rush of warmth reminded me that I had never finished my letter to him and it lay abandoned in my writing-case.

As soon as Jean came in that night I sensed his preoccupation. He was always the first home from school in the evenings and I looked forward to his return. It was the only time of the day we had alone together side by side on the settee in front of the fire. I liked to watch the hint of strain fade from his face when he kissed me. But tonight he was late and I had been anxious. We had finished dinner when he arrived and although he sat down beside me and kissed me as usual, it was only the briefest greeting.

"I am very tired," he said with a sigh. I accepted that he had perhaps indulged in some kind of hard physical training and went to fetch a cup of coffee for him. "You are kind," he said, his eyes expressing his gratitude. Puccini was blaring from the radiogram. There was quite a bit of rivalry between Jefke and the new boy Pierre. It was often a question of who could reach the gramophone first, and now it seemed, that the former in his after dinner triumph had turned up the volume. Jean spoke seriously, though with difficulty against the music.

"Excuse me - I have had a long day. I had to be alone to think. It was necessary for me to think very hard - a great deal is depending on it."

"Oh," I said. My mother brought his dinner to him on a tray and he started to eat slowly with one hand, keeping me near him with the other.

"There are some things I must tell you," he began, his mouth close to my ear. "Today - I know when I must go." I had not expected this while still in London.

"When?" I asked anxiously. "Perhaps a month - six weeks, a little more or less, it depends on the weather." His reply prompted me to breathe normally again.

"I have to go back to school next week," I said, making it sound equally final. He placed his cheek on mine and broke into one of his most hopeful grins.

"We shall be together for this week - long enough to tell you some things, but now - it is impossible," he suggested, nodding in the direction of the radiogram.

"I wish I wasn't going back to school."

"We can write some letters - perhaps I will come and see you in your countryside and, it is possible - you will come back here to see again your mother - and me?" he encouraged.

To hear him making plans ahead opened yet another dimension of our love. My nerves tingled so that I found the courage to ask the question which had niggled in my mind for a few days. "Is it going to be dangerous - for you?" I said, working my finger into a little round pattern of inconsequence on the arm of the settee. He looked down pensively at his plate and as soon as he spoke I rested my hand ready to take in what he said. *"Non Chérie,"* he replied, but his manner was too nonchalant, too cheerful, too blatantly self-deceiving to be convincing. I had guessed it was going to be such a dangerous undertaking that he dared not admit it even to himself. We looked one another in the eye and it told me everything. The mood of the music seemed to match my changing feelings, and as Gigli's lovely voice broke into its characteristic sob before fading into a long, slow diminuendo, it was impossible to talk anymore.

With Monsieur Gobeaux's last allusive standpoint fresh in my thoughts I wanted to know precisely the nature of the work going on with the boys. There was a camaraderie which I sensed was slightly forced. It was unlikely that an engineer, a classical scholar, a policeman, farmer and professional soldier, not to mention the Count - or the Baron who were to turn up later - would come together so naturally in peacetime, so it was as if they must lose their identity behind a common front to hide their deeper feelings. One could only guess at this from hints of their conversation in their own vernacular; by the frequent use of such words as *Patrie Résistance, sacrifier*, *liberation* and *clandestine*.

I lay awake a long time before falling asleep. Jean and his departure were on my mind. I knew that whatever had happened that day had been critical. I would have liked him to be able to take me into his confidence to help shoulder some of the burden but I knew that was impossible.

My mother had told me that her boys, all volunteers, were hand-picked for the Job; that those who had evaded the German Police in their escape to this country were particularly well qualified for the courage and the initiative they had already displayed. As I lay in the darkness, turning and sorting the pieces of the puzzle I had so far - the Morse Code and transmitter, the BBC messages and the disquieting inference to be drawn from the dramatic warnings of Monsieur Gobeaux and Peter, things began to slot into place. Jean was training to be sent back inside occupied Belgium as a spy and to transmit information back to this country. No wonder Monsieur Gobeaux should feel that the finer feelings of his *protéges* were well-accounted for at this moment. Was he right? With the war and the uncertainty as it dragged on from year to year, surely an emotional relationship could not have been all bad? Someone to confide in as far as possible. Someone to love, someone to live for! My adoration increased a thousandfold as if Jean's safety depended on the strength of my love. What I did not know was that Jean, in undergoing his specialised training, had been studied and assessed as to his suitability to work as a secret agent. Now, his superiors, their scrutiny complete, had reached their verdict. He was to continue training for definite departure. Like Roll before him, he would be sent on a mission. The moment to turn it down had come that day and passed.

PART SEVEN

PROMISE

It was getting late. I looked at my watch in the department where we had come to choose some material for a new dress. Jean, overhearing our plans to go shopping in Harrods, had invited us to lunch with him. My mother noticed my agitation.

"I think I'll go off now, you have lunch with him on your own," she said, astonishing me with her wish to back out of the arrangement. I turned to her.

"Are you sure?" fervently hoping it would not persuade her to reconsider.

"Yes, it's all right," she said, buttoning her coat and fussing with her parcels, ostensibly to make them easier to manage. "I still have things I want to do," she added, casting a meaningful wink at the salesman standing by with her change. "And you can't keep him waiting. Here, carry your own material," she ordered me brusquely. The salesman, self-important and obsequious, made his own interpretation of things.

"They grow up so quickly these days Madam. Not like the old days, oh dear me no, they have to be heard as well as seen now," he lamented, not entirely displeased with the attention he was managing to wring from the transaction.

"You're telling me," she laughed. "But you see - it's a special occasion, not the place for an old mother this time."

"I don't doubt mothers can be very useful at times, Madam," he retorted as he rolled and humped the bolts of cloth ostentatiously back into order to emphasise the time and trouble he had taken to suit us. "No Madam, they are not children long these days."

Annoyed at being made to feel guilty by yet another who automatically heaped on me all his disapprobation of youth in a mixture of scorn and envy, I was glad to escape, happy beyond description with the last minute change of plan. To be alone with Jean once more, freed from the censures of the household was a bonus I had not expected.

We had arranged to meet in the Banking Hall at one o'clock. The two rows of green leather armchairs on either side of the central aisle were always full of people. I had the uncanny impression they were always the same ones sitting there, forever watching and waiting, having secured their vantage point to scrutinise in comfort the rest of the world at large. It was intimidating to walk between them. But today my concern was to distinguish one person only and finding him there ahead of me was gratifying.

Jean was restive as he came along caring not one whit for the inquisitive eyes on either side of him. He examined each newcomer with myopic precision as if expecting to meet someone only two feet high. Yet unnoticed, I watched him from a distance and it was very forcefully impressed on me just how noticeable he was in a crowd. One only had to glance along the heads of everyone to pick him out as the tallest and straightest, and his movements, though not flamboyant, could not be described as self-effacing either. He was wearing the dark civilian overcoat I didn't like much. It made him look so long and narrow, divesting him of much of the dash his uniform enhanced in him, but it did not matter. As he spotted me and we made those last hurried steps towards one another, I did not care what he wore or who was watching us. I was proud of him and his wish to show the world he loved me.

"My mother still has some shopping to do and isn't coming, I hope you don't mind," I said, freed from his embrace.

"Ah yes - your mother," he said, as if he had forgotten about her. "I am sorry, but I am also happy to be alone with you, you understand?" he continued courteously with eyebrows raised and lips pointed. "Where shall we take some - lunch? I have something to say to you."

"Here, upstairs in the restaurant?" I offered, for I had imagined it had been predetermined that we would lunch in Harrods.

"No," he said with resolve. "I know where we shall go." And taking my hand he led me out of the store and in the direction of the Brompton Road. I was glad he was not in uniform and could keep a protective arm around my shoulder. As we swung along in our joy at being together I had the marvellous feeling that I was the only one in the world who mattered.

We went into a smallish restaurant passing through heavy black-out curtains at the doorway. It was dark coming in from the January daylight. Inside the atmosphere was warm and comfortable with that appetising smell of coffee, food cooked in herbs and wine, mingling with the smoke of natural tobacco only known in foreign restaurants. Music was playing softly, soothingly out of sight in contrast to the general bustle and activity evident. It soon became apparent that this eating-place was a rendezvous for many areas of the war with a predominance of Free French Army and Air Force personnel being so near to South Kensington and the Headquarters of General de Gaulle. The tables had been arranged in little alcoves for two or, at the most, four people, and nearly all were occupied by couples as *tête à tête* as was physically possible over the top of them. I was thrilled to be here alone with Jean and while we stood a moment at the entrance to acclimatise ourselves I tried to assume the air of being used to coming to such an establishment every day of my life. A waiter came and spoke in French; he and Jean were not strangers to one another and as he led us to a reserved table at the far end, the babble of a hundred urgent conversations rivalled only the clatter of knives and forks as we passed by.

I sat down with slight misgivings for being at a table for two when there might have been three of us. The whole vibrant influence of the place, the chic, semi-luxurious internationalism would have seen my mother in her element. It did not last. I looked at Jean who passed me one of his encouraging smiles and knew that it was more fitting for me to be here alone with him. There were some pretty, well-groomed women, mostly in uniform, sitting nearby and I could pick out random words in more than one foreign language. Jean helped me off with my coat and after hanging up his own, he sat down, adjusted his loose watch-strap, pushed his glasses more securely on his nose, assured himself I was comfortable before handing me the menu written in French.

"You are happy?" he enquired and I realised this was his way of asking if all was well with me.

"Yes, thank you," I replied, at ease for having something to say. "Do you come here every day?"

"Not every day - *de temps en autres* - you know? They still have good wine here, the food also - but *surtout* the wine," he declared with a wide-eyed nod as he took hold of the menu to peruse alongside me. From sheer relief to be sitting down, merging with the other lunchers, soon to be confounded by the prospect of having to choose something to eat from the incomprehensible list before me (no doubt purposely unintelligible to disguise the mediocrity of rationing and the repugnant sounding food such as snoek and whalemeat dredged from the depths of necessity) some of my excitement broke through my control.

"Golly!" I exclaimed, "What does it all mean?" feeling it more honest to own to my confusion.

"You are angry? - I mean to say, you are hungry?" he corrected himself taking care to aspirate the aitch the second time.

"Yes," I laughed nervously, and on an impulse to immerse myself totally in everything going on around us, I echoed. *"Est-ce que vous avez faim?"*

"Mais oui, j'ai faim," he responded. *"Et vous, Mademoiselle? Qu'est ce qu'on va manger?"* What will we eat? That is good English?" I nodded. *"Pâté Maison* - you know what it is?" he asked, scanning the menu with his finger.

"I'm not sure. I know *maison* means house."

"You know much French," he praised and translated, *"Pâté -* that is - er pastry? or Paste? Do you say this?" he asked like an enquiring schoolboy. I shrugged.

"Uh - could be either," I said doubtfully. He involved himself more deeply. "A paste or pastry made with *foie* - liver? Liver pastry?" I winced. He thought again.

"Paste of the House," he announced in schoolboy triumph.

"*Pâté Maison* sounds better," I assured him. "What's this?" I asked running my finger down the list.

"*Cervelles au beurre noir,*" sparked off his tongue, rippling an exquisite shiver down my spine.

"It sounds pretty," I said.

"*Cervelles* how you say that in English?" He searched for the words with his fingertips. "It is something inside the head of a sheep or, little cow. You know it?" He scratched his own head trying to release the correct word. "The mind - no, not the mind, the cleverness inside the head, the intelligence," he suggested laboriously, dismissing his lack vexedly with a nod while tapping his temple sharply.

"Brains?" I offered, turning up my nose.

"They are good if they are well-prepared," he assured me a little fretfully, emphasising their delicacy by forming his thumb and middle finger into a round O, almost kissing the air. "*Très bonnes!*"

"Brains in black butter! Sounds awful," I frowned. "*Formidable!*" I gibed pronouncing the word, he often used, in French. He chuckled. "What is black butter?" I asked.

"Perhaps it is black market butter," he teased. We giggled.

"Then it will be terribly expensive," I retorted.

"Formidable!" he retaliated in English and I was aware of his legs under the table gently encircle mine. I blushed and engrossed myself further in the menu. "Perhaps you will prefer some fish?" he said, tackling the question with more seriousness.

"Yes please, I like fish."

"Soup before?" he offered. "Soup or - you prefer dessert, we cannot have both." In wartime one could only have two courses in a restaurant.

"No soup, fish - this - *sole à la bonne femme,*" I pointed out. It sounded simple and wholesome. "And I don't mind which dessert, as long as it's nice," I said relinquishing my hold on the menu. "Do you really eat frog's legs in Fr - oh no, of course you are not French," I teased.

He sat upright, seemingly affronted. "And if I am speaking to you - in the language of the *Chinois* you will think I am a man from that country?" He pulled up his eyes at the corners. *"Un Chinois* - a Chinese man?"

"I'm sorry," I said.

"It is nothing, excuse me - frog's legs, what did you ask?"

"Yes, frog's legs and snails, have you eaten them?"

"Ah yes, I know it - yes they are good, you like that? No - I think not," he said, amused by my expression.

"Today I shall take - Paste of the house, Brains," he eyed me wickedly, "in Black Market butter and for you after *Crème Brulée, what is that?"* He was ready for more fun. I sighed with delight.

"Crème - I suppose means cream. *Brulée* - I am not sure."

"Brulée signifies when something - *quelque chose,"* he remembered the words with a grin, "Was cooking too much, it is good, I know *Crème_Brulée* and I am sure you will like that."

"If you say it is nice, although if it is cream cooked too much —it can't be real cream," I added as an afterthought. He held his head back to look at me down his nose, first passing his tongue over his lips, mouthing his fascination with my expression.

"You are uncertain of so much, life is not so fearsome as your face is sometimes indicating," he said with an affectionate grin, the corners of his eyes wrinkled into smiles.

"Oh," I let out lost for words although I could not help smiling for in order to be helpful he had made most things sound disgusting.

"I make a foolish mistake in Spain!" he announced, as though reading my thoughts. "I ask for a knife - to remove the skin of a spider. The word for an orange is very similar to that for a spider in the Spanish language, just the difference of one letter or so," he said making a quick verbal illustration.

"What a coincidence that it should be a spider," I said.

"I think your mother knows this, that is the reason she has given to me this name." We both giggled. "She wishes - that I do not forget that foolish mistake. Marjorie," he spoke out, his expression undergoing a rapid change.

"Yes?" I said in surprise.

"I must make a confession, I have been sinful."

"What have you done?"

"This morning - I ask your mother not to come today."

"Did you - why?"

"Be-cause… " He always said the word 'because' with a pause afterwards as if he expected me to know or guess what was to follow. I thought.

"Because…" he repeated, "I wish to be with you alone. It is natural and reasonable - no?" I nodded, flattered.

"She didn't tell me," I said.

"No, I ask her not to - am I very evil?" he said, placing his fingers to his lips to suggest it had been a deadly conspiracy between them.

"I-see," I responded slowly for it explained my mother's behaviour in the material department.
The waiter took the order and Jean asked for the wine list. "I will choose some wine - you will see if you like it."

"I only drink wine on special occasions," I said, "Though in Germany when I was very small Robin and I sometimes drank beer with dinner!"

"Ah but wine is not the same as beer, wine is light, it goes up to the head and stimulates the brain. Beer is heavy, it remains in the stomach - the Germans get very fat. With wine it is always a special occasion!" He smiled and we both relaxed.

I was hungry now that it had come to the moment and also so warm that I could feel my nose throbbing. I was also immensely fascinated by the life going on around us, then I remembered Jean said he had something to say to me; obviously something private if he didn't want my mother here. I looked forward to hearing it and remained silent, hoping it would encourage him to speak. I did not think he could talk about his job in a public place, perhaps he was going to reveal more of his past, and while I sat expectantly, he reached across and took hold of my hands.

"I love you very much - more than I can say it to you, but, you have not said to me positively that you feel the same?" His eyebrows raised themselves quizzically. I was startled and shy of replying. "I think I know it - not so different from me?" he stated softly to draw some hint of accord. I turned away, wondering if the occupants of the nearest table could hear us. I remembered my mother's caution, 'always keep a man guessing, for once a woman admits her love the chase is over and his interest will flag.' I had never liked this cat-and-mouse approach to love but took notice of it now in my confusion and withdrew one of my hands. He held on to the other as if he feared that might slip from his grasp too. Then reaching to my chin, he lifted it so that I should face him again. From the corner of my eye I was relieved to notice that all around us were too engrossed in their own private dramas to bother with us. In fact the Free French Air Force Officer at the next table might have been posing exactly the same question so intently was he gazing into his companion's eyes, but she looked more adept at handling the situation. I kept my eye on her in the hope of a clue to resolving my dilemma. I was therefore all the more amazed to see her accept a cigarette from her escort, which he lit with a quick flash of his silvery lighter, briefly illuminating their profiles and then blow the smoke from her first inhalation back into his face.

"I think it has been a great surprise to you because - not one of us thought it would happen, yes?" he said and I knew he was not talking about the couple at the next table who held not the slightest interest for him. There was no need for me to reply, he knew everything. I saw my own twin reflection in his glasses, very tiny and far away. "I never believed love at first sight was possible," he said, after a few seconds.

"It wasn't, not first sight," I said punctiliously, remembering the first evening I came home.

"No? I think so."

"Not the first evening I came home," I censured him.

"Well —" he shrugged, "Then it was the second-sight - so that I am twice sure, and with you - it is the same?" he responded with a twinkle.

"Perhaps," I replied provocatively. It was exciting to be hinting so intimately in public.

I felt at one with the rest of the diners. We smiled again and not afraid anymore to meet his eyes, I looked beyond the glasses. I admired his nose, mouth and as the tip of his tongue pointed between his teeth to moisten his lips, he whispered, "I wish to marry you."

My stomach turned completely over or so it felt. Everything seemed to go quiet as if he and I had been transported a thousand miles away.

"It is true what I say." I heard him through a mist. "Don't you wish it also? I should like to marry you tomorrow but I know that is not possible."

"Yes," I agreed.

"You are annoyed?"

"No." He closed his hand over mine so that it numbed and burned into not feeling part of me the deeper his words seeped into my consciousness. Not that marriage had never entered my scheme of things. Several times I had imagined myself married - to Tony, to Errol Flynn, but these were only the wildest daydreams. Now, it was real life — I was nervous.

"Why are we here together? Why are you coming, why am I coming? It is for the same purpose. I know it, I am sure you know it. You must answer me only if I am wrong. We have fallen in love and when two people love each other they wish to marry and live together - to live for ever." I heard him continue calmly, reasonably and persuasively.

This affair of ours, and I had not the slightest doubt it was a love-affair which deep down I had considered impossible, now assumed gigantic proportions. That it would end in marriage had never entered my head. His over simplification of the reasons for our marrying only skimmed the surface. They did not explain the mystery of why two such unlikely people should have fallen in love in the first place. His eyes simultaneously pleaded and comforted. There was no scheming, he seemed sure. I was nearly sure. My heart almost leapt out of my body and over to him.

The hum inside the restaurant switched itself on again. 'Jealousy' twanged assertively from behind the scenes. A waft of cigarette smoke from the next table blew across my face. I felt small and out of place. It would take only one more exquisite stroke to crumple the framework of my body completely. Jean drew circles on the back of my hand with his finger.

"May I ask your mother for her permission?"

"Haven't you asked her already?" I said, certain she must have known all in Harrods.

"No, I have told her only that I was wishing to speak with you alone, it is not very difficult for her to guess," he said. "And do you expect her to have some objections?" "I am too young to marry," I informed him without much grace. He studied my face so that I shivered, and had to do it again, consciously to pretend the first was on purpose and that I was in command of myself.

"You will not always be fifteen," he said. "After the war I shall come back, at sixteen you will be old enough or must you wait until eighteen in this country? If so, I can wait," he suggested, sitting back as if to begin there and then.

"Oh no, sixteen is old enough," I assured him.

The waiter came to prepare the table. The *sole à la bonne femme* smelt delicious but my hunger was not so immediate. I was uncertain whether Jean assumed I had accepted his proposal or was waiting for an answer. I made up my mind that if he asked again I would tell him I needed time to think. My mother could not grumble at that, but the waiter poured the wine and upset my resolve. Jean lifted his glass.

"To us - to the future!" The habit he had with his lips took on another significance. It was if he was blowing me a secret kiss. He looked so expectant that at this moment there was nothing in this world I wanted more than to live for ever with this kind, discerning, very human being who understood me better than I did myself and I did not care if he knew it.

"Yes," I responded shyly, picking up my glass. "Good luck for the future."

The first sip went down the wrong way. I coughed, tears welled in my eyes and the most agonising pain spread across the back of my shoulders. I had never imagined that a proposal of marriage could engender so much discomfort. Jean took hold of my glass. *"Pauvre Petite,"* he commiserated, his eyes moistening. I watched his arm in the pinstripe sleeve reach again to his glass and the strong, graceful hand slide up the stem with a delicate caress. Everything was so different from the shining armour of my dreams - the glasses to counteract Myopia, the short back swept hair - which I discovered was not kept in place with oil - yet he was more captivating than any film-star, more tender and compassionate than any poet.

"To the war ending quickly," he toasted. We began to eat and I changed the subject.

"Do you like London?" I said.

"At first - I am not sure," he answered, wavering his hand above his plate. "But now, yes, I like London very much."

"Why not - to begin with?"

"When I was just arriving it was from Gibraltar. It was a sad time for me. I did not know anybody in England."

"My mother told me you were sad."

He nodded as he swallowed ready to speak again, softly with feeling. "Yes, I was very sad - your mother knows it. She was very kind to me - I will tell you myself. It is better that you know these things about me." He lingered a moment in consideration, mopped his lips with his napkin, took a fresh gulp of wine and passed me a tender smile before he relaxed. No doubt prompted by the food and the alcohol and the intimacy of our little table in the alcove, he began the story which I had so longed to hear from his own lips. He spoke slowly, forming each phrase into a question to be continually reassured that I understood. With his imperfect English, he seemed once more to over-simplify the whole episode. "When the Germans were invading Belgium I was in the army. You know that? I have to fight."

"Yes," I nodded eagerly.

"It was an impossibility, the Germans are too strong. The war was not lasting long for us - it was a hard combat - we are quickly defeated."

"Weren't you relieved in one way?"

"The Germans have the most powerful army in Europe, even with France and England to help, we are not strong enough."

"Was it terrible - to fight?" He shook his head signifying that now was not the time or place to describe it. "What did you do next?"

"I go back to my home in Brussels - it is an unhappy time. The Germans are there, life is difficult - very *triste*. We think the war is finished - the Germans will soon invade Britain. Anita, you know? She is going to England, at the start of the invasion." I was glad that he could talk to me about the girl he had loved. "After some months, we hear on the Radio from your Mr. Churchill asking that all the young men from Europe must try to get to England to continue the fight. Then some *copains* - chums? and myself were looking for the occasion to escape from Belgium to this country where we can fight the Germans once more, so we start on our long travels through France. It takes some weeks and many adventures. And then we have to cross the Pyrenees - very high mountains into Spain. That is difficult because there are not good roads and the Frontier Guards will not permit us to go in Spain so we must go in secret. We have to pay much money to *un guide* and *avoir confiance*. We can easily lose ourselves and the roads are not good - you understand?"

"Yes, trust him," I offered. The longer his sentence lasted the slower and more obscure his English became but I wished to take in all he said and make the least interruption.

"It takes many days! Then we come in Spain and we are captured, arrested and we go in prison!" He paused, smiled and poured himself more wine.

"What was it like in prison?" He shook his head.

"Not one prison, *Enfin* - we arrive in Miranda and we must stay here. We must say we are British from Canada. Like that we can make appeal to the British Embassy in Madrid for our release.

"Miranda! What a pretty name."

"Majala!" he exclaimed. "It is not a pretty place, it is a *camp de concentration!*" he stressed. "A very bad place."

"*Formidable?*"

"*Epouvantable, dégoutant, affreux!*" he said. "There were many people here and we live like animals."

"All Belgians?"

He laughed. "No - *Canadiens*, from every country in Europe, French *Canadiens*, *Hollandais*, *Polonais* - even German *Canadiens*," he wisecracked, "And some British *aviateurs* from the RAF. We suffered much in Spain – *des souffrances physiques et morales* - you understand? The Spanish are very cruel." Distracted by my expression, he blew his breath out of barely open lips and reached for my hand. "Is it too sad for you?" he asked softly. I shook my head, enthralled.

"Are the Spanish worse than the Germans?"

"The Germans are clever and good soldiers; it is only Hitler who is *maniaque*. The Spanish are nearly not human. I have seen them kill one man - I cannot speak about it - it is too awful but I am always confident that one day we will come out. We must hope! We did not know anything. We must trust in God - I have prayed much during this time. *Enfin* we are released after many months and I come to England and you see me here." He seemed to want that to be the happy ending to his story but I wanted him to tell me everything and, with the wine giving an extra boost to my nerve, I reminded him.

"Anita made you suffer?" He dug the base of his wine glass into the white starched cloth making a deep indentation, then drew it down in a line, carelessly flicking off dashes so that some wine spilled in pinkish drops. He dabbed at them with his finger, trying to obliterate them.

"Yes, very much. It is a great disappointment for me when I see her and she tells me she wishes to *rompre nos finçailles* but she was perfectly right. It was I who was trying to force her love where it was not existing. Now you know why I am sad in London - no mother to console me, no home in which I may go to *pleurer* - alone in this big city."

"So what did you do all alone in this big city?" He gave an amiable chuckle.

"I must distract myself but first - there was the Patriotic School!" he said ominously.

"Whatever's the Patriotic School?"

"The Patriotic School," he repeated. "All the people who are just coming from Europe must go in the Patriotic School to answer a lot of questions. That is not nice - first one thinks we are spies, sent by the Germans, we must convince them we are not - it is hard work."

"Then - how did you distract yourself?"

"I have spent a lot of money. I have been a silly boy." He smiled apologetically.

"What did you spend the money on?" I persisted.

"Oh - too many clubs, too much drinking - many things - too much - *apitoiement sur moi-meme* - you understand?"

"I think so," I replied, not at all sure I did.

"Well," he said cheerily, "It is finished and I am here with you - *mon coeur est queri et mon âme est recomfortée* - and now I am very happy. You believe it?"

"Umm. You like the English?"

"Yes, of course, very much. The English are nice - polite - gentlemen. They love dogs and horses and fairplay," he asserted humorously.

"Oh and I forgot to ask - you like this wine?"

"Yes, it's very nice."

"That is something I can teach you - the English are not so good about. Good wine is like love, it enchants the spirit." He raised his glass, his spirit positively gleaming with enchantment.

"Is it because of Anita and everything that you are doing this job?" I challenged him warily. The question took him by surprise and prompted a moment's deep thought. Perhaps he wondered how much I knew and understood of the Job. At any rate he was not stationed with the Belgian Forces like most of his compatriots who had escaped over here.

"I was in the Army when I first arrived but she was not fighting. I wish to be active - to do something positive for the peace. I was waiting in Brussels - I do not wish to do that here. Now we talk about us, you and me - it is the future which is important."

"I like this burnt cream," I said. "What else did you eat in Spain besides peeled spiders?" He giggled, the memory amused him.

"The food in prison?" He shook his head. "Soup made from *rutabaga* and potatoes and bad bread. Every day the same. The spiders I had as a luxury in Madrid when I go out of the prison!"

He lit a cigarette and once it was going it seemed an embarrassment to him, as if he had not yet learnt how to cope with it. He was more at home with a pipe. As I watched him holding it alternately between his fingers and in his mouth with his head tilted back to prevent the smoke from rising up behind his glasses, while he toyed with remains on the table, I was evermore baffled why a man of his age and experience should have fixed on me. Was it because I, so little, lovesick and malleable, would be less likely to hurt him again? I felt very loving and protective towards him.

"I wish you weren't going away," I said.

"The time will pass quickly - you will see - the war must end soon," he replied.

"Do you think so? Suppose it goes on for years like the last war?"

"Then I shall come back after only one year, my job will not take so long."

"How can you come back?"

"I have done it once, I can do it again," he replied.

"But-" I stopped myself. He read my thoughts.

"There are better ways, ways we did not know before," he comforted me, and with a sidelong glance, he mimicked the posters. "Careless talk costs lives, walls have ears!" and he drew aside the curtains behind us pretending to look for them.

"Is your journey really necessary?" I retorted.

"Unfortunately, yes," he said firmly and we both dissolved into soft laughter. He poured the remains of the wine into his glass and reached again to my hand. The loose watchstrap, like a silver bracelet around his wrist, heightened his masculinity and I manoeuvred my hand so he could hold it more firmly. With his eyes on mine, he raised it to his lips and kissed my fingers. *"Ma petite fiancée - je t'adore,"* he whispered.

"I had a letter from Anita today," he remarked as we came out into the daylight and retraced our steps towards Knightsbridge station.

"It upset you? You are going to see her?" I asked with some misgivings.

"No," he replied calmly. "Nothing is changed, yes, everything is changed. My whole life is changed, but it is a good change. I shall live a better life." He squeezed my arm. "Anita was writing to give me a letter she received from my sister who lives in Africa. She has a baby son - I have a nephew," he said proudly.

"You are an uncle - how lovely! Is your sister like you?"

"No," he laughed. "My sister is very beautiful."

"I should like to know your sister."

"Surely you will. Come, I shall be late," he said, consulting his watch. "Goodbye, until later. Cheers, Cheers, I've got my wings, now we can look at some Bravington rings!" he recited and was gone.

Wherever we walked in London we were jostled by uniformed troops of every country and colour flocking here en masse to spend their leave. With so much manpower aligned on our side, surely, I cheered myself on the tube journey home, the war must end within the year.

***

As Jean and I took the next step forward in our quest for all that was good and beautiful, so the rift between Gobeaux and Peter widened. They even vied with each other how to put an end to our betrothal.

"Of course you know he is no position to offer marriage to your daughter," Peter proclaimed loftily to my mother. "A Belgian Officer cannot marry whom he chooses without first obtaining the permission of his Commanding Officer and, as you know at the moment, that is impossible!" But rather than put her off by laying emphasis on the exclusiveness of the young professional soldier, it only heightened in her eyes his eligibility as a prospective son-in-law. Whereas Monsieur Gobeaux, not entirely convinced of the sincerity of his youthful protegé conversant with his recent personal history and fearful of him reacting too hastily on the rebound, resented Peter's interference and loyally defended her *"Donc qu'est-ce qu'il fait pour aider son pays?"* was his constant plea behind his rival's back, while throwing up his hands in complete mystification to the heavens. *"Sh'ais pas, sh'ais pas,"* he would mutter to himself, his mouth set in a firm downward curve of disapproval. If my mother made the slightest attempt to justify the Captain's behaviour as well meaning, Monsieur Gobeaux would then accuse her of playing into the hands of the very one who was generally coming to be regarded as the dark villain of the story.

It was obvious that our affair was beginning to uncover something of a more worrying nature than mere childish vexation over whose right it was to be addressed as Captain. There was an atmosphere in the house and the boys, who had so far remained impartial, showed signs of restiveness. They were frequently heard to be conferring with the Chef often with anxious, raised voices, the Officers not least amongst them. Monsieur Gobeaux had not yet breathed a word of any further trouble with my mother, which was uncharacteristic. It was not in his nature to brush aside adversity once it had penetrated the obdurate covering of his brain. Perhaps this only accentuated its seriousness. We did notice, however, that he watched Peter like a hawk and often asked my mother to repeat to him all the Captain had said to her in English. The two sides thus embroiled, so our love with its new promise deepened and quickened under their noses and, like the best love-stories, it was individual, rich and beyond the reach of anyone.

***

"I wanted him to fall in love with you," my mother said while supervising our packing on the day before we were due to return to school, as if she had arranged the whole thing. I changed into my new dress she had rushed through for me to wear before I went back.

"I'll wear this tomorrow," I said.

"I wonder what Lady Lever is going to say? Will you tell her? Do you think she'll approve?" My mother bristled and raised herself to her full height.

"Of course - I think she'll be jolly relieved," she said, although I was not so sure.

The Levers had been threatened for the last year of having their house requisitioned for the duration to be turned into a Fire Station. They had put in a plea that as they had taken in two evacuees they should be exempted. At the same time they had been looking out for another house and had found one suitable nearer the city of Winchester. Lady

Lever had written to say their plea had failed and that it had been an opportune time for them to move while we were on holiday. Thompson had also left to take up war work and there was now a Parlourmaid Macdonald instead of a butler.

Jean and I contrived to be alone on our last night together after everyone had gone to bed. We sat on the floor of the drawing room in front of a mound of grey ash in the fireplace. I took the poker to stir some life into its heart and Jean placed some tiny lumps of coal strategically on top and blew on them to set them glowing. I shivered while we waited for the flames to rise and Jean unfastened his tunic and placed it around my shoulders. We sat lax, pensive, leaning towards one another, talking only when we had something to say. Thick greenish smoke issued up the chimney.

"I wish I wasn't going back to school tomorrow," I sighed.

"It is necessary for you remain in school - you must learn French. Do you take that at school?" I nodded wanly. "Will you do that for me - while I am away?"

"Yes, I'm quite good at French," I said, as it would give me the greatest pleasure to do something for him. "When are you going?" I asked casually.

"Perhaps March, if the weather is good."

"Are you going back to Belgium?" He nodded.

"What for? What are you going to do?"

"*Chérie,* I am not allowed to speak about this to anybody but we must go, to encourage the poor people there - to help them resist the Germans." I thought of the 'Piano'.

"Will you send messages in morse code?"

"To do this also," he said humouring me.

"Do you want to go?" He changed his tone to one of flippancy.

"I must," he stressed, wrinkling his brow as he studied my face.

"Isn't it dangerous?" This time he was honest.

"A little - yes. But not too much," he added.

"How are you going - by parachute? I heard you and Bunny talking about parachutes." He nodded.

"Isn't that very dangerous? The Germans might see you."

"Non *Chérie,* that is not the danger, unless I break my legs but if I have some practice that will not be possible. First I must go to take some training."

"Will you go in the night?"

"When there is a big moon - so that we can see that it will be safe." How conspicuous it sounded, to be dropped by parachute in the light of the full moon.

"Where will you land - in Brussels?" He laughed.

"No, that would be foolish and very dangerous. But you know - you must not speak about this to anybody - that is dangerous for me. You must promise that and you need not worry. The more quickly I go, the more quickly I will return - understand?" I nodded and watched the fire.

"Nobody thinks we should marry," I said.

"Everybody knows more about us than we know it ourselves."

"They think I'm too young," I said.

"Is it too much? *Non Chérie* - it will matter less as we grow older. The important thing is - that we love each other. We need not listen to these people - oh yes, Monsieur Gobeaux is kind, but he is old and knows nothing of us and how we feel." He caressed my arms. "I find my English not good - if you can understand French there are many kind things I am able to say to you. There is much for you to learn - of love - we shall discover that together. It will be marvellous you will see."

"You could look up the words in the dictionary," I suggested archly.

"I have already done so - this English language is so funny - *chou* in the dictionary in English is - cabbage, and *cher* is written dear, expensive - which are you?"

"Both," I smiled, snuggling closer to him.

"Ah," he sighed, easing his long back against the settee as he took off his glasses. I knew this was the sign that he was going to kiss me and I leant my head against him in anticipation. I liked him without glasses, very short-sighted; he was disarming himself. He looked vulnerable, mysterious, more ardent like this.

The flames erupted spasmodically and began to dispel the smoke, their red and orange light flickering on our faces as we stared into them. We were growing warm again and Jean enfolded me in his arms.

"Why do you like me?" I asked for it never ceased to puzzle me why he should want to love a schoolgirl.

"Oh - because - you - are - you and I - am - me, because - you are very – nice," he replied, punctuating his words with kisses.

"And you - what do you like about me?" he retaliated, the firelight sparkling in his eyes.

"Lots of things," I said, playing with his tie.

"Which things? Tell me those things," he said loosening the knot and unfastening his shirt collar. I admired his long neck.

"Many things - because you are tall." I said.

"But I love you because you are small," he replied, taking my hand to measure against his. "My dear, expensive, little cabbage," he laughed.

"*Mon Grand araignée noir!*" I retorted. He smirked.

"It is feminine, *araignée is feminine*. You must say *ma grande araignée*" he corrected, annunciating the difference with thrilling precision.

"Not a very suitable name for you then, if it's feminine - *ma araignée noire!*" I tried again.

"No, you cannot say *ma_araignée*," he laughed. "You must say *mon araignée* - not two vowels together - *mon_araignée noire* - or *ma grande araignée,*" he said hugging me.

"And you say English is difficult," I despaired. I moved my head so that still resting against him I could see his face. "Do you think the war will end soon?" I asked him.

"That is my best wish," he replied.

"Then what will happen?"

"First I shall come back to marry you and after I must find a job and we have got to make ourselves a home."

"But - I thought you were in the army - even in peacetime?" He shook his head.

"That was before the war, but when this war is finished, I think - I will have had enough war. The Belgian army was a defensive army only, to protect against invasion and I believe that possibility will be ended forever. I hope to find another job, something *paisible*, and to live in perfect happiness with you always." That he was contemplating a change of career came as a surprise. He did look very handsome in uniform.

"Don't you like the army?" A hint of strain passed over his face.

"It is not such a good life - a lot of exercises, we have a job only when there is war," he expressed naively, "And that is always for destruction and killing."

"Why did you join?"

"I was very young, it was my education. I went from school into the *Ecole Militaire*. I enjoy the training very much, the sport and the discipline, it has been hard but also good for me. I have been thinking about this during a long time. I was never wishing to remain in the army." He sat relaxed, watching the fire, the muscles above his jaw occasionally tensing as he mulled things over as he spoke. "When one is a good soldier," he began again, "One is no longer a human being - he must lose all his *sensibilité* - feeling? Otherwise, it is becoming insupportable. *Au même temps* he is also very human and very weak. The war has taught me much - it was my *baptême de feu!* Understand? Before it - I was full of myself. *Egoisme!*" he stressed. "But when I see so much suffering, so many good people killed I realise I am one very small man on the earth with no power and I feel very *impuissant.*"

"Were you afraid?"

"Of course, I did not wish to die but at those times one must forget himself - one must obey orders. I am thankful for much and, also that I was not taken a prisoner of war, but," he asserted cheerfully, "If I am successful in my job I shall have good recommendations."

"And if you are not successful?" I don't think I knew what he meant by success at this moment.

"There is no alternative," he stated undramatically.

"What do you mean?"

"I shall not get caught but if it will make you smile at me - I am still an Officer in the Belgian army and I would be arrested as a prisoner of war." The flames had gained control and were burning brightly. I nestled closer to him.

I had not yet been awakened by desire in the urgent, physical sense. My erotic imagination had been enough to contend with. Just beautifully content to have Jean's arms around me, to experience the delightful thrills that accompanied his kisses and pledges of love, I looked for nothing more. He certainly realised he must proceed cautiously and tenderly in his courtship if he was not to offend or frighten me away, even if sometimes he had to summon every ounce of self-control. Sitting inside his arms as he fondled the hair curling around my ear, silently, his eyes soft with undisguised longing as he contemplated my face and figure, I became aware of a power within me I had not known before. We moved ever closer and as he lifted my face to kiss him, long and sensuously I felt his hand warm and stirring steal over my breast. A great charge of intense feeling surged from the top of my head to my toes. I recognised myself as a woman, desired and desiring and I was very proud and happy.

***

I did not go back to Hampshire the next day. In the morning I awoke, conveniently, flushed and sneezing, with a temperature a little over a hundred degrees. This was too much of a temptation to keep me in London a little longer. I had known Jean for just over three weeks. Soon he would be going away and only God knew when we would meet again. My mother decided to send Robin back to the Levers with a note informing them I was undoubtedly contracting 'flu and would return when I was completely well. For two or three days I stayed in bed but once my mother decided to let me remain at home another fortnight, I recovered rapidly.

She was up early in the mornings which were very dark this time of year, due to the double Summer-time in force during the war to conserve the daylight for as long as possible in the evenings. On her way downstairs she usually gave me a call and switched on my light. I was not good at getting up in my icy bedroom but since my feverish indisposition I was lingering in bed longer than usual.

Roused by my mother, the light bright in the room, there was a knock on my door some half-hour later and I recognised it. Jean had been into my room several times to bring my dinner and to generally cheer me up as he put it.

"Good morning, do I disturb you?" he said kissing me and I breathed in the lavender-scented and peppermint wholesomeness of shaving soap and toothpaste. "Last night I forget to tell you - I shall come home late tonight - when you will be asleep. One of the boys is leaving and Bunny and I must go to a little party to wish him luck. I have come to wish you a happy day because - it is a long time until tomorrow."

"Which boy is leaving?" I asked concerned.

"Not one of the boys in this house, we see him only at school."

At dinner the following evening someone asked if they had enjoyed their party and Jean broke into a mischievous smile. "Oh yes," he began, "But after!" he exclaimed and set about describing what happened. "I was coming home very late, it was already tomorrow. The house was very quiet - everybody is in his bed. All the doors are - *fermé à clef!*" Here my mother looked puzzled for she always kept the back door unlocked to cover this very contingency, but curious to hear what he had to say she let him continue uninterrupted. "So-" he related, "I go into the garden to look for some stones to throw up to the window of Bear when I see - the window of the W.C. is open. You know that window? It is small and nearly two metres from the ground." He demonstrated with his hands. "*Enfin* - I go through this window - I am very quiet but because - I am in the W.C. - I was drinking this night so -! And then I was making the journey along the *couloir* into the hall." Spasmodically he broke into chuckles, increasing our suspense. "I did not wish to disturb the sleeping people but I must switch on the light to know where is the staircase. Majala! I got a very great shock! All the things are different and I ask myself - what formidable changes did Madame Rae make in this house today? Then, of course, I realise it is not the house of Madame!" Everyone gasped. "It is the house next door!" and he pointed to the side he meant which was identical in almost every respect.

"Whatever did you do?" cried my mother.

"I go out as quickly as possible!"

"The same way as you got in?"

"Ah no - I go out from the front door. Just one more gate and it is the correct house where, of course, I can some inside easily."

"It must have been some party! You should have taken more water with it!" exclaimed my mother and she burst into a fit of loud, abandoned laughter, her face twisted into a grimace of pain as her imagination ran riot. When it had subsided, which was nearly as quickly as it had developed, she said, "S'posing you'd gone upstairs and found yourself getting into bed beside old Mrs Fields - or even one of the daughters?" she surmised, almost starting herself off again.

"They would not have been complaining," interjected Bunny with his customary inscrutability.

"And when I was in the W.C. - I pulled the chain after! And it was making a formidable noise," Spider added with schoolboy glee.

The two weeks respite were passing all too quickly in retaliation for having been seized on a little deceitfully. It was certainly allowing me to know my betrothed, to see beyond the charm and superficial gloss of his personality to know and understand some of the character that lay beneath. Intelligent, uncomplicated and utterly honest, he was a religious man, though not in the regular church-going sense. There was no doubt that the long tradition of the Catholic church with its almost superstitious emphasis on sin and contrition had been fundamental to his upbringing and influential in helping him select those elements on which he placed high value and to form the principles on which to order his life. A romantic and idealist he considered little out of reach but, as with most irrepressible optimists, when disappointments came - as surely they did - he blamed only himself, his human condition and lack of adequate faith. It went without question that he had physical courage. To have come out of occupied territory showed bravery enough, but to go back inside again needed a special quality, hard to define allied to a youthful lust for adventure and an element of recklessness. His military training had instilled in him a strong sense of duty. Patriotism had infected him as much as the rest. Inherent in a cavalry officer of the time or perhaps it was simply the fact of being a tall man - the reverse of a small man's need to assert himself - went an air of quiet authority and a touch of arrogance, an insouciance, especially in the face of criticism. No-one knew better than he did his failure to come up to his own high standards. He had an almost naïve faith in the instinctive goodness of human nature, except for the Spanish whom he seemed, like most of the boys, to regard as a species apart. If excusable to an extent, it was a feeling that was already passing, for he gave the increasing impression that he would not have missed his Spanish adventure for anything, looking back on it as a testing time, he had a need to prove to himself something. To me he was a mixture of strength and gentility in equal parts, as though all his grooming for war must be weighed in kindness and compassion. He taught me we had hearts and souls both of which needed their correct nourishment just as much as our stomachs. I soon found I could turn to him to help solve the private and exclusive complexities of growing up more easily than I could to my mother. His English, to which he had applied himself this last month with extra assiduity, was now practically fluent and when I complimented him on this, he patted my arm and said it would be another qualification for the future.

***

In the meantime, Bear had made contact with his English sweetheart. He must have quickly rediscovered his love for he came back from their reunion brimming with happiness and informed us he was getting married in February. He found my mother and me alone in the kitchen cutting up vegetables. He sat down too, glad of the opportunity to talk.

"Where are you getting married?" asked my mother, her mind racing ahead.

"Here, in London," he said. "It will be a civil marriage - is it the same custom in England?"

"A Registry Office wedding we say over here, if it's not in a church," she said with a slight sniff. "But you could have the reception here afterwards," she offered, excitement beginning to take her over. I felt only disappointment. There could not possibly be another excuse to keep me in London until February. "Where will your wife live while you are away?"

Bear gulped, took in a deep breath "There is something I must explain - I shall not be going away. I am leaving the Job," he said.

"Leaving! Giving up? Are you really - is that possible?" she gasped. She had not heard of anyone leaving before, but then she had not followed up any of the boys once they left her house.

"Yes, Marjorie, my *fiancée* does not wish me to remain in the Job and I must think of her."

I had mixed feelings over his excuse. It would be marvellous if Jean did not go in the end but I could never ask him to give up. I was legally too young for marriage. We sat talking about wedding plans, my mother wanting to take charge of the whole thing. "You'll have to have a couple of witnesses for a Registry Office wedding," she said. "Yes, I will ask one of the boys and Marjorie, my Marjorie will bring her friend." He turned to me. "Mam'selle, will you be here?"

"No," I sighed. "On Sunday I have to go back. I'm sorry I shall miss seeing your - *fiancée* after all."

At that moment Jean came into the kitchen and finding the three of us so seriously engrossed, enquired, "What is this conspiration?"

"Spider, have you heard the news?" my mother cried out, insensitive to the fact that Bear might wish to inform his colleagues of his intentions in his own time. Maybe because she had to keep so much to herself that which was not strictly secret she felt she could divulge more readily.

"What is this news?" queried Jean, popping a round of carrot into his mouth.

"Bear is getting married and - giving up the Job," she exclaimed dramatically. Jean nearly choked.

"*Non!* - *Pas possible*," he exploded.

"*Si*," responded Bear meekly and began to offer his reasons in French.

After recovering from the news, Jean enquired, "When will you get married?"

My mother could not resist answering herself. "In only about two or three weeks' time."

"I won't be here," I said, puckering up my face.

"Oh yes, you must come back - is it possible?" Jean asked.

"Could you have the wedding on a Saturday?" suggested my mother. "Then perhaps she could come back for the weekend."

"It makes no difference," said Bear easily.

"That would be marvellous," I exclaimed, delighted that arrangements were being made to bring me back before I had even left.

"I shall go to make enquiries tomorrow," said Bear. He addressed Jean. "It is necessary to have a *Témoin de mariage* - will you do that?"

"Of course - I shall be enchanted," he replied, smiling at me. He knew I was amused by the flowery and archaic words he often chose to express himself.

"I must go to see Monsieur Gobeaux - I have some explanation to give to him. Will you wish me good luck?" Bear asked, making for the door, a sheepish grin on is face.

"Well, what do you think of that?" my mother demanded of Jean. "Do you think he has cold feet?"

"Cold feet! What is cold feet?" he asked. "He has got warm socks," he responded waggishly.

"No, seriously Spider. I mean - quite frankly, do you think he's scared - frightened?"

"Perhaps - I can't know that."

"Well - what do you think of him? Can he leave just like that?"

"It is better," he assured her. "If he has doubts, it is better that he is leaving. One must be one hundred per cent sure for this job, otherwise it is dangerous."

"You don't blame him then?" she asked.

"No, I don't blame him, as you say. I think he is right. If he questions himself, he cannot be certain. That is not safe."

"You wouldn't leave?" she challenged him and I listened eagerly for his response.

"No, but I am not Bear. We have two separate characters. It is not a just comparison."

"I don't know," she sighed, "Can he go just like that, having gone through all the training, knowing all he does? All the secrets and - everything?" Jean raised both hands in a shrug of resignation.

**

Now that it was time for me to return to the Levers and there could be no further remission, I was overcome with

224

all sorts of misgivings. I was revolted by the prospect of becoming a schoolgirl once more. It seemed as if my infatuation was nearly over as if I must suffer a setback in growing up. In Hampshire I would be a child again and, as I sank deeper into despondency, so I incurred a loss of the self-confidence that had been so lovingly and tenderly built up during the past five weeks.

At school my engagement would have to be kept secret. No-one would believe it. I would only be accused of making it up to score some dubious attention. I even began to question its validity myself, even Jean's sincerity. Perhaps once I had gone I would be forgotten and the whole affair would undo itself equally rapidly. If there was something I had learnt from this homecoming it was how fickle the human heart could be given the opportunity. The doubts began to creep back and, in my craving for reassurance, I tortured both of us, accusing Jean of simply amusing himself to pass the time. I let Jean think I believed there had been a good sense behind the warnings of Monsier Gobeaux and Peter.

Since my indisposition Jean's early morning visits to my room had become an established part of our daily round. Within an intimacy fast developing in the chill, dark mornings, I often didn't know he was there until wakened by his kisses when, shining with early morning tenderness and innocent mischief, he would sit on the edge of my bed and woo me with sweet words of love. On my last morning I was awake and ready for him.

"How are you today?" he greeted me cheerfully and as usual I removed his glasses as he bent over to kiss me. His newly shaved face was soft and I put my arms around his neck and held him tightly. "I love you darling," he whispered.

"Say it in French," I said, stroking his hair which was still damp from his efforts in the bathroom.

"*Je t'aime. Je t'adore,*" he said while I played with his hair, pressing it into waves before combing it back into place with my fingers.

"I expect you say that to all the girls," I taunted him. He sat up and looked down on me with a despairing frown.

"Which girls, where are all those girls you speak about?"

"Girls you will meet when I have gone back."

"*Chérie*, why do you always say that? I do not wish to meet other young girls - why do you think that? Why can't you be sure I love you?"

I was ashamed of upsetting him and eased myself up to rest against the headboard and hoped to make amends with a smile while working my finger down inside his shirt collar to feel his skin. He caressed the hair from my face and assured me.

"One little girl is enough for me - I have no time to start all over again, Mayala I have forgotten all - I must say." Then slowly drawing back the covers, his expression admiring and seductive, he ran his finger down my neck to the ribbons on my nightdress which he loosened.

"You are naughty," I feebly protested, making little effort to restrain him.

"And you are so lovely," he said, bending forward and burying his face in my bosom. "I shall be desolate when you are away," he sighed. Overwhelmed by my love, I folded my arms around his neck and hugged him close to kiss his brow, his hair and his ears. He sat up again and reclaimed his glasses, and gently easing the bedclothes up around my chin, he tucked me in like a tiny child.

When he had gone I lay some minutes giving reign to the new, mysterious and wonderful longings which had taken me over mind and body.

PART EIGHT

COVERING UP

It was another bitterly cold day as I sat hunched in the corner seat of the carriage, my hands in my pockets, the rough moquette of the upholstery prickling through to the backs of my legs. There was a smell of fish and soot and, outside, the first flecks of snow were tossed hither and thither on the wind. It was exactly five weeks since I had made that fateful journey in the opposite direction but this time there was not the same expectation, nothing to look forward to except, perhaps, a letter! I remained frozen in the same position for most of the time, swaying rhythmically from side to side or buffeted by the occasional bursts of impatience from the engine as we steamed ever onwards, each mile as it flashed past taking me further away from my love. I was convinced the affair must be over, that thrown once more amongst his hot-blooded compatriots Jean would regret his promises and gently back out of them. The note of the engine changed key and I recognised the long slow run-down into Winchester station. Cold and miserable, I collected my things, feeling little cheer at the prospect of getting into the new house for tea.

Robin came to meet me from the train and as we walked to the car where Lady Lever was waiting.

"Does she know anything - about what happened over Christmas?" I asked him, not at all sure he fully appreciated the situation himself.

"About you being engaged to - Spider, do you mean?"

"Sh-yes," I whispered, taken aback at both his acuity and his bluntness.

"Doesn't seem to - that is, she's never mentioned it."

"Thank goodness. I won't either - so please don't say anything will you? I'll leave it to Mummy to break the news."

"Hallo there Marjorie dear," came the cheerful burr of Lady Lever from the depths of the car as I climbed in beside her. She kissed me affectionately. "What a stranger! Well, you did have a long holiday, quite fit now I hope?" I was already the reticent schoolgirl again as I replied.

"Yes, thank you."

She forced bright conversation as we drove out of the station precinct, the three of us under the cosy bearskin, tactfully recognising that after five weeks away I would need to re-acclimatise myself. "Robin has missed you," she said to make me feel welcome.

"What a shame," I responded.

"Charlie Chaplin's Great Dictator is on at the Forum and I thought we'd take a trip down on Thursday."

"That would be nice." I didn't feel like talking.

The clean, country setting came again in contrast to the excitement and homeliness of war-scarred London and, as we drove through the town to start the climb up to Northlands, the new house amongst the beech trees, the square cathedral pile rose up higher from the water-meadows to dominate the skyline. There was so much beauty here and I was in no mood for any of it. It only emphasised my desolation.

As we entered the house, warm and ordered, vases of hot-house flowers devoutly arranged on every suitable surface, I caught sight of the stand in the lobby with its macabre assortment of sporting tackle. Fishing rods, keep nets and the cases of shot-guns and cartridges underneath - all to do with the snaring and death of some helpless creature and I felt trapped too. Robin took off his coat to hang amidst the grisly paraphernalia while Lady Lever loosed hers into the waiting arms of Macdonald.

Sir Hardman had heard us come in and sauntered into the hall, watch in hand, his thumb keeping his place in a book.

"Good afternoon Sir Hardman, Happy New Year," I greeted him dutifully.

"Hello, young lady, Happy New Year to you too - had a good journey? Train on time I see."

"Yes, thank you."

"The two-thirty's always the best on a Sunday. Get a seat? Many troops about?"

"No - I mean yes, I got a seat, the carriage was nearly empty."

"All quiet on the Western Front?"

"Yes, thank you, what about down here, any warnings?"

"No, but we had a spot of bother here last week, don't you know, what!" he exclaimed, eyeing Robin. "Ask your brother to tell you about it."

"What happened?" I asked him. Sir Hardman cut in impatiently.

"Smile at your sister -"

"Oh - you've broken your tooth, I never noticed."

"He can tell you about it himself later, now hurry up and get yourself washed and brushed up young lady - we want our tea don't we Robin? It's nearly five," he impressed on me.

Lady Lever ordered Macdonald to put a match to the spirit stove on the tea-table and Sir Hardman folded his glasses away in his top pocket. After carefully marking his place with a piece of folded paper, he ambled into the dining-room, his hand on Robin's shoulder. I heard the lustres ring out as I climbed the stairs unfastening my coat as I went, where Cannon was waiting to show me to my new room.

"Hallo dear, better are you? A bit pale still, but I see you are wearing a nice new dress - turn round, oh my, you do look grown-up," she said as I obliged. "Flu was it? Or just a heavy cold?"

"Flu, I think. I had a temperature of a hundred and one degrees," I said, not wishing to underrate my symptoms.

"There's a lot about; I think it's the lack of proper food. You know soap's going to be rationed do you? How you

231

are expected to have clean white blouses for school with no soap to wash them, I don't know. Oh my - what's to become of us all? I've put TCP in your bathroom - I should gargle tonight after the journey. You've a lovely view of the city from here but it's not like the other house."

I was indeed back in this very English, yet alien, world. In bed at half-past nine with my bedside lamp switched off in my splendid new surroundings, I craved Jean's kisses and tried to recapture them in my dreams by imagining myself in his arms as I had been at Waterloo station until the train was due to depart.

"What will you do when you get back?" I had asked him.

"I will write to you a letter, also I must be very busy - I have a lot of work to do," he stressed with a smile.

"I shall not have time to enjoy myself - two weeks only and you will be here again."

Two weeks, two weeks! It sounded an age. How would two weeks ever pass in the slow pace of life here in the country, where we could hear every second tick, and where the only beautiful thing that came about was the passing of the seasons. Two weeks nagged at my brain for hours until it became like two years and my tears ran silently into my pillow.

I was up as usual, dressing in the black knickers, navy blue skirt, white blouse and gold house tie which made up my school uniform. It was back to the old routine of Cannon giving me a call at seven-thirty and checking at intervals to make sure I was getting up while running the bath and putting out the clean underclothes for her mistress the other side of the landing. For once I was eager and on time. I wanted to see Cicely, the only one with whom I could talk.

I was always a little envied by my classmates for my connection with London and they welcomed me back in the hope of vicarious thrills from tales of the havoc wrought by the bombs or even American soldiers. It was a bolster to my vanity I usually enjoyed but not today. I sat down on the seat of my desk which gave me splinters in my bottom and saw my initials and those of Tony, painstakingly gouged out last summer, separated by a dripping heart pierced by an arrow. Afterwards, as I was filling them in artistically with red ink, Cicely had pointed out that instead of a clean penetration, Cupid's arrow had made a stitch. "Looks as if he had a job to pin you down," she chuckled. How right she turned out to be I told myself and shamefully covered them with my books.

I was a schoolgirl again, to be ordered and corrected, to be receptive and obedient, or rather not expected to be obedient at all but disruptive and insolent. We were all cast in the same mould in the eyes of our teachers without exception, as maiden ladies. Whereas for five whole weeks I had been a young woman, loved, considered and praised. I studied our irritable form mistress writing equations on the blackboard and wondered if she had ever experienced the joy of a lover's kiss. She still kept her girlish figure but her wavy chestnut hair, now white-streaked, was cropped unbecomingly short and kept in place by an obtrusive Kirby grip.

As she worked away for our benefit, throwing an occasional glance over her shoulder to check we were ostensibly at work, I noticed for the first time a ring on her third finger of the hand holding the book from which she was copying. Was this a clue to her anxiety, her irascibility for which we all despised her? I was inundated with pity. Had someone once loved her, enough to want to make her his bride? If the engagement had been broken surely she would have returned the ring. Perhaps her lover was dead, killed in the last war. With a shiver I fingered the gold chain around my neck and pulled it up inside my blouse to fondle the little emerald ring hidden from the world which Jean had chosen for me because it was my birthstone.

Cicely was quick to sense my reticence and opened up conversation as soon as we were alone on our way down to the sketch club.

"You've hardly spoken since you've been back - why were you late back anyway? Were you really ill?" I deemed this was not the moment to take her into my confidence.

"Well - I was, and I wasn't," I said mysteriously. I wanted her to probe.

"Do explain what you mean, you're sort of different."

"Am I? In what way?"

"Well, I can't tell whether you've really changed - through illness or something or whether you're just being affected."

"I have changed - in a way," I said preciously. She summed me up quickly and her tone hardened.

"You are being affected. I thought it might have been something to do with those Belgians you described in your letter, the one you called Spider," she specified, to see the effect it had on me. I desperately wanted to tell her about him. In fact I felt fit to burst if I kept things to myself much longer. So, hiding behind the pretext of just another schoolgirl crush, I gave way to my true feelings.

"Oh he's marvellous, absolutely divine, he really is - I'm terribly in love with him," I raved.

"Oh really," she remarked in her calm, matter-of-fact tone, well-used to this kind of outburst from me.

"Do tell me what he's like."

"He is six feet four, two inches taller than Errol Flynn! He's an officer and he speaks with the most heavenly accent - everything about him is - well - perfect! He wears glasses, his ears stick out and my mother calls him Spider because of his long legs," I added deliberately, half because I was afraid she might just have taken me seriously and half in order to laugh myself, to relieve the tension.

Cicely slid me a pitying old-fashioned look and declared with stinging sarcasm, "He sounds perfect, I must say." There was a silence. I looked at her and she at me and slowly we dissolved into a protracted attack of the giggles and we continued laughing until we were crying with big tears rolling down our cheeks. But it resolved the situation and we were back on our old footing.

"Oh he is, he is - really he is, though he's nothing like a real spider," I continued as we blew into our handkerchiefs.

"I should hope he isn't," she said, stopping dead to laugh again loudly with her head back.

"I saw Tony last week and he asked when you were coming back," she said, sobering down equally rapidly.

"Gosh, did he really?"

"You haven't gone off him, have you?"

"I think I have a bit."

"Oh you haven't," she scolded and we continued in silence pre-occupied with our thoughts.

"And what did this handsome, foreign giant think of you?" Cicely enquired derisively as we turned the corner of the block.

"I think he was quite - keen," I said, wishing to drop the subject. "Look it's beginning to snow again," I cried and we started to run, clutching our berets, our gasmasks and satchels flapping against us as we attempted to catch the large wet flakes before they reached the ground.

I hurried up the drive of Northlands against the driving sleet and wondered what was going on at home. I picked up the letter on the hall table as I came in and closed my eyes with both relief and dread. I guessed the identity of its author as soon as I spotted it through the glass inner door, lying boldly there on the silver salver, addressed to me, with its London postmark, for all the world to see. I shivered as I read the unfamiliar writing and decided to take it up to my room to read alone and hopefully undisturbed. My inside began to tingle as I climbed the stairs, clutching the precious, portentous envelope against my satchel.

"Hallo," called Cannon from her vantage point on the landing. "Seen your letter?"

"Yes, I've got it, thank you."

"I expect your mother's anxious to know how you got on after the journey." I couldn't bring myself to deceive her; neither could I tell her the truth.

"I - I don't think the letter's from my mother."

"Oh?" She pretended to be unconcerned.

"No, it's from - a friend, I think," I said, knowing full well that she was perfectly aware it was not my mother's handwriting on the envelope.

"You haven't opened it then?" she declared in surprise. The letter began to burn my hand.

"I thought I would take my things off first, my hands are freezing - it started to snow again and my hair's quite wet," I said.

"Shall I come and rub it for you? You don't want to catch another cold."

"No – no," I said quickly. "It's hardly anything, really - it was only my beret which got a bit damp." And I took it off and knocked it against my side to demonstrate the fact.

Inside my private sanctum at last, I shut the door and stood against it a moment as if someone might have been going to force an entry. Then I propped the letter prominently on the dressing-table while I changed my shoes, hung up my coat, and went to the lavatory; in fact saving the moment until, settled in the armchair at last, nothing would mar my peace of mind or comfort of body. I was also putting it off because I was afraid. Even now I let the letter rest on my lap while I warmed my hands under my armpits - treating it almost with contempt - then suddenly, sticking my nail under the corner of the flap, I eased it open, ready for anything.

The large untidy writing had the same ingenuous quality as his early attempts at English conversation and as my eyes moved ardently over the words and my worst fears were immediately allayed, I could hear his voice, with the accent that thrilled me to the centre of my being speaking to me once more.

Beloved Marjorie,

I miss you very much. During all the day I am thinking of you and your cherished image is steadily in my mind.

Now you are away, I get a clearer picture of my love for you. One thing pains me, it is that you don't believe me, you don't believe in my faithfulness, you are afraid that I shall meet one pretty young girl with whom I shall be flirting and like her better than you.

Non Chérie that shall never happen. If you knew me better, if you knew my life you would surely lose that silly fear because one of my qualities is the constancy of my love. Only twice before you I have been really in love and I remained faithful notwithstanding the very little hope I had to see the girl share my love. Perhaps fear you that I still love Anita? Non petite Chérie it is ended, completely terminated. I should lie if I said that it has run out when I just met you. I must even say that I still loved

*her a few days before you went back, but today I may write
sincerely that I love you Darling more and better than I ever
loved anybody. The love I had for Anita made me suffer very
much while ours is lucky and happy. We love each other! And
that is very scarce on this world. Chérie I wish not that you
mistrust me, because in love doubt is painful and also if it is not
well-founded it is an offence against the suspected one.*

*I love you Darling with all my heart. I don't only love you
because you love me and because I delight in being loved. No, I
love you because you are you. I guess many qualities of your
brain and your soul, for instance, a keen sensibility and a great
delicateness, just that one I prefer.*

*I don't want to flatter you. I know also your sins, not all of
them, I shall not talk about them, you know them better than I
do.*

*Chérie I must finish my letter although I have many nice things
to say to you but the dinner is ready and M. Gobeaux is not
waiting!*
*I love you with all my heart darling, I cannot love you any more
than I do.*

I adore you.
Jean.

P.S. I hope see you again in a fortnight.
P.P.S. Kind regards to dear Robin
P.P.S. Forgive the mistakes, my bad English, et ma sale écriture.

I had a wild desire to rush about, to sing aloud, to take off
my school clothes and put on my best ones; to dash from
the room and acclaim the truth to Cannon; to sit down and
write back to him at once to tell him I believed

wholeheartedly in all he had written. But, instead, I tucked the letter into the pocket of my blouse under my cardigan, nearest my heart, walked over to the dressing table and took a long look at the image the other side of the looking glass. The stranger, as she appeared to me, with the small pointed features of her father and the dark Mediterranean eyes of her mother, brighter and more liquid than usual. I brushed my hair as I did every day on my return from school, straightened the tie in its anti-feminine collar and went downstairs, trying to show as little emotion as if I had received a letter from my music teacher reminding me to turn up for my exam with clean fingernails.

"You look a little flushed this evening Marjorie dear," remarked Lady Lever at the tea-table. "I should gargle before you go to bed - just to be on the safe side. We don't want another flare-up of your flu."

"Oh I feel perfectly well, absolutely all right again now," I said. All the same I did gargle that night, like mad, and I said my prayers. No new indisposition must be allowed to prevent my trip to London for the wedding.

On Saturday the first post brought the letter from my mother informing Lady Lever of the engagement and requesting her sanction for me to go home for the weekend of the 7th. Macdonald brought in the mail while we were still at breakfast. I should have urged my mother to keep things secret from this corner of the world. Lady Lever was disapproving enough of my friendship with Tony, a mere boy of fifteen. Could we really have imagined that an impromptu love affair culminating in a promise of marriage from a comparatively unknown foreigner, twelve years my senior, would meet with her more ready approval? In putting an end to one worrying relationship this was the last thing she would have bargained for in acquiescing to my mother's wish to have us home for Christmas. Her reaction to the news before her was one of complete and utter stupefaction as she read on. I could see all respect for my mother drain away with the colour in her face. For a few moments she was distraught. Her anxious, unbelieving eyes moved rapidly from the letter to me, the window and back again. She appeared to look right through me, as if she hoped for one mad moment I was not there. After reading the letter once more she placed it at the bottom of the pile and made no intimation to us that she had received word from our mother as she usually did, knowing that Robin and I could recognise the writing on the envelope. Her expression became calm again but I could sense the storm gathering as with great self-control she immersed herself in the rest of her correspondence. Sir Hardman, engrossed in his own mail, noticed nothing.

"Anything of interest, my dear?" he enquired as usual, straightening himself and pocketing his glasses. Lady Lever fussed consecutively with her cup and saucer, butter knife and pearls.

"Erm - no - Sammy, not really, one or two bills - and things I'd better attend to right away," she said, carefully gathering everything to her bosom.

"What sort of things?" he asked, alerted.

"Oh - silly things," she answered irritably, shaking her head. "I'll go and do them right away. You children," she stressed, "have plenty to occupy you this morning and Oh Marjorie, when you've tidied your room I would like to see you in the study," she said and waved us from the room.

"Sammy - something very tiresome has cropped up," she said, walking over to his side of the table, then, thinking better of it she stopped, scratched her head and continued forward. I overheard the words 'weekend' and 'wedding'.

***

It had been an unusual week in many respects. I had work to make up at school and now that we had moved away from the village where Tony lived I didn't see him except at church and there we always behaved as strangers anyway. Most of the time I moved around in a daze, reading and re-reading my love letter which I kept with me the whole time. It had certainly added another new and wonderful dimension to our love. At others I was strung up and on my guard, extra-sensitive to the moods of everyone while waiting for the first crack of thunder which I was certain would come. It was a relief that Lady Lever had been informed. I was glad she wanted to see me, that everything would be out in the open.

She was sitting in front of her typewriter when I entered the study and she got up and closed the door behind me. "Sit down, Marjorie my dear," she began kindly, and sat down herself in the armchair opposite, crossing one of her long shapeless legs over the other.

"I expect you can guess why I have asked you to come, why I want a little private chat with you," she said, busily fitting a cigarette into her long silver cigarette-holder which she lit up from her table-lighter. I waited until she had sensually breathed out her first inhalation before replying.

"Yes, I think so." She cleared her throat.

"Your mother has written me this morning to say she has given her consent to your engagement - to an officer in the Belgian army!" I could not help but feel proud on hearing this but the coldness of her tone put me on my guard.

"Yes," I answered, smiling in an appeal for her not to be too harsh.

"I can tell you it has come as a great shock - but as I know nothing, no-one has told me anything until now, you must forgive me if I seem - well - surprised. I would like you to tell me what you have to say about it." I hung my head hardly knowing how to begin. Why should I feel so guilty, and why should the one who loved me subject me to this cross-examination? He should be here to speak with me. "Have you known this young man long - had you met him before the Christmas holiday?" she offered to help me along. She tapped her ash into a little dish at her side and furtively removed a speck of tobacco from her tongue with her thumb and middle finger and flicked it away.

"No, I haven't - I had not seen him before," I said as if it would somehow make it sound better than worse. She eased the holder back between her teeth with a tiny nod of bewilderment.

"Are you in love with him, my dear?" I flushed. A little robin hopping outside the French Windows in the remains of the snow caught my eye. Lady Lever frowned.

"I - think so," I said, my eyes on the robin. She gasped open-mouthed.

"You only think so!" she exclaimed with a scornful chuckle. "My poor, dear child, there is no happiness in marriage

243

without real, incontrovertible love. Do you want to marry him?" I knew I was condemning myself with every word.

"Yes," I said and coughed, trying to speak out more positively, "But not for at least a year."

"So your mother tells me - and you think that during that year you will grow to love him, sincerely?" Realising it was hopeless, I made no attempt to redeem myself.

"I was really rather surprised he wanted to marry me," I confessed, and she seemed relieved and softer.

"Marjorie, my dear, how did this young man - what is his name?"

"Jean – it's French for John."

"How did - Jean behave towards you - do you feel he loves you? Tell me about him."

By encouraging me to talk she hoped for a clearer picture of my feelings. My top lip quivered and I took out my hanky to cover it. The little robin - a small natural mercy - kept hopping on to the same stone. I did not know how to answer my wartime guardian. I could not tell her that Jean was loving and demonstrative, that he had come secretly into my room each morning to wake me with kisses and, at the end of the day, had often carried me upstairs to bed. Yet I wanted to give her a good impression. I wanted to stress his tenderness and protectiveness - him treating me at times as a father might his child of which my own experience was so incomplete, and which, I imagined, was one of the most perfect of all relationships. "He must have made some impression on you - if you have agreed to become his wife!" she prompted impatiently. "It's a very big step to take, the promise of a lifetime together - you do realise that?" My hands felt moist and awkward and I put them behind me.

"Yes. He was very nice, very kind to me - he seemed to behave in a fatherly way." Lady Lever brightened. Was this the clue she had been waiting for? "And you feel that is a good basis for marriage, where you are to live with and love someone despite everything for the rest of your life? You know what marriage is all about my dear, the intimate loving and giving of one's whole self - children. No, of course, you can't possibly understand all that yet."

She closed up and became unrelaxed, searching for loose hairpins in her hair which she pushed back so that it looked almost painful. "Suppose you are in love with Monsieur - Jean, which I don't believe you are. I believe - as you say yourself - that you are thinking of him as the father you sadly lost and goodness knows what that poor man would think of all this - however you are only sixteen, not even that! It's not to say you will feel the same at twenty-one. At twenty-one you will be free to marry whoever you choose. You have the whole business of growing from a child to a woman between now and then and, my dear child, those few years can make a world of difference, believe me. You won't be looking for a father's love at twenty-one!"

The robin was watching me and seemed to cock his little head in sympathy. "Marjorie, sixteen is a very beautiful age. At sixteen you have the world at your feet and you can fall in love with who you like," she soliloquised. "Be careful, is all I can say. Oh yes, I was the same at your age. I too was in love at sixteen, seventeen actually." She stopped speaking to look at me full in the face as if I might have difficulty believing her. "With my German music teacher - my parents warned me and of course I didn't want to listen - but they were right and when I was twenty-one I understood the mistake I might have made if I'd followed the dictates of my childish heart. You see, we were all ready to run away together - we knew there had never been love quite like it before." She had cheered herself up and I hoped the interview was nearly over. "Marjorie dear, I want you to promise me something," she said. "Will you do that?"

"Yes," I said, willing to promise almost anything to get away.

"If ever you feel you cannot go on with this engagement because you have stopped loving Monsieur - Jean, or for whatever reason, will you tell me? It's up to you, not your mother - nor anyone else, not even Monsieur Jean. For one thing it wouldn't be fair to him, to let him think you were waiting for him when you weren't even sure - would it?"

"No, it wouldn't," I agreed, wishing she would not call him Monsieur Jean.

"So you will make that promise?"

"Yes."

"Good child. Have you thought what it would mean to live in another country, speaking a foreign language where you had no friends or family of your own?"

"I have a little."

"And is - Jean a Roman Catholic? That's another important consideration."

"I don't really know but I believe he is; most Belgians are."

"And do you realise what that will mean, being married to a Roman Catholic? You would have to change your religion and promise to bring up your children as Catholics and there might be quite a family," she added wryly.

"Would you like that?"

"No, not very much," I answered truthfully. I was rather afraid of Catholics and the idea of having to confess one's sins to a priest filled me with unholy dread.

Lady Lever uncrossed her legs and folded them over the other way and still managed to keep both feet touching the ground. It fascinated me how she could do this for when I tried one foot always bounced up in the air. My mother had been brought up a Catholic but my father was not one, neither were Robin and I. Lady Lever was not necessarily right about everything.

"I shall write to your mother. I'm glad we've had this little chat and don't forget your promise. Oh, and there's one more thing," she said ominously. "We shall keep this as our little secret. It's our little confidence," she stressed guiltily, "From everyone, even Sir Hardman, is that understood?" She got up and came and placed her arm around my shoulder. "Think over what we've said, there is all the time in the world to fall in love - you don't want to rush into it. I am fond of you and want you to have a happy life. Perhaps you are a little infatuated with your Belgian Officer, after all it's very flattering to have a proposal of marriage at fifteen isn't it?" she added with surprising understanding. "Alrighty - then off you go," she said and ushered me from the room. "We'll have to see about re-organising the Squad when the warm weather comes," she called after me.

I went to my room to begin my reply to Jean, as far as I could in French, simply to convince myself that his nationality, another language, had absolutely no bearing on our love. Lady Lever went back to her typewriter and placed a piece of paper ready for a letter, then with a firm shake of her head she took it out again and picked up her pen. Her indignation was returning. How could Mrs. Rae be such a silly woman? She wrote hurriedly in large uninhibited writing, not even beginning the letter 'Dear Mrs. Rae'.

I feel more and more appalled when I think of your consent to Marjorie's engagement. I have spoken to her and the child is not the slightest bit in love. All she would say was 'he seemed nice and that she was surprised he wanted to marry her as he acted towards her in a fatherly manner.

And she underlined 'fatherly' three times.

I have not dared tell Sir Hardman for I know how angry he would be and not with Marjorie. If Lieut. Cornez comes down here with you I cannot receive him. Have you thought what his mother will say and has he her consent? To send a child of seventeen to Belgium without a single friend! England will be a poor enough place after the war but I cannot imagine what Belgium will be like. Also, he is an R.C.

Lady Lever was from French Huguenot extraction.

Marjorie said she would not like to change her religion and what will his mother think of that? I can't see much happiness for the child without deep, real affection for the man she is going to marry. As for her coming back for the wedding on the 7th, I really feel this is an unnecessary extravagance, especially as it's not a family wedding. Sir Hardman says will you write to the Headmistress yourself to ask permission. She will have to take a very small bag as she will have to walk back from the station on Sunday. The chauffeur is away at present and the gardener is off duty on Sundays. Altogether, it is most inconvenient.

My mother enclosed the necessary note for me to take to the Headmistress in the second letter I received from Jean.

My beloved Marjorie,

I was very impatient to receive your letter and nearly becoming to be angry but it happened with the war, the snow and the black-out, the post was very slow.

You were so kind to write in French and I hope you will be quickly improving - each time just a little. Do not be angry if I give you some advices for your French - I trust you'll pardon my correction, that stuff is there for your instruction! You have written j'était, j'écrit. The t̲ is the mark of the third person - il était - you must write j'étais, j'écris with an s̲.

But let us speak of other things, I do not want to be like a teacher for you.

I prefer to tell you how much I adore you.

I am glad you found my letter like a good whisky and a hot fire.

I see you cannot understand. It was so because when you received it you were wet and frozen. Maybe my letter, it was like a dry, hot towel! Was it not?

I do not think Lady Lever is very fond of me but I hope she will change her mind if she knew me - am I conceited? And I think she will certainly change, when after the war, I shall come back and marry you.

Darling, let us do not take care of the opinion of the world, our love is great enough to do so. You know Chérie everybody may say what he likes, if we remain honest and if we love each other as we do, we will certainly live in the most happiness and God will bless us - as your mother did on Christmas Eve, do you remember? We have stayed together during only a month but it was such a good time that we have a big lot of memories.

I shall never forget how kind you were when you brought me a cup of coffee because I was tired. Also I shall never forget how sweet and nice you were in the cosy living room and in the mornings when I came to wish you a happy day. We have a big lot of memories but haven't we an unlimited lot of hopes and projects?

I miss you Darling, and when I am writing to you it is nearly like a conversation, I feel you near me, and therefore I like very much to write long letters. Perhaps they are stupid but it makes me so happy I can't finish them.

Darling all the things are so lonely and the house so empty without you.

I enjoy myself with the idea that soon I shall see you again. You are for me more than all the rest of the world.

May I know at last which things you say you love in me? Please tell me.

Do not answer a lot of things - as you did so often. I want some precision, to know what you like in me and to be able to love you better if it is possible.

Ma Chérie, I adore you more every minute, may I kiss you - X. That is only a kiss through a letter. I hope soon to give you real ones.

Goodnight Darling, happy dreams - I believe you will receive this in the evening.

Jean.

P.S. I adore you.

I longed to sit down and write back, to tell him what I loved in him. His tenderness above all, his vulnerability and his strength; the candour in his eyes which were the windows of his soul; his smile which every time it shone touched the bottom of my heart; his ears which gave him that earnest, enquiring look of a little boy. I loved his hair with its tendency to wave that he brushed back so severely in his efforts to look a soldier. His graceful hands with their so gentle caress and his long, sensual back, the embodiment of all that enchantment. But there was not time for another letter for better still, in two days' time, I would be there, in his arms. First, with the help of my mother's note, I must convince our almost senile headmistress that my journey was imperative.

***

I took my place in the queue to go on the platform after prayers to see our headmistress, a big woman and a veritable dragon in her time - who would have retired but for the war - was inconsistent and unpredictable nowadays. She was slow in dealing with the various items of business brought to her attention, mostly in the form of notes to explain absence or permission to keep dentist appointments and the like. I grew more apprehensive as my turn approached in case she reproved me for wanting to take part in such a frivolous activity as a wedding when there were serious matters like School Cert. in the offing. One got the feeling that for her weddings, or any occasion that pandered to feminine vanity, were all rather infra dig. Even at the best of times.

"Right, next," she croaked, her right arm outstretched and I realised it was my turn. She opened the envelope and read through the contents hurriedly, making little affirmative grunting noises while I, hardly daring to breathe, contemplated the parting in her thin, grey hair, her years' old threadbare gown, turning brown in its folds and the coffee-coloured stains down the front of her white, tucked blouse covering her very ample, low-slung bosom. I felt sorry for her. She was a mass of contradictions. Easing herself back in her chair, she took off her glasses with a quick, mechanical movement as if wrenching sticking plaster from her eyes, coughed into her chest and drew her lips back from her teeth in a kind of depraved smile.

"Marjorie Rae," she said with some relish and my heart felt as if it had dropped into my shoes. "Marjorie Rae," she spoke out again as if playing for time or had taken a sudden fancy to my name, "of the lower fifth? You're the gal who's come to us from London are you not?"

"Yes, Miss," I answered quaking.

"Um, Marjorie - hope you're happy with us?" she muttered, seeming to have lost her train of thought, and after reading the letter again she thrust it aside and offered me another toothy grimace.

"So you want permission to leave after morning session on Friday?"

"Yes, please Miss."

"To go to London for a wedding?" I crossed my fingers behind my back.

"Yes please, so I won't have to travel in the black-out" I said, taking a gamble on her compassion. She turned and frowned, focusing her eyes on nothing in particular as if about to lecture on the evil of boys in dimly-lit railway compartments, one of her pet topics.

"Marjorie," she began ponderously, "You may go to your wedding. I think it is important to keep up with friends these days for one never quite knows when one will meet again." I could hardly believe it. God seemed to be blessing us already.

"Thank you Miss," I replied and prepared to leave the platform. "One minute - will you tell Lady - er Rae that for such a minor deviation from the school rules it was extremely gracious of her to write a note. Of course I grant my permission and I hope you have a happy weekend. Give my respects to Lady Rae - tell her another time a 'phone call would have been quite in order," she drooled unctuously, the corners of her mouth shooting up to meet the two wrinkled slits that were her eyes.

***

The wintry trees stood out very black against the cold, moist sunset as the train rattled on to leave the countryside. The evenings were drawing out and the blackbird was singing again in the cottage gardens. Hope was already to rise up in another day over and away behind the bright, pinkish horizon. Christmas gave the impression of having passed a long time ago. Two weeks had been an age and now, on my way at last, urging the train on faster, I worked out every permutation of my reunion with Jean. Would he be there at Waterloo or would it be my mother? Would he be at home or still on his way back from school?

Just after we left Woking station I paid a visit to the W.C. to comb my hair and to apply a trace of lipstick. Released from the Levers and school, I felt grown up and self-possessed.

I was positively trembling with joy as we drew alongside the platform at Waterloo where I soon spotted Jean, alone and hatless, above the heads of most. Then all at once I was there in his arms, completely safe, caring nothing for the opinion of the world as we embraced one another affectionately and passionately. The separation, the new opposition of Lady Lever, had not made one scrap of difference. If anything, it had only strengthened our love and confirmed our need for each other. He took over my small bag, and with his arm around my shoulder, one finger inside the collar of my coat fondling my cheek, we walked to the Underground.

I was beginning to learn that with the capacity to love intensely there comes the agony of suffering with great depth of feeling. One cannot be without the other. Ecstasy must be balanced by anguish. All around us were the harrowing reminders of the war, sandbags, first aid posts, placards marshalling and directing troop assembly and displacement, and there were the people, dependent, clinging and driven. Men weighed down with cumbersome packs, weary and unsettled; tearful women overwrought after frantic leaves seeking solace in cups of tea, bewildered and tired children, doomed to long and often final separation. In spite of my happiness with Jean at my side and the weekend before us, I was touched with compassion on passing them by.

The tube-train was packed with rush-hour travellers and we stood near the door ready to get out as soon as we came to our stop. Jean steadied himself against the glass partition and encircled me with his arms to keep me balanced as the train whistled and jolted us along the track, bumping us ever closer in its impatience to get us home. It was too noisy to talk and we could only look shyly to refresh our memories of all we had missed during the previous fortnight.

The searchlights were active over the common, their long, smoky beams criss-crossing the sparse cloud in the sky. "What are they looking for?" I remarked to Jean. He looked up so that I caught a glimpse of his noble profile silhouetted against the bright air.

"It is a practice - or perhaps they wish to find heaven," he suggested whimsically.

"Do you believe in heaven?" I asked.

"Of course."

"What do you believe is up there in heaven?"

"The angels, the stars," he said lightly.

"When I was a little girl I used to think the stars were the souls of all the dead people who had gone to heaven - I thought my father was a star, the biggest and brightest in the sky - heaven doesn't look very far away tonight."

"*Ma Chérie,*" he said, restraining me with his linked arm, "For me tonight heaven is here on earth," and he put down my case by the gate and hugged and kissed me before we went up the path.

My mother, one of our few sympathetic well-wishers, opened the door eager and smiling.

"Hello Ducky, back again," she said, embracing me fondly and using it as an excuse to kiss Jean too. "You're warm, both of you - as warm as toast. Bless your hearts, my children," she said with affectionate understanding. "Come and meet the other Marjorie," she said, leading us towards the drawing room.

There was a lovely smell of roasting chicken. A bird of some sort was generally her way of marking a celebration. Here at home it was always Christmas and I noticed with surprise the evergreen still festooned around the picture-rail. I began to wonder.

"I left them there," she said, spotting me looking up. "They were so pretty, Bear and the boys had taken such a lot of trouble, I thought they would be nice for the wedding."

"It's supposed to be unlucky," I said.

"Fine time to tell me now - look who's here," she announced to the room.

"Ah Mademoiselle Marjorie," exclaimed Bunny, jumping up to embrace me warmly on both cheeks, "You have come back to dance? Ho ho," he chuckled and, humming a tune, he swept me up in his arms and waltzed me round the room.

"This is - or was - my daughter," said my mother, addressing the two girls on either side of Bear. "Marjorie, the *fiancée* of Spider, come here and meet Marjorie the bride of Bear," she quipped. "Oh, and this is Kay her friend who has come to be chief witness," she added. "Want your fortune told? Kay will do it for you!"

"What's happened to all the others?" I asked my mother later, having noticed some new faces at dinner.

"Which others?"

"Mr and Mrs. Peter, Jefke and the one with the spotty face." It was different now; I wanted to keep track of them all.

"My dear," began my mother ominously "haven't you heard? Didn't Spider tell you?" I looked at her blankly. "We had a terrible row here after you left."

"What about?"

"Well, Spider had a real showdown with both old Gobbo and Peter - I think the letter from Lady Lever was the last straw - I'll show it you later. Then Gobbo and Peter had a big set-to that had been blowing up for some time." I was too astounded to interrupt. "Spider was right - Peter had no right to be called a Captain, he'd never been in the army and for reasons I don't properly understand, he's been interned in the Isle of Man, suspected of being a German spy or something!"

"A Germany spy?" I repeated aghast.

"Oh, I don't know there have been some funny things going on for a long time. Anyway Spider and Bunny insisted that old Gobbo got things sorted out or else they said they weren't going, it wasn't safe. It's a funny thing. Old Gobbo never liked him from the start and Spider and Bunny always said he was a great big phoney."

"Did Mrs Peter go too - to the Isle of Man?"

"She's gone but not with him - that's another thing," she added indignantly. "They weren't even married. She said Peter was very cruel to her. I couldn't help feeling sorry for her. I think she was trying to get off with Spider to escape Peter and when you came along it upset the applecart. Oh well, we live and learn. I've never seen Spider so angry - he was furious to think Peter had the audacity to criticise him when he was doing far worse himself. He looks lovely when he's angry - so full of pride and authority," she said. "I don't suppose she was all innocence - Dinah. As for Jefke and Feather they've gone - don't know where." She changed the subject. "You're going up to town with them tomorrow evening, you know. Hope you've brought your new dress. The wedding is at twelve-thirty, lunch here afterwards, then dinner in Knightsbridge in the evening."

"Are you coming?"

"No, it's only for you young ones - the Count's coming," she announced proudly, "And the girl next door" she added pulling a face.

After that first trip to the cinema, Jean had needed no further persuasion to put on his uniform. Whenever we went out together and it was practical, he wore it simply because he knew it pleased me, although he had often intimated how he preferred the casual anonymity of civilian clothes.

We got up early on Saturday morning - the weekend must not be wasted - and went up to Harrods to buy a wedding present. That in itself was enough to make my day. We ambled through the various departments and took coffee like habituees in the restaurant. In fact we were so absorbed in ourselves and our multifarious surroundings that we almost forgot our purpose in coming out, and eventually arrived at the Register Office where Jean was to be a witness, nearly a quarter of an hour late. The bridal pair had almost reached the point of plucking a complete stranger in from the road in order to proceed with the ceremony and they showed their relief by taking a firm hold of Jean and marching him straight to the Registrar. Because no-one seemed concerned with me for the moment, had made no indication that I should follow once the door had swung to behind them, I, no more familiar with the spartan protocol of an English Civilian marriage than they, stayed where I was. It was a large, bare room and outside the grimy windows snow began to fall in large wet flakes silently, relentlessly.

A noisy, jolly group of six or seven came in and I was glad. A young private in battledress, his forage cap tucked into his epaulette, had one arm clasped around the neck of a thin, pale girl dressed in a light blue costume with a pink carnation in her buttonhole. They were presumably the bride and groom. Hardly aware of me, two of the men began to crack jokes and a woman, supposedly the mother of the bride, for it was an action my own mother might have done, took out her compact and began to powder the nose of the girl. She did not look much more than sixteen. I watched the little wedding party with a mixture of fascination and envy. I was three months too young for lawful marriage, three months too young to make legal love! No-one had come in search of me. The hands of the big, round electric clock had already ticked away ten minutes at two minute intervals and I was overwhelmed by the lonely feeling of being left out which almost amounted to panic. I stood up and walked over to the door just as it opened and Jean looked in. Everyone stared as he took my hand and I hoped they thought I was a bride too, being claimed by my handsome bridegroom.

Jean took Kay's arm as well as mine and the five of us came outside where the snow was rapidly turning to slush under the influence of the weak sun. We walked a little way along the Broadway, mingling with the Saturday crowds out shopping. But cold, hungry and impatient to get into the warm house where we knew my mother would have made an extra effort with the lunch, we finally took a taxi.

In the afternoon, dizzy and aglow from the after-effects of some spurious black market Champagne, we went outside in the pale sunlight to take photographs. Afterwards we lit a bonfire with the old Christmas tree and brought down all the greenery from the picture rail to pile on top. The dry, dusty foliage made an easy crackling blaze and the excitement of the flames took hold and we danced around it in a sort of rite, holding hands, prepared to slough off the past and attack the future with all the passion we felt surging within us.

***

I awoke, my bedroom full of daylight. It had been so late when we returned from the dinner in town, just Jean and me, the others having gone on to a nightclub called Coconut Grove which Jean considered was not for us, that, when I eventually got into bed I undressed quickly without drawing the curtains or switching on my light. It was still relatively early for I could hear the clink of bottles on the milk-cart out in the road and the milkman, eager to finish his round, gently ordering his horse on as he hurried from doorstep to doorstep in the semi-comatose avenue.

Directly under my window, the restive clop of the horse's hooves on the ground made the universe, that Sunday morning, sound such a small, hollow world. In the same way as the searchlights last night had linked heaven to earth, bringing it so much nearer than it looked to be when blinking up into the blue infinity of a summer's day.

Sunday was the one day when everyone slept a little longer, and the only morning my mother did not give me a call. I turned over and closed my eyes again in the half-conscious endeavour to continue the very pleasant dream from which I had been roused. A trick which was often successful. Dozing off once more, and in that fitful state between sleeping and waking, it gradually penetrated through to me that there was a very real, though hushed fumbling outside my door accompanied by the satisfactory tinkling of crockery. An early morning cup of tea was reserved only for my birthday and anyway my mother would have walked straight in. But during that second of coming to and working all this out, the door opened and there was Jean beside my bed carefully balancing a cup and saucer in each hand.

"Coffee is served," he announced with a smile and I sat up, delighted he had not abandoned his early morning custom of coming to wish me a happy day. I took one of the cups while he went to close the door and then I saw he was dressed only in blue, cotton pyjamas with nothing on his feet. It was a cold morning with the remains of the snow outside and, feeling only for his comfort as I might have done for my mother, brother or any of my friends coming for a cosy chat, I automatically drew aside the bedclothes for him to get in beside me.

We sat drinking our coffee, eyeing each other over the cups like two bold children who had stolen together to hold a midnight feast and I hoped the warmth of my body would filter through to him via my leg which I moved alongside his.

"You are up early," I said.

"I had a very uncomfortable night, not much sleep," he replied running his hand down his back to emphasise he was suffering an aftermath of discomfort.

"Why - what's the matter?"

"I was sleeping downstairs on the couch and it was not long enough for my body," he said, giving a groan as he stretched himself so one foot stuck out of the side of the bed.

"Sh-sh" I rebuked him, fearful we might attract notice, adding in delayed astonishment:
"Why? Why ever did you sleep downstairs?" I derived a secret pleasure from knowing that his room which he shared with Bunny was next to mine and if it had not been for the wall in between we should be lying within touching distance all night.

"Because - Eve was sleeping in my bed. That is the reason I am dressed so - I cannot fetch my clothes."

"Oh!" I gasped. "Did you have to get up in the middle of the night? And where did Bunny sleep?" He did not answer immediately but raised his eyebrows and smiled in consideration of my puzzled expression.

"Well-" I repeated.

"Why? Where?" he mimicked me seeming to dodge the question and firmly closing his lips he ran his finger down my nose. I shivered and waited. "Well?" I asked again.

"Bunny was in his bed," he said again slowly and it took me a full second to gather his implication. I went hot and cold, only too aware of my own weakness in permitting him access to my room dressed as he was, let alone the shameless invitation to come into my bed. With a peremptory turn from him I asked,

"Are you the first up?"

"No - your mother is downstairs - she has made the coffee."

We finished drinking and he deposited my cup and saucer with his own and his glasses on the table beside the bed. Sitting back again he put his arms around me and drew me to him.

"Are we naughty?" I asked.

"Perhaps a little," he replied, pursing his lips and stroking the hair back from my face as he offered his eternal excuse.

"I love you."

It was delightful to be so intimate and cosy and as I lay in his arms I acknowledged that I loved him too and hoped that would make everything good in the eyes of God. We sealed our pledge with a loving kiss.

It was the first time he had come unshaven and it invested him with a new attraction, a reckless abandon, a disreputable charm, a proud flagrant virility that caught on to something deep inside me. I kissed his rough complexion, his eyes, nose and mouth as if to have every feature impressed on my lips for all the time we were going to be apart. I outlined his chin idly with my finger and drew it down over his throat. I thought of the other Marjorie and Bear in their marriage bed, of Bunny and Eve! And on an impulse to know him more intimately and see his body, it was my turn now. I unfastened his pyjama jacket and smoothed my hand over his bare chest. My hand was not cold, yet he gave a shiver and his skin broke out in tight goose pimples. He lay back against the pillows taking a passive delight in this new expression of my love which had come in its own time and seemed, by the new brighter look in his eyes, to be enciting me to go on.

I remembered the photo he had shown us, taken just after his release from the Spanish prison camp in which he had appeared so thin and where he was wearing a beret to cover his head because his hair, infested with lice, had been shaved from his head. Surely now, I marvelled to myself, he was in the peak of condition after six months in England and I allowed my hand to stray further down his body on which the Mediterranean sun had left its legacy in an enhancing, though fading, tan. I caressed my finger in the hollow of his navel.

"You have been beautifully made," I whispered with some considerable awe.

"And you equally," he said, reaching to the ribbons on my nightdress which he slowly untied. Carefully he eased the silk over my shoulders until it fell to my waist. We were on equal terms.

"You are beautiful - all of you. A man is not beautiful," he murmured, kissing my breast. I was happy and proud that he should take delight in my body. This and my reverence for his made me more adventurous. He stayed submissive, teasing, explored and exploring rather than excited and exciting, sweetly titillated, two innocents seemingly.

"You have been a man a long time," I spoke out softly.

"Umm," he shrugged non-committally.

"Were you a man at fifteen?"

"Perhaps, I have forgotten, and you? You are a woman since - one year - or less?"

"Three years, four years in June," I let him know.

"You know exactly - the year, the month, the day - the hour? How can you be so sure?" he teased.

"It is easy for a girl to know when she becomes a woman and that was when I was twelve!"

"You are already an old woman!" he exclaimed with the most ravishing grin.

He was the first man, indeed the first person ever with whom I had come in such close, naked contact and I laid myself against his warm uncovered body which complemented my own so beautifully. It was the culmination of the spring erupting on that first country year when I watched with awe the skeleton trees flush reddish at their tips before burgeoning into impressionist spots of purest green. While the shafts of sunlight shot through their trunks, growing longer daily, spotlit the snowdrops, primroses and bluebells successively upstaging each other at their feet.

"Am I really a woman?" I asked feeling myself, soft, desirable and exquisitely feminine in contrast to his man's body, my cheek finding its own natural repose in the curve of his throat.

"I have no doubts - I think it is most likely."

"Not a child?"

"My darling, I adore you whether you are a woman, a child - or are existing only in my imagination," he said, pulling up the covers to bind us even closer and through my body I could feel his heart beating with my own.

"I think - *nous sommes très* naughty," I said.

"*Très* naughty," he echoed, his accent crisp with love and a little mischief.

"Do you like being naughty?" I asked.

"Yes," he murmured into my hair.

"Have you been naughty before?"

"Yes," he whispered with some reluctance.

"Very naughty?"

He hesitated.

"Have you?" I persisted.

"Yes."

"You've made love - properly?" I charged him and when he didn't reply I lifted my head to look at his face. "Have you?" I persisted and his eyes answered with frank liquid contrition. It was a blow and I slipped down in the bed until my face was against his chest. "You are a very naughty man," I scolded, my heart pounding. He enveloped me in his arms and held me tight.

"*Chérie* - it is better that I am honest with you - no?" I nodded.

"Was she amusing?" I asked through barely open lips. He kissed the top of my head where his cheek rested and took one or two breaths.

"*Ma petite Chérie,*" he breathed into my hair, "I am ashamed of grieving you," he soothed remorsefully. "Did you love her very much?" I asked, my voice muffled by our closeness, for then I reasoned it might not matter so much.

"I owe you the truth," he said, "It was not so much a question of love. I love you better than I did anybody, nothing for me was so good as my love now. When I was loving before those young girls were not loving me and the ones who loved me I was not loving them. But we love each other and that is rare, it is precious like a great treasure and we must keep it safe. But you are of more value to me even of this - you have given me faith again - and hope, faith in myself and hope for the future." He kissed my lips. "You are my future. I promise to you to try to live a good life - with you and for you," he said, and

267

seeing tears running down my face with gentle, soothing words, he wiped them away with a corner of the sheet.

"I don't think it should be called making love unless people really love one another," I remarked pettishly, still smarting from the blow which in some ways was also beginning to excite me.

"You are right, it is something different..." "What is it?", I asked, he shrugged, searching for an easy explanation. "It is called many things - perhaps it was for me a concern to prove to myself I am a man, but it is really weakness, human weakness," he qualified it as if it made it more forgivable.

"I don't think I like weak men," I said.

"Let me tell you something. When we are young we believe that the world is made for us and that we can do all which we desire but, as we grow older, *plus sage* let us hope, the values change and we realise those which are worth more and those which are worth less and we must choose which we want. It is difficult for me to explain this to you. But I hope you will understand as you grow older because we can learn from our weakness, nothing is ever without some importance - you will see."

I looked down proudly on my pale bosom compressed against his tanned body. "Do you mean you believe in love at last?"

"I have always believed in love but it is sometimes difficult to find. It can be *une illusion*, we think we have it and we have not. To make love with somebody we love sincerely and who returns that love is the best - and that will be marriage - it must be so, don't you think that?" He kissed me. "We shall discover that together," he added comfortingly. "I am also human - a little *egoiste* - I tell you about myself because - I wish that you love me for my weakness and my strength. What is passed is finished."

I was sad that he would not share with me those first tenuous raptures of physical consummation, that someone else, however unimportant to him had stolen that from me. That I was a virgin, whereas he was not, inflamed me with the urge to have him possess me there and then, to cancel out all that had gone before so that at least we could continue as equals. As I nestled closer to him, tense and excited, I think I was aware of the first stirrings of desire prickling through my veins and that he, the man of experience, recognised them.

"Would you like to make love with me?" I tried him, with only the most elementary grasp of how incautiously I was reacting. He kissed my brow and shook his head slowly from side to side without a word, replaced my nightdress primly over my shoulders and retied the ribbon. "You are cross with me?" I suggested.

"No - you know I look forward to making love to you - but we have time and," he quipped with a twinkling smile as he reached for his glasses, "I don't want to be arrested as a criminal!"

"Must you go away?" The question slipped out as I thought of Bear and his new wife, secure in the knowledge that there would be no separation for them. He creased his brow in mild distress that I should still feel doubtful and unhappy.

"You think I will not come back, that I mean nothing of what I say?"

"No - not really, I-I just don't want you to go, that's all," I said, picking at the eiderdown, "like Bear."

"You must not ask me that. You would be angry with yourself if I did not go. It is the best like this, it is better for you - for me to go and come back, better for convincing Monsieur Gobeaux and your Lady Lever. That separation will be your security - your assurance that you can have faith in me, that I speak the truth - you understand? Of course I shall come back," he stressed in one last soothing embrace.

He got up and pulled the covers snugly up to my chin and with his pyjamas still unbuttoned, sat down beside me and smiled. "When I am with you it is such a nice, beautiful world and one that I hope to share with you forever - you know that? Since I know you it makes me more certain that I must protect this life for you, therefore I am not sad to be going. You must not be sad. You will be busy while I'm away - and don't forget the French," he stressed, willing me to be confident and forward looking.

"No," I said.

"I hope it will make you happy to do that for me?"

"Yes," I replied.

"I think I will buy some records for you - Linguaphone? Do you know it? Like that it will be easier for you, you can hear the words as well as to read them and the time will pass quickly you will see - we will both be working hard!"

As he sat on the bed and put his pyjamas to rights I caught a glimpse of his long naked back and it reminded me of a picture of Christ I had seen in the National Gallery which had aroused in me a similar awe and reverence.

"Are you a Roman Catholic?" Lady Lever asked me."

"Yes, I am Catholic, not very devout - I think Lady Lever is not very fond of me, she doesn't like Catholics?"

"I don't think she does, I'm glad you are not a good Catholic."

"You are?" he queried in surprise.

"Catholics are a bit frightening - always going to Mass and Confession with rosaries and things." He patted my hand.

"Lady Lever is Christian?"

"Oh yes," I assured him.

"*Eh bien* - what is the difference? No, I think for Lady Lever, nothing of me is good."

"Oh - it's nothing personal, after all she doesn't know you, it's just that she thinks I'm too young to be engaged. I wonder what she would say if she knew you had come into my bed!" A flash of impish delight lit up his face.

"She will say - first, I must have the permission of my mother!"

***

Jean never referred to his job or his departure more than necessary but we both felt it looming dangerously there ahead. I was ignorant of any battle that might have been going on inside him as the day grew nearer. Could he face prison a second time if things went wrong? Would he be likely to betray compatriots or give away secrets under cross-examination? Torture, one heard stories, and death were a possibility. The strongest man would have misgivings until he had mustered the necessary faith in himself. The element of challenge would have appealed to Jean when he had needed to find new meaning for his life after the battle for his Country, his escape and the privations in Spain, when his love for Anita had kept him going only to find it rejected on his arrival here. The move of a proud, self-respecting man nonetheless, not of one broken irrecoverably by defeat. But things had changed. To make promises forever was to acknowledge the future. I was that future. He had told me. He needed me - here - waiting for him. I felt strong. Jean could depend on me. I knew too that he a man of action was committed from the beginning. Like Bear he could have turned the job down - there would be others ready to take his place - but it was not in his optimistic nature to consider failure. He would depart confidently and he would succeed! I longed to know about his mission, not from idle curiosity, but in order to visualise him at work, to comprehend some of the dangers and to be with him always in spirit.

Over the weekend I sensed that departure, the future, even death were on Bunny's mind which revealed itself in a light-hearted session of fortune-telling embarked on by Kay, the friend of the new bride. After perusing the lines on his with a near-professional scrutiny, she pointed out that his life-line was unusual in that it was broken in half, both halves being well-defined. On hearing this he sprung up, making his own predictions as if he was afraid of her continuing to do it.

"Tiens!" he exclaimed and showed my mother. "I die half-way in my life and - then I am born again - and live for many years," he said, inscribing the course of the offending lines with his finger nail, deeply, trying to weld them together. My mother laughed aloud.

"You're all right then my dear boy, what are you worrying about?"

"Anybody else want their hand done?" Kay offered.

"You, Mrs. Rae?"

"No fear, I'd rather not know what I'm in for, thank you very much."

"I won't tell you anything nasty, just the nice things," coaxed Kay.

"No - no thanks - I couldn't bear it, anyway I don't believe in it," replied my mother, making her hands into two tight fists and hiding them behind her. She was in fact very superstitious, never walked under a ladder, always threw spilt salt over her shoulder and was forever touching wood. She thought that merely contemplating the future was enough to tempt fate. Bunny offered his hand again.

"What is going to happen - in the second life?" he asked, winking at us. Kay took hold of it and caressed the bumps and studied the lines languorously.

"I see a dark woman," she spoke out slowly, "Yes, an alliance of sorts - with a dark lady."

We all looked at Eve with her blonde hair and made grimaces of sympathy. Kay continued, "A love affair perhaps?" rather fancifully.

"Tiens!" he exclaimed again, stroking an imaginary beard and striking a good imitation of Methusulah. "A love affair! But I shall be too old."

"Well, if it's not a love affair it's some sort of relationship that's beneficial to you both, a reunion maybe!" She looked up to see if this registered with him. "She's a pretty strong influence - this person, and she won't be young either." Bunny was intrigued. No-one spoke for a minute. The atmosphere tensed. My mother coughed "It can't be Eve," she pronounced, tactlessly.

"Continue," Bunny instructed Kay. "The dark woman - who is she?"

"Do you know a dark woman?" she asked.

"It is possible," he replied mysteriously. Kay concentrated.

"She could be a widow - older than you - quite a bit," Kay said but Bunny shrugged and sat back, interested no more.

"A strong character - dark - older than you, a widow?" reiterated my mother, her eyes bright. "Well, you know who that is, don't you? Why it's me, of course, who else could it be?" Bunny's mind began to work.

"Of course Madame," he said. My mother winked broadly at Jean. "A real *entente cordiale* - you and Marjorie, me and Bunny!" Bunny slapped his knee with delight and turned to his friend. *"Mon Dieu,"* he ejaculated. "I shall be his father! Ho Ho! You will have to take notice of me! Stand up and salute when I come home. Oh yes - you must behave yourself, oh my boy, I shall make you suffer." He relapsed into his chair making some remark in French *"Ton pere - nom de Dieu!"* he rasped, *"Quelle affaire!"* and they both broke into fits of laughter.

"Do Spider now," my mother ordered Kay. "Shall I?" she invited and he knelt on the floor in front of her and offered his hand. I watched his face as Kay made her inspection. "Make your hand into a fist like this. Now open it. There again, it's different, the light's not too good." He did as she asked. Kay looked puzzled. "Oh Lord!" she gasped. "I'm looking at your left hand, it's always the right hand which shows your prospects - what you make of your life. You are right-handed, I take it?" He nodded.

"Prospects?" he repeated quizzically, offering his right hand.

"That's better," she said, "Quite a family there," she prophesied relinquishing her grasp and I felt myself blush.

"Any more prospects?" he enquired, relishing the word. She gave his hand another cursory look over.

"Uhmm," she hummed, "A swift blaze of glory, either past - or to come," she pronounced airily. "Let's have a record on," suggested my mother, bored with it all. "What would you like?"

Quick as a flash Bunny said, *"Danse Macabre!"*

I had become fond of Bunny. Despite an inscrutability which I found disconcerting, he was always kindly disposed towards me. A practical joker, quicker than Jean to seize his chance, he was an altogether a more guarded character, a realist with a cynicism one suspected might have come from adversity. One could be completely disarmed by his wistful charm and he made women feel protective towards him. My mother, Eve and now Kay: he had them all in thrall. In civilian life he was a farmer which gave him the bucolic look of one used to the open air. He was never to gain the same fluency in English as Jean - Eve was too accomplished at French. With Bunny, too, khaki was a wartime expediency and, in spite of a sharper crease in his trousers, a newer shine on his brass buttons, he didn't display the same elegance, the ease and the more casual decorum of his friend used to uniform.

Just before I left after lunch on Sunday, he placed his arm affectionately around my shoulder with a new fatherly concern. "It is good to keep your husband always a little afraid he will lose you - make him suffer for his love, play a little game but," he added close to my ear and I suspected from the heart, "Remain always faithful - it is the best way of life."

***

'Parting is such sweet sorrow,' Sir Hardman might have quoted and it would have expressed exactly my feelings when I said good-bye to Jean for the second time at Waterloo station. We had arrived just in time for me to go inside the compartment and claim a seat and release the catch on the window before the whistle blew, catching us both unawares. "I shall come to see you soon," was all he had time to say as he kissed my hand through the window before the train started. And although I waved to him and he walked right to the end of the platform, he was soon cut off from view by the carriage curving round like some great articulated creature.

This time I was not so unhappy to be leaving Jean. I knew he would keep his promise and see me before he went away, that this short separation was nothing like the one that was coming, and I was hopeful too that some satisfactory adjustment could be arranged to meet with the blessing of Lady Lever. I did not mind going back to school either. I was eager to tackle the French and the weekend which had taught me much had left me confident and self-respecting. I knew that a year would make all the difference. That at the end of it I would be on the way to making a better wife and that part of the maturing process had already begun. This time the two-thirty was moderately full and I smiled at the lady sitting opposite.

PART NINE

THE GO-BETWEEN

Lady Lever welcomed me back and asked after the journey, but otherwise wanted to hear nothing of my weekend. I was happy for it to be so and hoped life would proceed as before. However, I was very surprised when Cannon, waiting for me on the landing, followed me into my room and closed the door behind us.

"I hope you had a nice weekend?" she said, perching herself on the arm of the chair in a hitherto unknown mateyness.

"Yes thank you - I had a lovely time," I said, taking off my coat.

"How did the wedding go?" she asked, reaching for a coathanger from the wardrobe.

"Well, it was quite a plain wedding in a Registry Office. I didn't like it much. The bride only wore a navy costume."

"Still, I expect your young man was pleased to see you," she said, and I was dumbfounded by her reference to one I thought was supposed to be kept deadly secret.

"Her ladyship told me in confidence about the engagement - she knows she can trust me. I shan't breathe a word to a soul," she assured me.

"Actually, I don't mind you knowing. Yes, he was pleased to see me I think, and I was pleased to see him."

"Her ladyship says he wants to come down here with your mother." Even more astonished, I repeated his last words on Waterloo station.

"Yes, before he goes away."

"He's going abroad I hear - in the forces is he?"

"Yes, an officer in the Belgian army - and it will be a year before he comes back," I said, pleased to talk about him.

"My friend's husband's gone overseas, to the Far East. She went to Liverpool at the weekend to see him off. Two thousand of them altogether, right to the other side of the world. Destination secret of course! To fight the Japs no doubt. Goodness knows when she will see him again." Cannon was trying to win my confidence as she probed and prattled on. "I've put your clean blouse in the top drawer. We had a bit of snow here at the weekend." She walked across to the window to look out over the garden and, catching sight of herself in the long looking-glass, she turned sideways, smoothed her hands down over her stomach and went out of the room saying: "There's no hurry - you've high tea today, they've had theirs downstairs. Sir Hardman couldn't wait."

Three days later I received a letter from my mother with a note from Jean folded inside.

My Beloved,
    I have not written to you, because I was very busy these last days and also because I don't know if Lady Lever likes that you receive letters from me, therefore I put this in one of your mother's.

Darling, I shall never forget the lovely days we have just spent. I feel my

English not very improving. I bought the records I promised you. You will receive them in a few days with the books. I send you with this letter a paper, will you fill it up and post it back quickly. I think you will receive a correspondence course at the same time as you learn with the records and the grammar. Will it be too much work for you, little busy girl? I hope it will be useful for you.

I hope to see you again soon Darling, as soon as possible. Do you think I may go down there? It will not be for a fortnight or three weeks because I am on duty for that time. So you have a long time to prepare Lady Lever for that!

I miss you very much Chérie. I feel I have not kissed and caressed you enough.

I want to feel you so little and so sweet in my arms. You were so lovely when you said I was naughty! Darling I love you better than I did ever in my life.

I have to end that lovely conversation with you because it is late — already tomorrow - and in eight hours I must be at school and so must you.

Darling my dreams are full of you.

Kind regards to Robin and all my love for you.

Sincerely yours forever.

Jean.

At school I began to confide more in Cicely without actually telling her about the engagement, hoping she might come to suspect it for herself, and until she did, I felt she was not yet ready. It was a relief to talk, no matter how frivolous she thought me or how inconsequential she considered Jean's place in my life.

It was Cannon who was rapidly winning for herself the position of confidante. She was always inventing excuses to come into my room – ever-ready to dally and ask questions. I had never been so well-groomed, so pressed and polished. But I never gave her the chance to find my letters. I made a little bag for them, embroidered with the flags of all the allies, so that the Belgian tricolour should not look overstated, and took it everywhere, tucked in my pocket, handbag, or satchel when I was at school.

"Here's a letter from Stockport," she said one morning when she came to make sure I was getting up. "Who do you know in that part of the world?" I was curious and took the envelope to discover his writing. What indeed was he doing in Stockport? I asked myself. "Is everything all right?" she enquired.

"I hope so, it's from my - er friend," I said, impatient for her to go, while it flashed through my mind that he might already be on his way and this was his method of breaking the news, after he had gone. Cannon left and I tore open the envelope.

Somewhere in England.
Petite Marjorie adorée
    Thank you so much for the love you sent me. I am glad that you do not hide your love for me, I do not. I am proud of you and of loving you.
    I started from home a little after your letter arrived and after a quick and comfortable journey I reach this place. I am here with Bunny and several other boys for the Parachutist Training!
    This morning, Monday, we have had a blooming P.T. and after a little ride in an aeroplane we saw an exhibition from the Paratroops. It seemed to us very attractive but we feel a little apprehension - fear - for our first jump.
    Just after lunch we had it - the first drop from a plane! It has been very easy and we were not at all afraid! And I must add

that the aeroplane - only a small part of a bomber's body - remained still, suspended from three yards high above the ground. There has been no casualty! Now I have to go for another exercise.

Good night Darling.

It is 4 p.m. I continue my letter. We have just seen the packing of a parachute and why it must always open itself. We have great confidence in it. As you can see our first training was full of exercises. Now we rest in the lounge of the Officer's Mess. It is very cosy, a good fire, but also central heating! It is frozen hard all day and to sit near the fire in a comfortable armchair is a nice feeling for my tired body.

But my mind is always restless. You are always occupying it, is that poor English or Shakespearean? Ça ne fait rien Chérie because it is surely very rich in feelings and sentiments. I miss you so much. But I am not sad, for I know the day will come from which we will never more be separated from the other.

Bunny was just trying to do some work too difficult for his little intelligence - brain! And he just interrupted me asking for help. He just said 'Mayala' because I read that to him - and he sends you all his love - a father's one indeed!

Darling I can't post this letter today because nobody have got a stamp. I will send it tomorrow. I am very tired and I must go to bed, I will surely have the nicest dream. I am sure I will see you with me under the same parachute.

Good night Darling.

The 17th just before dinner.

Today has also been tiring. This afternoon we must have our first jump but the wind was too heavy, it has been 'partie remise' understand?

I shall write another letter soon. Do not answer me because I am not allowed to give my address. Darling I stop. I love you more than I can say it to you.

Jean

P.S. Soon you will be smiling and telling me 'You are naughty'!

Learning to drop from a plane by parachute was the only element of his training which I understood and therefore it seemed to me the most dangerous one. I had a vague story-book idea of espionage; spies living by their wits lurking darkly in a cloak and dagger world of intrigue and graft! Yet I could not fit Jean into this fanciful concept. What he would do once parachuted back inside his own country I had no clear picture. Nor could I tie in the Morse code and the sending of messages with any kind of practical arrangement. I was completely ignorant of radio-transmission or its dangers, fortunately. Yet the idea of dropping by parachute in the light of the full moon sounded the most reckless folly. Suppose he did break his legs, or even his neck? And the possibility conjured up some painful images in my mind. The moon shining on his parachute marking it like a silver beacon, as he drifted defencelessly to earth, only to be left a broken wreck on the cold ground, or worse, falling into a German trap! The enemy were not fools, he had conceded this himself. Surely they would be scanning the skies with searchlights for this very contingency? Suppose he was fired on and killed on his way down?

Before I got into bed that night I switched off my light and peeped through the curtains. It was very dark outside. The moon was almost new. It was impossible to tell whether it was going towards its last quarter or just beginning a new phase. Whichever it was I knew the next full moon would be the one to direct my love miles away on his dangerous mission.

Lady Lever called after me on my way to school and she was agitated. "One minute Marjorie, come in here," she said, furtively directing me into the lobby and pushing the door to after us. "Did you get a letter from your mother this morning?"

"No," I replied, anxiously.

"Well, I did and she is coming down next weekend." Her eyes darted to either side like a cornered animal as she stood with her back to the gun cupboard.

"Oh - is she?" I said, pleasantly surprised.

"Yes, she says it's a hurried, last-minute decision, no doubt you will be hearing yourself."

"Is she coming - on her own?" I enquired guardedly.

"No - and that's what I want to arrange with you," she said. "Your mother says they will put up at a hotel in town but you could book rooms at the Abbey Hotel. I will tell Sir Hardman that she particularly wants to come this weekend as it's your half- term - and that it's not convenient for her to stay here at such short notice."

"Yes - I see," I replied, hardly able to contain my delight. "And I thought you would like to spend the weekend with - them, you could book the rooms on your way home from school, it will be nice for Robin to have you close by."

"Yes, shall I book a room for Robin too?"

"No, no not Robin," she said quickly. "He has football on Saturday afternoon and the cross-country on Monday morning early."

I brimmed with joy at this unexpected move and also because Lady Lever seemed to be making it easy for me to have probably my last weekend with Jean; entering into conspiracy with me by inventing excuses for her husband so that he would not think it odd if my mother did not stay in the house as usual. But over one point she would remain adamant. She had made up her mind she could not receive Jean and by this resolution she would abide. She was clearing all trace of me from the house too, but not so far away! The Abbey hotel was the next establishment up the hill from Northlands. Was it a last, desperate attempt to keep me under her diminishing control?

Jean and my mother arrived in Hampshire after lunch the following Saturday and I was there alone to meet them at the station, Robin having been dispatched to his football match much against his will. I met our biology mistress by the booking-office and we cordially greeted one another as we found ourselves making for the same platform. I, buoyant with excitement at the prospect of meeting the two people who meant most to me in the world, while she was all set to get on the train coming from London, to continue with it to Bournemouth. Overtaken by the urge to have the arrival of my betrothed witnessed by someone, I kept close to her, even if she was never to know who he was, or why he should be accompanying my mother down here.

The long, green Southern Railway train, full of its own powerful importance, steamed into the station exactly on time. Miss Edmonds and I parted company and I looked eagerly at the groups alighting from the carriages. Then all at once they were there, together, in front of me, walking along side by side. The tall elegant officer in khaki greatcoat and cap dwarfing the neat, dumpy woman of the world at his side. So different in appearance and yet so strangely alike in many ways. Both a little larger than life, both endowed with more than their fair share of fantastic pluck, and both loving me! As I saw Jean again - no foreigner to me any longer - attentive and considerate towards his travelling companion, my love intensified. He looked so attractive, so masculine and fine, I felt so proud. I watched his long legs as he came forward and felt more elated with his every step, but suddenly my self-confidence ebbed away. I had just spotted Miss Edmonds, having secured herself a corner seat, happily waving in our direction and I dreaded that Jean would take me in his arms and embrace me in her full view. Always a little less demonstrative in uniform, he seemed instinctively to have sensed my misgivings for as we came face to face he smiled and only took my hand, leaving my mother with her generous endearments and kisses to supply the physical expression of love. It was not until we were safely concealed inside the back of a taxi, on our way out of town, that he took me in his arms.

The Abbey Hotel, only five hundred yards or so up the hill from Northlands, was virtually the house next door. Yet today I must pass by my second home as if I did not belong there. Robin could easily have missed the football match and the cross-country for once. An unexpected visit from a parent was a good enough excuse in wartime to drop out of a school function. No, it was as if Lady Lever wanted him kept apart, untainted by the eccentricity surrounding me. I was hurt too, that my mother herself must suffer ostracism - or was it punishment? this weekend on my account. She, however, judging by what her own reaction might have been in the circumstances, expected that once Jean arrived, Lady Lever would have been unable to contain her curiosity and make some last-minute excuse to see things for herself. But when she realised there were no such plans, that I had come with my dressing case packed for two nights and definitely no invitations, not even to inspect our clothes, she was disappointed more than offended. Yet as the afternoon wore on and the receptionist ushered Cannon into the lounge, my mother and I regarded one another, realising all was not imbued with the indifference it might have seemed.

Cannon, who had come ostensibly to make apologies on behalf of her mistress - inextricably committed to a Bridge party and jumble sale for the Red Cross - was visibly overawed by the appearance of Jean, who stood up as she stepped nervously into the room, so that pink with a new youthfulness she could not help exclaiming,

"Oh, what a tall gentleman!" Before even my mother had the chance to introduce the two of them. Delighted by her perfectly natural reaction, my mother invited her to stay for tea, discerning that a little literal sweetening would not go amiss in helping to flavour the report for the mistress on whose behalf she had so transparently come as an informer.

This was to be our last weekend together for a year, perhaps less if the war ended sooner, but twelve months was a good round figure to reckon with. And although today it seemed an eternity, Jean assured me it would pass quickly. On one thing he was resolute: he did not want this last precious leave to be a sad occasion and so referred to his departure as little as possible. I was delighted to have him here, coming to see me in my headquarters so to speak, and it gave me great pleasure to show him the countryside I had grown to love. After lunch on Sunday we went for a walk, alone, along the less trampled paths, my mother and Robin spending time together.

It was a fine day, full of hope, and with more than a touch of spring in the air although we needed to wrap up warmly, for the wind was keen. The sky above was very blue with some cloud high up blown about in streaks, and we could hear the drone of an aeroplane engine far off and out of sight. The smoke came racing from the cottage chimneys, billowing in all directions, and the tits and hedge-sparrows, seduced too by thoughts of love, were hopping cheerfully from branch to bush and back again, exploring every nook and crevice in which to build their nests. The magpies were already paired - 'Two for Joy'. The leaves occasionally set to life by the blustery wind got up and danced along the path in front of us.

We walked fairly briskly; it was too cold to dawdle. Sometimes Jean placed his arm around my shoulders and I would lean towards him but it was difficult to proceed clasped together. The thaw had left the rutted track muddy in places and we needed to pick our way, jumping over the worst of it. Sometimes we flushed a pheasant out from the undergrowth which alerted the jays who signalled the alarm like the sound of linen tearing. I was alone with Jean for the first time for a fortnight and the emotion uniting us was matched only by the beauty of nature surrounding us; the notes of the blackbirds and robins, the warmth of the sun we felt now and again on our heads, the gorse bushes flecked with yellow. 'When gorse is out of bloom kissing is out of season'! Every nerve in my body was in tune with the afternoon. We came to a birch tree. Jean took my hand and leaning his back against the trunk, pulled me to him and hugged me tightly. A gust of wind blew my hair across my face and he picked the strands from my eyes and kissed me with more passion than before. It was a new experience to embrace in the open air. And to shield me from the wind, he unbuttoned his coat and I snuggled into the warmth inside, even closer to him.

We lingered some moments, braced together against the tree, but it was too raw to stand still for long and reluctantly he released his arms and we moved away, my cheeks burning, the rest of me shivering visibly so that we stopped again and he turned up the collar of my coat around my face before we walked back into the wind.

Along the bridle path ahead were two horses, their young riders at their sides, and as we came closer I recognised the daughters of a local farmer. The younger one appeared to be having difficulty in getting up in the saddle for every time she made a more determined effort the pony backed away leaving her helpless at its side. Jean strode to her assistance. He held the reins, patted the animal on the nose and, after a firm but natural command in French, the pony calmed down and he helped her remount. Astride and confident once more, impressing their thanks and smiling, the girls trotted off in the opposite direction.

"You were good with that pony, do all horses understand French?" I asked.

"Oh yes," he replied with an oblique smile, "Just - in the same way as all horses, French and Belgian, understand English - animals are superior, they can learn languages without Linguaphone records," he said squeezing me to him.

"I go riding sometimes," I said.

"Then one day we shall go riding together, yes?" he asked.

That will be nice?" I nodded in agreement.

***

Tucked into one of the twin beds in the same hotel bedroom as my mother, and stupidly happy that the three of us were all under the same roof again, I was excited and in no mood for sleep. When it finally overtook me it was fitful, intercepted by much extravagant dreaming and I awoke very early the next morning. I lay some time in the darkness and the stillness, only just aware of the sleeping body in the bed next to mine. My thoughts at first diffused and fuddled by inadequate rest, gradually formed themselves into conscious order. Jean was leaving for London later that day and yet the weekend had given us little opportunity to be on our own. We could not have had a more sympathetic chaperone but the expression of our love was ours, alone. One desire superseded all others. I wanted to be close and intimate with him once more. To look into his eyes without his glasses. To be kissed and caressed without the constriction of too many clothes, to feel myself 'so little and sweet' in his arms, despite my age, these were the first stirrings of the desires of a woman, albeit as yet with little urgency, and what about him, lying in bed in the next room? Had he not similar and more sophisticated longings? He could not come to me now, as in London, with my mother beside me. I would go to him.

I got up silently and let myself out of the room holding my breath. My mother made no sign she was disturbed and would surely assume I had gone to the bathroom if she were to awake and find my bed empty. I did not intend to be away long.   Satisfying myself that no-one was about, I moved silently the few yards along the corridor to his room, opened the door with no noise and stood there on the inside, my heart thumping.   In the darkness all was silent. He did not wake immediately. When the door had been briefly open, the landing light had illuminated a narrow wedge of the room, enough to show me the layout and I groped my way to the electric fire and switched it on. I stood by while it slowly began to redden, my arms folded around my frail, girlish body, now wishing I had not come. At that moment, acknowledging the deep-seated spark of wantonness within me which the world seemed to have been afraid would be prematurely set alight by this liaison, I was ashamed of my vulnerability. I owned too that it was much less fair to him to have come like this.

Soon there was a warm, mounting glow in the room and very sleepily Jean raised himself in the bed and peered at me, rubbing his eyes to convince himself he was awake. "I thought it was - *un ange,*" he whispered, half getting up and guiding me back into the soft, potent aura of warmth surrounding him in the hollow of his single bed where I had ached to be.

We lay in each other's arms, tense, inert, hearts racing fearfully conscious that between us we possessed everything necessary to carry us over into ecstasy. Instinctively we clung to one another, trying to escape ourselves.   I, contrary to all desire to give my love generously, knowing I should resist while he, always responsible and protective, now barely awake to this new temptation, was unable to help himself.

"Je t'aime, je t'aime," was all he said, repeating it over and over between kisses and the most tender caresses as love,

and charity, triumphed. We were closer than we had ever been. For a few sublime moments I hugged my love to my breast. I fondled his ears and combed my fingers through his hair, and with my heart beating under his hand, I let them stray on over his neck and along his spine until finally I spread them out to lavish all my passion on the beautiful long muscles of his back.

On the threshold of Paradise, the metamorphosis of maiden into mistress, mother even to the child within the man pressed to her heart, there came a sudden, loud purposeful knock on the door as if fate itself had taken a hand in forcing us down to earth and our responsibilities. Startled beyond description, I retreated under the bedclothes and lay as if turned to stone. And during that same brief second my lover, abruptly relinquishing all his love, conspired to keep me hidden by pulling the covers over my head - the only deceit in which I knew him participate.

There was a clanking of pans outside the door and a female voice announced, "It's eight fifteen, your hot water Sir." A long moment elapsed before the door was thrown wide open and a brisk set of footsteps entered the room to place the enamel jug with a clatter inside the bowl on the washstand. I had forgotten that we had asked for an early morning call! "Shall I draw the curtains?" The footsteps enquired while moving towards the window before turning back and going from the room closing the door noisily behind them. I surfaced for air. The room was flooded with admonishing daylight and we both breathed again. I wondered if the unseen visitor had noticed that two bodies were heaped in the bed and what she would make of my empty bed when she went next door to give my mother a similar rude call. Without another word or kiss I slipped from my lover's arms and crept back into the bed beside my mother.

***

After an unmagical English austerity lunch at the Cadena accompanied by three determined lady musicians armed with a cello, double bass and a piano, plus a bottle of third-rate Algerian wine to wash away all trace of the experience, Jean and I left my mother and Robin and moved on to the cinema in the afternoon. It was somewhere to go to be, if not alone, unseen and warm. We sat holding hands, mesmerised by the flickering images on the screen. I was too aware of the real and substantial presence at my side, who was finding it difficult to sit comfortably, so cramped were his legs, and who would not be here much longer, to take in much of the fiction unfolding before us. Yet the gloom and the occasional swell of the music heightened my fancy so that I had a sense of taking part in a film myself. The tragic heroine who must pass through much drama and tribulation before the triumphant chords would herald in my happy ending.

It was therefore some comfort to emerge blinking from the Forum, the glaring daylight mollifying my darkest feelings. Outside, jostled by the late afternoon shoppers, everything seemed less grave and I surreptitiously dabbed my eyes. A year would eventually pass - another two terms at school, three more holidays in London - and with a lighter step I led Jean to my favourite tea rooms at the bottom of the town - an old Medieval Rectory where the beams were so low that he had to stoop as we stepped inside to find a table.

The atmosphere was cosy and provincial. Well-heeled ladies in stitched felt hats, looking content and prosperous, were quietly sipping tea from flowered cups on pretty print cloths. For despite being rationed to three half-slices of bread and butter and one piece of cake, it was still a treat to come out to tea. Jean was the only man present and because of this and his inconvenient stature, we attracted some sympathetic notice. We sat down and waited in the tranquillity of our sedate surroundings and Jean removed his cap which left two indentations in his hair above his ears.

Our pot of tea for two was soon brought to us by a smiling waitress. It gave me great pleasure to take charge of the occasion, to render him this last rite of English domesticity and I poured the tea with extra loving care. I watched him pick up his cup, his lips poised ready to sip the hot liquid, my eyes only leaving him fleetingly to locate my own cup and saucer before they were back ready to see the sensual movements in his throat as he paused intermittently to swallow. The tea brought a flush to his face and he unfastened his greatcoat, revealing his tunic with the insignia of his elite calling, which did not seem important any more.

The sanctity of the moment overcame the need for words - there was too much to say, we had barely begun - though time was becoming precious. There was just enough to take in one long, scrupulous regard from his eyes and lips - ever ready to blow their last secret kisses - down over his body and legs to the toe-caps of his shoes dulled and spattered with wholesome Hampshire earth. Intimately sharing our concerns we lingered in the hushed peace of the Chesil Rectory for as long as we dared, making love to one another with our eyes, deepening our memories to carry us through the coming year.

The last customers to leave, we came outside ready to walk back through the town. Now as we made our way along the streets practically deserted after the homeward rush, the chill twilight breeze sending a shiver through the urban gardens, I began to feel the heaviness of my heart. We walked on cutting through the back streets past the cathedral. It was one of my favourite walks in summer when the lime trees were in flower, making a fragrant shady avenue, their honeydew sweetness deposited on the flagstones beneath. Cicely and I referred to it uppishly as 'Unter den Linden' and we passed here every Monday afternoon on our way to a big warehouse where we would make camouflage by weaving strips of earth-coloured hessian in and out of enormous nets strung aloft. My thoughts went over to its namesake in Berlin, and the Germans amongst whom Jean would be operating undercover in a week or so. Back in the front line of war, where I would be remote to him, neither of us able to draw any comfort from the other. Completely cut off with no occasional visits or letters, and when even the telephone for emergencies would be denied us.

Jean, having made an effort over the weekend to remain cheerful, was quieter now. He put his arm around me and the extra effort of keeping close as we climbed the hill slowed us. He and my mother had a train to catch that evening so we kept on going right back to the hotel.

My mother was already packed and waiting and Jean left us together while he hastily collected his things. Alone with my mother, I kept a distance knowing that any show of emotion on either side would tip me to breaking point. We talked banally about the weekend, the comfort and convenience of the hotel, the weather and the film - which I could not remember - its title nor the stars - and he was back again his face strained, but he managed his smile as he suggested my mother should telephone for a taxi to take them to the station after he had seen me back to the house. I said goodbye to my mother summarily, as though I would see her again the following week.

It was quite dark and we kept close and silent on our way down the hill. My heart was nearly overflowing. There was that same chill unearthliness over the black landscape I had remarked on the first time and which made every footfall along the pavement echo eerily away into the darkness. The night was beautifully clear and dry, with that crispness in the air that heralds a frost, while overhead a million million stars illuminated the heavens.

We came at last to the two stone pillars marking the entrance to Northlands where the gates, ironic as it seemed now, were always kept welcomingly open. Like two fugitives, we crept inside a little way along the drive on tiptoe in order to muffle our footsteps on the gravel. The stately country house to which he was barred loomed darkly, implacable, at the curve of the lawn some fifty yards off, and there was enough moon to catch the slant of the roof and lighten the sills to define its character in a ghostly glimmer. It was time to say *Adieu*, and stopping where the low hanging branches of the weeping beeches would conceal us, we turned to face one another.

Jean removed his glasses and placed them within the safety of his cap on the stones of the rockery at our feet. He loosened my coat and slipped his arms inside and around my body, and stood hugging me without a word until he took my face in his hands and lifted it to him. My cheeks were wet.

"Chérie," he soothed with his infinite cheering tenderness. *"Il ne faut p-"* his words tailed off as he kissed my eyes, my mouth, and holding me tightly he laid his cheek on my brow. I tried to dry my face on his coat where it had come to rest but the thick woollen stuff, smelling so slightly of tobacco and the world, only smudged my tears so that they felt wetter and cold on my cheeks. I put my arms around him, and standing there locked together in the stillness, my head pressed to him, I felt the rise and fall of his chest breathing in my native air, and I heard his heart muffled but steady transmitting not only a message of life but of love. And then it seemed as if our hearts changed places and our souls welded themselves together.

"Goodbye little Marjorie, I love you," he said. My tears welled up again and looking through them I saw his face dark against the sky and I made myself say, "Good-bye." We kissed one another, not desperately, not even as though it was the last time for a year, but with lips trembling with meaning so that if necessary this expression of our devotion would remain with us for ever. "Goodbye," he said again, releasing his arms, for we had run right out of time. He fastened my coat and in one last effort not to leave in sadness, added - as was the custom of the time, "Keep smiling - one year is quickly gone, you will see - I will write when I get back." He let go of my hand and I walked about twenty yards up the drive away from him and turned. He had moved out from the shadows but was still there, watching after me, his straight, proud military figure silhouetted against the trees and I waved before continuing on my way. The kiss which he had impressed indelibly on my lips was cooling and I covered it with my fingers to keep it warm and fix it there.

Just before I reached the house I turned once more, but this time no-one was there. Only the weeping beech trees with their sad branches drawn down to earth in their eternal gesture of despair were gently rustling in the cold air. For one terrifying instant I had the pronounced feeling that this was the end, that he would not return and I should never see him again. Tears streamed down my face. I was so utterly alone. The severance of his soul from mine had left a raw wound which was beginning to ache. I felt sympathy for those poor wild creatures we sometimes heard in the darkness - a snared rabbit, a fowl prey to a fox - issuing their last piteous cries as they were wrenched from life in the vicious shades of the night. Instinctively I turned towards heaven and there rising up was the half-formed moon, mysterious and beautiful, bright and menacing, defiant as a rival sure in her power and shameless in her purpose. Had she come to stake her claim so soon? I wanted to go after him, to call him back and then I heard the unmistakable approach of the taxi and I waited to listen as it changed gear to chug its way up the hill and past the house, and I knew it was too late.

***

"You and your Belgian Officer were seen over half-term - at least I presume it was the Spider," Cicely announced in her stylish manner at prep time.

"Who by?" I asked in proud astonishment.

"Daphne Parsons. She said she came out of the pictures behind a very tall Army Officer and a girl and when she turned round she was never so surprised to see it was you. She didn't recognise you out of school uniform."

"I didn't see her," I said.

"So she said, you were far too engrossed to notice anybody, otherwise she said she might have spoken to you."

"Did she say anything else?"

"That you were walking along like the cat who'd swallowed the canary!"

"What cheek, what did she mean?" I said. "But she liked the look of him!"

"Well," she replied tantalisingly slowly, "She said he looked interesting and that he held your hand when you crossed the road by the Square."

"The Square! She must have kept a pretty good eye on us right down there! Did she say anything else?"

"She wondered if he was a relation of yours."

"Did you enlighten her?"

"I just said he was someone you knew in London."

"I'm glad she found him interesting. I've got a photo of him I'll bring it to show you. I'm going to marry him in a year's time," I said, for her to make of it what she liked. Cicely sat watching me with her vague, elfin scepticism turning up one corner of her mouth and she began to doodle a large spider wearing an enormous pair of spectacles on my rough book.

"That's a very optimistic declaration - I shall remind you of it next year," she scoffed putting the finishing touches to her drawing while I sat watching her, going over the weekend in my mind.

"There's a lovely picture in the National Gallery," I said, in an upsurge of emotion.

"Oh yes - what of?   Who by?" she quizzed me, amused by my sudden change of topic.

"I've forgotten - but I think it's my favourite picture."

"Picture of what?" she insisted.

"Oh - a naked man, an angel - or Christ or someone. Someone with the most heavenly body." She resumed work on her drawing, blackening the legs and making them hairy.

"Not hairy," I said, "But smooth and firm - and quite brown."

"What on earth's that got to do with your Belgian or Daphne Parsons seeing you in town?" she asked, holding her head back to admire her handiwork.

"Oh - I don't know," I said. "Except, I think my Belgian might look like him, rather saintly with a long beautiful body."

"No doubt you will find that out when you marry him!" she taunted amidst snorts of mirth.

"Yes," I said, "I shall marry him - just you wait and see."

"You were going to marry Lord Lovat last summer - remember?"

"He's a Sagittarian too, by the way," I said, hoping to win her more favourable regard as I snatched back my book.

"Aspiring in an honourable way at high matters - eh?" she teased emphasising 'high' and she dissolved into heaves of suppressed laughter, her hand covering her mouth.

***

Jean and Bunny were to depart together, weather permitting, in a little over a week's time, by the light of the next full moon. All kinds of last minute preparations were taking place. With characteristic optimism Jean ordered a new suit and had just time for one fitting so that it would be almost complete when he returned. He also bought new shirts, socks and ties to match the fawn Prince of Wales check he had chosen with the expert help of my mother. "His *trousseau*," she declared later.

She was very preoccupied with the departure of her favourites and managed to persuade Jean, who had developed a bad head cold, to stay in bed during the last weekend he was to spend in her care. It gave her great pleasure to cosset him, while he too relished these last hours of homely comfort and motherly attention. "He was so sweet, he let me tuck him up just like a little boy," she told me on the phone.

At the training school there was much to finalise. Those last essentials of the Morse and other codes to be perfected. There were photographs to be taken for the forged identity papers each agent must carry with him. Their new identities and cover stories had to be memorised as, for obvious reasons, they could not go back under their own names or to their previous occupations. All clothing had to be scrutinised for glaring details of British manufacture. In short, all the English influence of the last few months, often so loving and painstakingly acquired, had to be obliterated. The Germans were on the look-out for telling signs just as much as the British had been alerted by the foreign accents and the berets.

All this of course was completely unknown to anyone outside the service including me, to say nothing of the emotions and the anxieties crowding the mind at such a time.

Jean's written English, not yet fluent enough without a dictionary, meant his letters to me took him a long time to write - my mother described them as 'a real labour of love' - with him sitting in the evenings poring over the big red Cassels dictionary he had bought especially. The letter he had promised me on his return was late as a result.

> *Ma petite Marjorie adorée*
>
> *Will you forgive the worthless, nasty, lazy boy I am? I promised you a letter last Monday and only on Friday evening I send this letter. I have been busy all the week. I wrote you a letter in French but thought it easier for you to understand my bad English than my academic French so I have not posted it.*
>
> *There are reasons for the delay of my letter.*
>
> *Beloved, have you thought about the marvellous succession of events that*
>
> *God arranged for us and our love? How can I meet you without the war, without the invasion of Belgium, without my long travels through France and Spain? A few months ago only it was silly to pretend we will love each other. If Monsieur Gobeaux was not coming in England, if your mother did not*

nurse him, if the Belgian army was fighting, if I did not hear someone speaking about the job, if this, if that, if one of the least things did not happen, what would it be with us?

I met you in the precise moment I needed it. They were sorrowful days in my life. My heart needed your sweet smiles to be healed and my soul needed your bright eyes to be recomforted. Is it not quite marvellous Darling? I think God himself wanted to create our love and our happiness and that gives me great confidence in the future.

I like very much your sensitiveness Darling and I hope you will always keep it because without it the life is monotonous and valueless. Perhaps was I naughty, too naughty with you, perhaps did I sometimes hurt your sensitiveness? I am not so evil as you imagine, my age and my just formerly life are for the most part of the cause of that. But I do not regret to have been such a naughty boy. Those lovely hours we spent together will remain my best memory. And you Darling, do you regret something? Don't you hope such a lovely time to come again soon?

Chérie you must not be sad if we are separated! Our love annihilates distances and time, every evening we are together again, both only. My heart and my brain are full of you and I believe at the same moment you are dreaming of me, aren't we together in such moments? Darling we will be - only bodily - separated during a long time. I have to fight, it is my duty, also it will be good for me. After that struggle I shall be stronger-minded and also if I succeed in my job I shall win the security of our future estate.

I must do my duty because my poor invaded land needs me. I will certainly be faithful and our love will sustain me and help me in the accomplishment of my job. You also Darling, you must not be moping - keep smiling and laughing - I ask only that you keep for me your heart. You have to be cheerful and smiling sweet Darling because you know I accomplish my duty and because you know I love you.

Later if God allows it, we will reach the greatest happiness - the fulfilment of our dearest wish, we will get married. You will be my cherished wife and I will be your husband! We will be travelling together, enjoying ourselves in the cities - not too much - practising sports! What about riding together in the fields and the woods. But also we will have a home   Surely I will be very fond of staying there. I will revel in the happiness to be loved and to cherish. I will worship you Darling and our home will be the Eden.

Perhaps we will have the happiness of having some children - not too many - let us take it easy and not think about that yet!

My mother will be very glad to know you and she will love you surely. You will see how sweet and kind she is. You will love her, I am positively certain about that.

So the life appears to us to become marvellous after a little while of sorrow.

Yes Darling, it will be lucky and happy, surely we will have some misfortunes and chagrins, but our love will always be strong enough to recomfort us and make us happy.

What is important? We love each other! People may think, people may say, people may do anything, we do not care!

Darling I can't tell you how much I love you. Même en francais je n'ai pas assez de mots pour te dire combien je t'adore.

Sincerely for ever

Jean

P.S. Dear, Expensive, I forgot my pipe in the Abbey hotel last weekend. Will you ask for it please? Thank you and I hope you will not mention the trouble I give you.

P.P.S. Dear Cabbage, will you say for me many things - kind ones - to your brother.

P.P.P.S. I will write before I start. Perhaps more than once it depends on the weather.

P.P.P.P.S. Cheerio!   Keep smiling for victory. Ta grande araignêe noire.

Knowing that time was running out from my nightly inspection of the moon growing bigger and more threatening, I wrote back immediately but even this I feared might not be soon enough. So on the excuse of going down to the village to post my letter, I took all my pocket money and rang home from the public call box to know exactly how things stood. It was a comfort to hear his voice once more, to tell him my letter was on its way and to say goodbye again.

Still in school uniform I went to reclaim his pipe from the hotel and, on being shown into the lounge, came face to face with a pert-voiced chambermaid with a familiar step who I recognised, with some dismay, as a frequent associate of Cannon. She offered to help in my search as nothing had been handed in. She said she remembered me and the tall gentleman who had occupied rooms twenty-one and twenty-two, adding disconcertingly, "Well you could have knocked me down with a feather to discover you was one of the evacuees from Northlands!"

We eventually found the pipe down the side of a settee and I took it back to put away with his letters which amounted to quite a bundle. Too cumbersome to carry about, so I placed them in my handbag which I concealed under all my clothes in the bottom of my chest of drawers.

The next evening my mother made an emergency telephone call and Lady Lever instructed me to take it undisturbed in her bedroom.

"Hello Darling," came the far-away greeting. "I thought you'd like to know the boys went off this morning," she announced with anxious excitement. The skin all over my body tightened.

"Already?" I asked. "What's the weather like there?"

"Not so cold today, rather a fine evening, bright moonlight and no clouds. I think things should go well."

"I hope they'll be all right," was all I could think of saying.

"I hope so too," she said. "You should have seen them, they were up and down the stairs a million times before they finally went out of the front door. Bless their hearts. They were so sweet, they took me out to dinner the night before last - insisted I left the cooking to Marie for once and we went up to a posh restaurant in Knightsbridge. They were in marvellous form and we drank two bottles of Pommard! Spider said it was his favourite. He'll make a marvellous husband, knows all about food and wine and how to look after a woman - you'll have a wonderful life with him."

I let her talk on. "Oh! And before I forget, Mister Gobeaux says that from this morning he is promoted to Captain." A new surge of pride helped lighten my sadness.

"That's nice," I said, my tears beginning to prick. "Did he say - anything?"

"He said he was very sad to leave you, of course, and he took two or three of those little photos of you and tucked them deep in his inside pocket - next to his heart, he said."

"Did he get my letter?"

"No - it didn't come until after he'd gone, he was disappointed about that but they had a car waiting for them. They both hugged and kissed me as they left. I could cry this evening, really I could. The house isn't the same at all."

"Was there a message on the wireless?"

"Oh yes, we heard it - at least I think we did, you know old Gobbo. Something about the Three Musketeers. I've forgotten exactly - in French of course - something to do with musketeers, anyway."

"When will there be any news?"

"Mister Gobbo hasn't come in yet, but as soon as I hear anything I'll let you know."

"I hope they'll be all right." The pips went.

"I'm sure they will, I'll have to go now, I'll write the minute I hear. Goodbye," I said goodbye and replaced the receiver. The moment I had been dreading had arrived. He would be in this country for only another few hours, if he had not gone already, and then I would never know where to look for him.

I went straight to my room and, without switching on the light, closed the door and walked over to the window to look through the curtains. There above, perfectly round and beautiful, was the full moon sending its cold unearthly radiance over the world. I gazed, transfixed, eyes wide and unblinking. No wonder it could turn the mind! Yet there was a hopefulness too in the way it lightened the darkness, an ally for the lost and errant. Wishing to solicit help, to appeal for protection for my beloved, I pulled the curtains round my face and stood in full communion, pleading for his safety and praying silently that he would have a nylon parachute - which Lady Lever said was stronger than silk - until my tears had dried on my cheeks and my brow pressed to the windowpane had grown numb with cold.

***

That night at the airfield, after the last check-up to make sure no forgotten cigarette packets lurked in pockets, no stray bus tickets were trapped in trouser turn-ups, Jean sealed two letters. In the first, addressed to my mother, he inserted one hundred and twenty one-pound notes, all the money left in his London bank account which he had withdrawn that morning. The other to me, he had written at the last minute, and he directed that both letters were to be handed to Monsieur Gobeaux for delivery.

Dear Mrs. Rae, may I say dear Mother?

You were always so kind to me and it is a great pain for me to leave you and

Marjorie and also dear Robin.

Nobody can say what will happen and therefore I ask you to accept this.

Because of your situation and that of my cherished Marjorie may change - it is wartime - you must not refuse it. Because I knew you would not accept it, I asked Monsieur Gobeaux to give you this after I have gone.

May I ask you to fetch my suit from the tailor's shop. I owe him five pounds but I think it is preferable to keep it with my things. Will you go after next Tuesday when it will be ready for the second essayage. Thank you for that and all you did for me.

I hope you will not be too sad after Bunny and I have left. You know it is our duty, our country is invaded and suffers from the German domination and each one of us has to work for the liberation. I hope you will also console my poor beloved. She is so sensitive, if she can be happy for the least thing, she can also suffer very much for any unlucky moment. She is so sweet and nice. I cannot tell you how much I love her.

God will help us in these difficult times. Pray for us and the success of our job.

Goodbye dear Mother, I will not be so long, a year is quickly gone away and perhaps I will be back before that!

Remember me

Yours truly

Your son Jean

His last letter to me which I received when the moon was on the wane was written in pencil, in French, on a piece of foolscap paper. The handwriting, unlike the large untidy scrawl of his previous letters when he had been searching for every word and phrase, was spontaneous and controlled. Gone were the wild flourishes, the alterations and the endless postscripts. Although it took me many days to work out fully what he said I was glad he had written to me in his own language.

Translation.

'Somewhere in England

Bien Chere petite Marjorie

The moment of my departure has come. When you read this letter I shall be far away. My feelings at this moment are very difficult to describe - joy, at returning to my own country and of being able to fight the Germans, mixed with a slight sense of danger (Oh don't worry, I shall be careful) and above all, great sadness at leaving you, of being so far away without much chance of seeing you for what seems today, such a frightfully long time. Certainly if I'd stayed in England we should also have been separated but from time to time we would have met and we could have corresponded. That hope has gone, most probably. But our final reunion is not so far off. The war could end soon, that I hope with all my heart, and then the happiness in store for us

*after our marriage won't it be all the greater, all the more
beautiful, the best. For a happiness that is difficult to find or
slow to come by is always more intense than one ready-made. We
will quickly forget this sad time you will see.*

*My Darling, promise me you won't be sad after I've gone.
When you telephoned yesterday I was very upset because I could
hear and sense you were sad. You mustn't be. You know the love
which unites us dear little sweetheart and you have faith in me,
why be unhappy? Could you love a man who was not prepared
to do his duty? That is all he could possibly do for his country
today. Darling if I am incapable of serving my country I should
also be incapable of sacrificing myself for you. Love makes
sacrifices easy and I love my country, not as much as you
certainly, but for our own happiness, our love, it is better that we
take on ourselves the sacrifice of the separation. You will be
proud of me and I shall be proud of you because you will have
suffered for my country as well as your own.*

*I will not receive the letter you sent yesterday. That I regret
very much because I am always so happy to read what you have
written. It is so nice and so good and it brings me close to you.
When I am writing to you or when I am reading what you have
written it is as if you were there (or nearly) as if we were speaking
to one another. I can see and hear you and feel you near me.*

*Darling a new phase of your life has just begun. You are in
love! You love me. Love engenders much unhappiness but also
exquisite joys, undreamed of by insensitive people. You will see.*

*We are suffering now because it is a painful time, but it is
painful for everyone and we are the least to complain. What
about the mothers who have their sons at the front, the fiancées
and wives who have the men they love at the front? My job is
not as dangerous as theirs, we must keep things in perspective.*

*And then Darling, as I told you in my last letter, we love each
other and that guarantees our happiness, and no-one can break it
and events can never reach it.*

Trust in the future - it is for us!

Excuse the pencil and paper but the circumstances...
Adieu mon amour, I adore you.
Jean.

A few days later my mother rang to say that everything had gone according to plan, that Spider and Bunny were now safely back in their own country. From that moment Belgium became for me the most precious land on earth.

***

The spring came and the first winter aconites tucked deep in the woods, the chiff-chaff and the fluffy yellow chicks newly-hatched in the kitchen garden. As they shook the last drops of moisture from their tiny wings their timorous chirpings rejoiced, they were newborn and already in love with life. There had never been a spring like it. I was of the same generation as the birds and the trees.

The morning shadows darkened and shortened. The days grew longer. Cicely and I made a pact to get up at dawn on May 1st to bathe our faces in the dew. The chalk streams swelled in the water meadows and the amorous frogs generous in their love-making, allowed the evidence to spill over into puddles. Sometimes the sun was so warm it gave a false impression of the time of year. Soon the meadow beyond the garden was golden with daffodils. Surely they grew by divine order, for no matter whether Easter was early or late they were always there, ready in abundance for the decoration of the church. Lady Lever and I picked armfuls and tied them in bundles which we took down after tea on the Wednesday before Good Friday. We stood them in tall enamel jugs in the darkest part of the Vestry for the ladies who would come in their aprons and hats to 'do the

311

flowers' but Robin and I went to London the following morning to spend a week at home.

***

My mother had little time to mourn the loss of her two tall officers. She quickly had to make their room ready for the newcomers, and moved the blue cabin trunk which Jean had bought for storing his belongings into my bedroom. It was not long before she had a new boy to capture her affections, tall again, with blond, tightly-curled hair.

"You'll love Jean-Pierre," she assailed us at Waterloo station. "I call him my Greek God!"

My first enquiry on arriving indoors after shaking hands with Monsieur Gobeaux was for news of Jean.

"*Il va bien, il va bien,*" he insisted, knowing it was not much comfort but perhaps more of a reassurance if he said it twice.

I found my letter which had arrived too late, carelessly cast to one side under a pile of circulars on the hall table. I crossed out Lieut. and proudly wrote in Capt. over the top and took it to my room to put with the rest of his things. I gingerly lifted the lid of the trunk. I could tell my mother had been busy for expertly laid out in tissue paper was the new suit that Jean had ordered. I admired the colour and texture of the cloth which I reckoned would suit him better than navy-blue pinstripe. Loathe to disturb things too much, I probed in one corner just enough to get a fuller picture of the contents, and there safely stowed away were the new clothes in their cellophane wrappings and the beloved uniform. How marvellous it would be next year I told myself and slipped my letter inside and closed the lid, content that all his personal effects were near at hand. My mother came in carrying a small package.

"Darling," she said, handing it to me, "Spider left this for you - it's a birthday present. He didn't want it to go through the post - so you may as well have it now. It's a piece of jewellery, I think."

"Shall I open it?" I suggested, as curious as she to know what was making the hard little knot inside the envelope. She came close as I unwrapped the tiny parcel of tissue paper. "Oh isn't that sweet!" I gasped, to discover a small gold brooch in the form of a spider set with a pearl and green peridot. My mother took it from my hand to admire.

"My word! He never showed it to me, he must have bought it and wrapped it up in a hurry - at the last moment. He told me it was a brooch. A pearl! They say that means tears," she said, pinning it to my dress. "Well, you had those when he left," she added, redeeming herself. I took out the brief note enclosed to read.

Overseas May 9th
Dear little fiancée
    Now you are sixteen! I am sorry I can't see the pretty nice young lady I imagine you are! Sixteen, the most agreeable period in the life! Sixteen and already in love - since months!
    You started early didn't you, I think I got some responsibility for that!
    What about that stuff - the age? Never mind! We will remain young for more than a century.
    All my best wishes for your birthday!
    All my brain and my heart will be with you on this day, more than ever if it is possible.

A bientôt.
Jean.

"Did Lady Lever ever tell you what Cannon thought of him?" enquired my mother.

"No," I said.

"She must have told her what he was like," she replied. "You can't tell me she wasn't dying to know."

"Maybe - but Lady Lever never talks about him - ever. Cannon said she thought he was handsome and that he had nice manners and that was all."

"Never mentions him! Never asks how he is or anything - she knows he's gone - I told her," she responded.

"No - she has never once spoken his name since that day your letter came and we had that frightful talk. Anyway, Sir Hardman's not supposed to know anything about him." My mother stared at me, incredulous. "I think she thinks if Sir Hardman knew he wouldn't want me there any more."

"Do you mean to say - oh - how extraordinary! What a funny woman!" she exclaimed. "What was so frightful?"

"She was so shocked and disgusted I could tell, and with you, obviously, for letting it happen," I replied, feeling my mother's heckles rising.

"She's a bit of a hypocrite," she said. "Sir Hardman's mother was married at sixteen, she told me that herself quite proudly - anyway, my dear child I could never have prevented him loving you if I'd tried."

"But you needn't have been quite so pleased about it," I said, looking down to admire the brooch pinned over my bosom. She looked bewildered.

"I *was* pleased - I was delighted, you know I was - didn't you want me to be?"

"Yes - of course I did but you could have pretended you were a bit anxious or something. I am rather young."

"Perhaps for any other man, but not for him."

"Don't you honestly think he is too old for me? He will probably meet someone else, or his mother might put him off the whole thing like Lady Lever hopes no doubt," *or worse, he might go back to one of his previous girlfriends,* I thought, keeping it to myself. "I wish we'd kept the whole thing secret and never told anyone."

"That's just what he didn't want. He told old Gobbo during the row that it was a fact and there was no shame in it and he almost dictated the letter I wrote back to Lady Lever. His mother's permission at his age - that really made him laugh."

"Do you think he really loves me? Do you think he will come back?" My mother sighed wearily and shook her head while lovingly smoothing the hair off my brow.

"Do you know - he asked me the same question. It was the weekend we came to see you, when we were coming home on the train. He was very quiet the whole journey, looking down in his lap and not speaking - not like him at all, and when I made some remark, he looked up and his eyes were

315

full of tears - I knew what he was thinking - and he brushed them away with his finger and said, 'Does she *really* love me? or is it the glamour of the job and the uniform?' He told me you were the best thing that ever happened to him."

"You don't think he'll regret everything once he gets back?" I asked, craving constant reassurance. My mother spoke kindly.

"I trust that man implicitly, from the first moment I ever set eyes on him. Long before you came home, when I thanked him after he offered to fetch some coal and he said, 'It is nothing - that is the way I have been trained,' not like some of them I can tell you. Anyway who do you think your mother is?" she exclaimed, becoming suddenly uptight. "It makes me laugh sometimes - just as though I'd let you get into the hands of any Tom, Dick or Harry that came along! It's because I liked him and trusted him and knew that you liked him too that I thought things were all right. I would be most surprised if he never kept his word - most surprised."

I considered her words while she straightened the bedcover. "What's a mistress?" I asked warily.

"Do you mean a mistress of a house or a school mistress?" she replied, seemingly obtuse all of a sudden.

"I mean - when a man has a mistress," I specified and she braced herself.

"Strictly speaking - it's when a man lives with a woman as his wife when he isn't married to her," she said.

316

"Would you have called Mrs Peter 'Mister Peter's mistress'?" I continued.

"Put like that, I suppose you would."

"Why do men have mistresses?" I asked.

"Why are men – men," she chuckled.

I paused. "Don't men love their mistresses?"

"Some do, some of the greatest love-stories in history have been between a man and his mistress - Lord Nelson and Lady Hamilton for instance."

"Why don't they marry?"

"Perhaps they can't, perhaps one's married already."

"What about a youngish man who isn't married - who has a mistress?"

"With a young man I'd say it was more a question of sowing his wild oats - that he probably hasn't felt the need to settle down or hasn't yet found the one he wants to marry," she stated, eyeing me sideways.

"It's not very nice for the girl he does marry to know - he's had a mistress is it?" She gave a chuckle.

"It's always better to marry a man who's sown his wild oats. They're more ready to settle down and make better husbands. They have seen life, gained some experience and don't hanker for it later."

"I don't think I should like my husband to have had a mistress," I said.

"You'd be lucky to find a man who's never experienced life in that way." The conversation was beginning to irritate me.

"Oh," I groaned loudly. "I wish the war would end tomorrow."

***

On the morning of my sixteenth birthday I awoke unusually early, more eagerly than on any birthday before. I was now old enough to marry should the war end tomorrow. I thought of the one person who had written to say he would be thinking of me on this special day. But May 10th had sad memories for him. It was the day he had stopped playing soldiers and gone to war. The day his world had begun to fall apart, inflicting scars that would never completely fade.

Cannon came in as usual after a light token knock to signal time to get up.

"Awake already?" she exclaimed, seeing the sun streaming through the windows. "It's a lovely morning - many happy returns," she said, placing some envelopes on the end of my bed. "These came yesterday."

"Thank you," I said, reaching down excitedly to pick them off my feet. "Yes, it is a nice day - and do you know? I'm old enough to marry!"

"Glory be! Listen to her - they do say sweet sixteen and never been kissed!" She slid me a sidelong glance. "Don't they?" she probed, and I felt myself blushing.

"Do you think I'll marry at sixteen?" I asked. Startled, Cannon was cautious.

"We'll just have to wait and see," she said, fearful always of betraying allegiance to her mistress. "Nothing from your young man, is there?" she pointed out.

"No," I replied sadly, "But he gave my mother a present to give me - would you like to see it?" I swiftly got out of bed and took the little brooch from its secret hiding place and handed it to her. "There, isn't it sweet?"

"Oh my - yes, it's very pretty - what made him choose a spider?"

"It's his - sort of nickname, my mother gave him because of his long legs, doesn't suit him really." Then I thought for an instant. It suddenly struck me how suitable it was in more ways than one. When my mother chose it she probably saw it written as Spyder.

"I always call him by his Christian name which is Jean, French for John."

"That's better," she said. "Some people say a spider is an omen of bad luck!"

***

This was to be my last year at school. As the excitement of the winter months gradually subsided, and Jean ceased to

319

monopolise my thoughts, I was able to settle happily and enjoy the remaining period in Hampshire. I profited from the long solitary evenings in the playroom with the Linguaphone records and at school I pulled myself up in French to be best in the class. Latin and the Gallic wars also became a challenging subject with their reference to the 'Belgae in the North, the bravest of all the people of Gaul'. I was also pleased to learn that the Roman name for Winchester was Venta Belgarum, which I believed to be a good omen.

We were shuttled backwards and forwards to London pretty frequently these days and it always puzzled me that Monsieur Gobeaux never had any real news of the departed favourites. To my request for confirmation of their well-being his replies were always stereotypical and vaguely impatient - that everyone was in good health and working as well as expected. As he had never become resigned to my engagement so I tried to keep my queries general, not singling out Jean for special mention anymore but it made no difference. My confidence in the future came to depend more and more on the proverbial knowledge that 'no news must be good news'. It was therefore some uneasy consolation when we did receive apparently direct endorsement of his welfare and safety.

The day before returning for my last term in Hampshire, Monsieur Gobeaux invited my mother and me to lunch at his favourite restaurant - the Café Anglais in Leicester Square. Here, the waiters spoke French despite the name, and knew him well. It was a treat for him to come here, where he could converse freely and he took advantage, spending a long time over the menu and going into intricate culinary detail over each course. Lunch at the Café Anglais was always a long, drawn-out affair.

My mother and I took up our positions to wait for him outside his bureau in St. James, just at the same moment as Captain Conway, the one who had called on my mother in the early days, came down the steps. With an outstretched hand and a cordial smile he greeted us. "It's Mrs Rae isn't it - and Miss Rae, I presume, how do you do." We shook hands.

"Yes, this is my daughter, Marjorie, who is engaged to Captain Cornez, you knew that did you?" she put to him proudly.

"Yes, Mrs Rae, I had heard," he replied with a disconcerting half-smile while running his thumb and index finger up and down his nose once or twice.

"Oh by the way, have you news of Cornez? Is he well?" she enquired naively. The Captain, obviously taken aback, studied us both with a fixed expression as if some dark problem had suddenly clouded his mind. We were left suspended. However, he soon broke into a reassuring grin.

"Well, yes - fine. Everything's fine," he said pleasantly, "That is fine as far as we know," he covered himself.

"How do y-?" began my mother, slightly alarmed.

"We had one or two nasty moments in the early days. I won't pretend we didn't but that's all been sorted now." This was indeed news. Monsieur Gobeaux had never hinted at anything mildly amiss. I could feel my heart beating.

"Nasty moments?" my mother queried anxiously. "Y-es," he said, "One - or two cryptic messages - but they've all been cleared up I'm glad to say. Oh well, I must be off," he said, fidgeting with his watch and swagger cane at the same time, giving us no time to draw him further. "Lovely weather isn't it? Too nice to be in London on a day like this. Goodbye Mrs Rae, Miss Rae, nice to have seen you - we have to keep cheerful in this job. Incidentally, it isn't Captain for Mr Cornez until it's official, which won't be until after this little lot now." And with that he was gone, having said enough to set the fecund imaginations of both my mother and I working on almost identical lines.

"Nasty moments," I said, turning to her with a puzzled frown. "What did he mean?"

"And cryptic messages," she said. "We'll have to see what old Gobbo has to say about that, but they couldn't have been very serious or he wouldn't have said things were fine again now" she added comfortingly as Monsieur Gobeaux hobbled down the steps. For once, lunch at the Café Anglais passed unexpectedly quickly as the three of us thrashed out endlessly the Captain's implications as we ate.

PART TEN

VALEDICTION

When I finally left school and returned to live at home it coincided with the second wave of air-raids over London. To begin with, the bombs were spasmodic, scattered over a wider area, and with less concentrated fury than during the Blitz. At sixteen I was considered old enough to withstand the risk, though Robin was to stay on in Winchester to complete his schooling.

In many ways I think Lady Lever was relieved I had gone from her care. She no longer needed to live a lie, looking on me daily in front of her husband to be reminded of the deceit to which she had debased herself. Though, when it had actually come to the moment of my leaving she had seemed incredibly understanding.

I had arrived back from school on my last morning to find, to my surprise, my room cleared of all my possessions. My books and clothes had been packed and my handbag containing my letters and most precious and private treasures, was now perched conspicuously on top of my cases in the playroom ready for my departure later that afternoon. Lady Lever was waiting there alone.

"I do hope everything turns out for you my dear, as beautifully as you have it planned." She paused to lower some meaning into her voice, "I don't believe you had begun to tell me the half of it, had you? I do hope so - so very much," she said with moist eyes. "That this beastly war - let's hope that ends real soon." She always reverted to the transatlantic idiom when she was under any kind of duress. "I think the tide has turned at last. Don't forget - keep praying, especially for the safety of those we love - you never told me you wanted to change your mind - remember? We must all put our trust in God," she confided, picking up my bag and hugging it to her with feeling before handing it over for me to stow my ration book and medical card inside.

***

Back home in London, Christmas came and went, marked by no special festivities this year. Life had become a little more austere; the boys were not such a congenial bunch, and there was nothing much to celebrate. All the same I was overjoyed when Monsieur Gobeaux handed me another letter from Jean, the second of the two he had written in advance - 'so she won't forget me,' he had said to my mother - even if it told me nothing of his present welfare.

Somewhere loving you. Dec. 24th
My beloved Marjorie

One year ago already, both of us - we fell in love! Do you remember? We were only together a few months but nevertheless what a lot of memories!

Now the day of our greatest happiness is not far off - 'Happy days are here again' - you will hear my voice soon and I shall see your eyes and I shall feel you in my arms and I shall kiss you.

Darling if our souls during this long separation are always together our bodies are missing each other! Do you not think so?

Now the largest part of our unhappiness has passed! We must only take care of the future and it looks marvellous! My little dear sweetheart, keep smiling. I am coming back.

Cheerio! Happy Christmas and the most sincere wishes for luck and happiness for the next ninety-nine years.

Always worshipping you.

Your fiancé
Jean. And what about your French mon trésor adoré?

It was comforting to hear him reaffirming all our dreams even if they had been expressed in the heat of the moment nine months previously.

***

Suddenly it was spring again in London. The Edwardian suburban gardens were a riot of tastefully contrived colours as they had been for some years and would be, Hitler permitting, for a long time yet. Delicate clouds of frothy pink and white almond and cherry blossoms against the steely backdrop of the sky emphasised the drab condition of the houses in need of decoration, delayed by sheer force of circumstances these last few years. The neat hedges bordering the hard city pavements burst into new green life and it was sometimes difficult to believe a war could still be raging amidst so much hope and regeneration. The news was better. The Germans were in retreat in North Africa, the Russians had held Stalingrad and the heavy industrial cities of the Ruhr were being crippled relentlessly night after night by the RAF.

I had just celebrated my seventeenth birthday. Nearly fifteen months had passed since that cold unhappy night in Hampshire when Jean had walked out of my life into the moonlight. Three months longer than he said, but I made excuses for him. He could not have envisaged the war lasting so long when he made his blithe promise all those months before. Day by day, week by week, month by month, my love had remained constant but always with reserve. I did not dare let myself depend on his return. I had not known him long enough to be able to judge his reliability. As he said his return was to be my proof and so far he had not come back! People had stopped talking about him. Friends and acquaintances convinced, no doubt, in their own minds that they had won their early gamble on his real intentions, now afraid to add 'insult to injury', had stopped asking for news. In any case I had never welcomed enquiries, having always to respond with an unqualified 'No'. Even my mother had started to speak of her favourites in the past - 'Spider and Bunny - they were two of the best'. Perhaps therefore it was not surprising if sometimes he, of whom I had received no real or comforting word - directly or indirectly - since the day he had gone, should seem almost a stranger to me, and that my thoughts were often cast down in gloomy bouts of depression. In my heart I felt it was in his nature to have sent me a message by some means.

Fifteen months had made a lot of difference. I had read books on espionage. I had heard of Mata Hari and Edith Cavell. I knew of the dangers and exhilarations of working against the enemy in their midst. My imagination had taken over from where my senses had been frozen.

I tried to picture Jean wherever he was. I thought of the first time he had tuned his transmitter to England, if that was the expression - the crackling atmosphere, the suspense - and the thrill of making contact all those miles away. He would have enjoyed that, it would have appealed to his adventurous spirit - one of the peak moments of a lifetime as when a mountaineer reaches the summit, the first drop by parachute, or just falling in love!

I visualised the reunion with his mother and him recounting to her his suffering in Spain. I heard him going over the heartbreak of the love affair and I saw her place a comforting hand on his brow, kiss him and reaffirm that he was home again with all his suffering at an end, just as my own mother had hoped. Safely reunited with his family, he would have no need of me. I had been a comfort only when he was here in the uncertainty of a foreign country when there might have been some danger he might not get back to those who loved him. Monsieur Gobeaux had been right. For Jean, our romance had flared up from the chaos of a broken heart. Lady Lever was right. I could hear his mother pointing out the crass irresponsibility of him marrying a young English Protestant girl, little more than half his age, with no friends or family abroad, who could be nothing but a liability. I feared even if I looked hard enough that I might catch a glimpse of him planning to win back the heart of his former love.

But when I was in my darkest mood I would go up to my room and lift the lid of the trunk and peep at all the new clothes, and read his letters through again. Once more I would be infected with his reckless optimism and burn for the moment of his return, not at all sure how it would be. A telephone call from some English port to say he had just landed? A knock on the front door? At any rate the rush into his arms knowing he was here and that everything was going to be marvellous - secretly hoping he might come back in the night - even climbing in at the window - to be there the next morning to wake me with kisses.

***

It was an early summer morning after a particularly heavy night of activity by the RAF over Germany. A new kind of bomb had been invented which could bounce on rivers and canals and blow up bridges. The news was displayed proudly on the front page of *the Daily Mail* with aerial photographs of the resulting devastation, side by side with pictures of happy smiling people sunning themselves along the South Coast where the rolls of protective barbed wire had been drawn back for their enjoyment. Pictures of the relaxed and happy English, to throw up in sharp contrast the deserving, suffering plight of the enemy. I scanned through the rest of the paper at the breakfast table and finally turned over the last page casually, to complete my scrutiny, and to leave the paper tidily for the next person as we had been schooled in Winchester. I was folding it neatly in half when by eyes were drawn to a tiny paragraph at the bottom of the page in a space marked 'Stop Press News'. It might easily have passed unnoticed save for the arresting headline in small print.

BELGIAN OFFICER SHOT

I felt suddenly far away as I read on with unbelieving eyes. Lieut. Jean Cornez, a Belgian Officer who, after escaping to England, returned to Belgium on a special mission, has been shot by the Nazis.

For a moment I was completely disorientated and read it through again, whispering the words aloud. Jean Cornez - that was his name. Could it be the same person? My Jean Cornez was a Captain or was he? Might there be two? Jean was common enough. Both Lieutenants? Returned to Belgium on a special mission? It gave no dates. It was all so feasible and yet none of it fitted - or did it? It was frightening.

After reading it through once more, slowly, to wrest some hidden explanation from the words, I took the paper to show my mother. She studied it and like me, could not take it in at first glance. A nerve in her neck twitched as if her body must somehow adjust to the words printed before her. She cleared her throat and concentrated hard, and as I watched her, dangling over a precipice, the colour slowly left her face.

"Oh my God!" she gasped and almost staggered as she placed her hand over her mouth.

"Is it true?" I asked my incredulous eyes staring at the words, their meaning beyond my comprehension. She leant against the sideboard for support.

"It can't be," she argued. "Mister Gobbo would have told us," she added, inhaling through her nose deeply and shaking her head before releasing her breath more slowly the same way in an effort to calm herself. "No, it can't possibly be true - we would have heard something - surely?" she declared, looking at me seriously as I stood there, a cold feeling of despair creeping up through my veins. We spread the paper on the table and heads together studied the paragraph again.

"Why is it in the paper? How did it get in?" I asked with unbelievable naivety. I had slipped into a dream world. This was not happening to me.

"I'm sure it can't be true," she said, barely hearing my questions. "I'll ring the office." We both rushed to the telephone. Monsieur Gobeaux had left the house barely twenty minutes earlier, he would not have reached his bureau yet and as he had the keys he was the first to arrive. My mother let the phone ring on as though the sound of it would somehow penetrate through to him in the Underground and he would come all the quicker. Finally she gave up and tried again at frequent intervals, growing steadily more impatient and redder in the face. I went to clear the table for something to do. After another quarter of an hour my mother came into the kitchen, breathless and trembling, smiling with uneasy elation.

"Old Gobbo knows nothing, he was just as flabbergasted as us. He's going out to buy a copy of the paper and says the Major's going in later today and he'll ask him about it and ring us back - I shouldn't worry too much. Sometimes these things are put into the paper for a reason. Maybe it's a mistake or perhaps they want people to think he's dead as part of their policy." I realised my mother was saying whatever came into her head but I clung to every supposition save what was printed before us.

We talked of nothing else for the rest of the morning and by lunchtime I was exhausted from the strain of not knowing what to believe. One minute I was convinced there could be no newspaper report without very good grounds for printing it and the next, dismissed the whole thing as a crass impossibility too ridiculous for words. By early afternoon my mental vacillation was so profound I began to tremble incontrollably.

Monsieur Gobeaux telephoned as promised to say the news had been as much of a shock to the Major who would be starting investigations right away. This raised our hopes only to have them dashed when Mrs Fields from next door arrived with a copy of *the Daily Telegraph* in which she had ringed round a small paragraph. We welcomed her in and pressed her to stay. It was good to have the closeness of another at such a time, and silently we studied the second report with its disturbing addition of three extra lines.

According to clandestine reports he was kept in prison for six months before his final execution which took place in secret.

Imprisoned for six months and yet neither the Major nor Monsieur Gobeaux had known a thing about it! This was nearly laughable but from where had such irresponsible rumours emanated? We decided to ring the office of *the Daily Telegraph* to determine the origin of their longer report, and after some delay, they told us it had come from secret sources within Belgium passed on to them by the Belgian Embassy in London. The sort of messages he might have sent over himself? For one hopeful, though sad, moment I thought it might be part of his own special policy, to pretend to me he was dead.

Monsieur Gobeaux arrived home. The newspaper reports had been shattering news to him. He said the Embassy was going to send us a copy of their bulletin through the post.

***

It was a pleasant summer evening. The lilies of the valley had just finished blooming; their perfume lingered. The moss roses were in bud and the London swifts, overjoyed to be back, screeched and swirled like black sickles in the skies in triumph. As we sat in the garden, breathing in the warm flower-scented air, my mother, me, Mrs Fields and a very confused and silent Monsieur Gobeaux, it was difficult to believe that tragedy could be so close at hand. We sat grouped together until it had grown quite dark and the stars came out one by one like sequins to embroider the heavens, I, afraid to go to bed for fear of the terrors my imagination would conjure up from the loneliness and the silence of that long, black night of uncertainty ahead.

I got into bed eventually, hoping that oblivion would come quickly, but when I lay down rest was not easy. Torn between resignation to the worst and a conviction it was all part of some devious scheme or hoax, I turned these alternatives over in my mind for hours. But when I closed my eyes I saw jagged lights that spun and oscillated in the blackness, gathering momentum until I feared they would go out of control. I opened them again and lay there until my body began to feel as if it was growing bigger, swelling up like a huge inflatable doll, floating ever higher over the world. I wanted to scream out and in a panic I switched on my bedside lamp and remained with my eyelids open until I could hear the comforting notes of the birds and the early morning sounds of life in the Avenue below; my body exhausted, my eyes hard and painful and a deep ache in the centre of my brow.

The next few days were terrible days. We seemed to be on the telephone to every known official with none of them able to confirm or deny anything. Finally, we received the report from the Embassy. If it was true that he had been dead these last seven months and, if imprisoned for six months before that, he must have been arrested soon after his arrival. It sounded unlikely and was our only ray of hope. After all we had seen the Captain in early autumn who, filling us with consternation to begin with, had ultimately left us in a hopeful state of reassurance.

At the end of that long week the newspaper *'La Belgique Independente'*, printed in this country, was delivered as usual and there, smiling out from a large photo captioned *'UN HEROS'* was my Captain looking beautifully carefree and debonair. Front-page news for all the expatriot Belgians to read!   Surely no newspaper account of such reportage would be in print if there was doubt about its authenticity.

Lieutenant Jean Cornez, a Belgian Officer, who, after having escaped from occupied territory spent several months in England returned to Belgium on a special mission, was arrested in Brussels and executed by the Germans. According to the clandestine newspaper 'La Libre Belgique', Jean Cornez was not tried until five and a half months after his arrest and that the Execution which the Germans had kept secret took place fifteen days after sentence of death had been passed.
During his detention in St. Gilles prison he suffered from hunger. He died courageously as a soldier, assisted in his last moments by a German military Chaplain.
Jean Cornez passed brilliantly his entrance exams into the Royal Military Academy. He took part in the campaign of May 1940 where he fought valiantly and avoided being taken prisoner.
After spending several months in Brussels, he succeeded in reaching England even though he was arrested in the course of the journey and interned in a Concentration Camp in Spain.

My mother now took matters into her own hands and rang the Bureau demanding to speak to the Major himself. I could hear her voice, loud, steadfast in her wild and desperate conviction that she was going to hear a complete denial of the facts which had been printed.

"My daughter is absolutely demented by the reports in the papers during the week," she began, "and now, today, it's all splashed over the front page of the *Belgique Independente*. Please Major, can you tell us, once and for all, is it true or isn't it?" There was a fearful silence this end while he replied. My mother fidgeted with the things on the hall table, her head drooped, her tongue clicked against the roof of her mouth, her eyes saddened, and her voice lost all its officiousness as she spoke again.

"Oh, how terrible, poor boy, poor little Marjorie. Whatever happened?" I conceded all hope in her marked change of tone, thankful to know the truth. She continued talking, asking questions, resigned and subdued. Finally, she replaced the receiver and turned to me. I looked directly into her big child-eyes which were brimming with tears.

"He said," she began, "Everything we read in the papers is true, but beyond that he can tell us nothing - he won't even discuss it. Now we know," she said with a terrible ring of finality. Now I would never know if he intended to keep his promise.

He had been dead last Christmas when I received his final letter, dead even before I left school. In prison on my sixteenth birthday and probably under sentence of death last autumn when we had met the Captain. Never had I considered his death would be the reason to prevent him returning, that his was a suicide mission. I thought back to that crisp dark night under the beech trees. He had not seemed afraid. I think I must have known.

I looked out of the window. A couple of laughing schoolgirls were passing the gate. The man who lived opposite was standing on a chair clipping his hedge. A sparrow flew out of the lime tree. The sun dappled patterns of light reflections and dark shadows on the windows across the road. The bread cart rumbled past. Nothing special about any of this but together it made up the rhythm of life which now had to go on from day to day in its own orderly fashion. Tears, which until now I had refused to allow, began to sting my eyes.

"It was all that greenery - I knew he shouldn't have given you a pearl or - an emerald," sighed my mother as she enveloped me in her arms. "I'll always remember him that night - when we came back after seeing you. I think he was wondering then if he would ever see you again, poor boy - after all he was only a boy. He was my son - he said so himself." My nose felt hot and distorted. I began to shake on stifling my sobs. I was helpless. Tears streamed from my eyes, there was no stopping them. They ran down my nose and over my chin. I could not contain them with my hands and they trickled through my fingers and on to the floor. "Oh my darling," cried my mother, a catch in her voice. "Cry, cry as much as you can, it's the finest thing," she urged almost joyously, taking off and throwing me her apron to mop up my tears. With this encouragement I sat down in the nearest chair and buried my face in the cushions and wept, loud, uncontrollable tears of anger, self-pity and despair. Not only did I cry for my lost love, but for my father, those gentle honeyed days that would never come again - for Cicely and Tony, a lament for and on behalf of the whole world.

Now that I had broken down, got my grief out so to speak, my mother felt she must make a further effort by referring to the past as little as possible and by insisting that everything had come about for the best. Her remarks only hurt and mystified me. I could not understand her rush to eradicate the memory of one she held so dear. That is, until enough time had elapsed before she would be able to look back through her rosy lens of nostalgia and dig it out again. "Well it's over now - you always thought he was too old, perhaps you were right - anyway you were only fifteen. I don't suppose you knew what love was really about, did you?" She was joining the ranks of the others. I did not contradict her, never argued if that was truly her belief then she had been most irresponsible in encouraging us. In fact I abetted her by my silence. The shock, the heartbreak, the humiliation, I coped with by enclosing them within me, locking away my passion and my memories. Our love had been ill-favoured and ill-fated from the start. It was too late to protest.

I received two letters of condolence. The first from Cicely came by return of post to my confession of the truth at last.

I received your letter an hour ago and you have not been from my thoughts since. I feel so sorry for you and I was happy you had written to me so soon.

As for the engagement I can say nothing - except that I turned it over in my mind for over a week and finally dismissed it as impossible and dared not ask you. I should like to be nearer to you...

Lady Lever wrote:

It does grieve my heart to learn of your sorrow. I do send you my deepest sympathy and pray that with the conflicting news it may not be true.

Do not give up hope until you have official, written information. So many have turned up who have been posted missing, or even dead.

Your Jean has been so brave and courageous that you must feel very proud of him. If the news is true then you must realise that he has done the greatest thing a man can do and that is to give up his life for his country. This does not make it any easier

for you, my dear child, so you have my loving sympathy. I hope
you will come down here to see us soon.

I never lived on false hopes. There would never be any
written confirmation for I was not his next of kin, not
related to him in any way that counted. I took his beloved
uniform from the trunk and hung it amongst my own things
in the wardrobe.

As the endless questions offered themselves and remained
unanswerable, his image as I had known him, vital, dutiful
and loving, impressed itself more securely into my
memory. In retrospect it seemed ridiculous. How
unsuitable he was to be a spy. It was not in his nature - he
needed cunning and caution, to temper the idealism and
settle the courage. How could he move discreetly amongst
a suspecting factor in the population when he stood half a
head taller than the ordinary man in the street? Any
counter-espionage group furnished with his description
could not fail to track him down. I had read how spies
went to great lengths to disguise themselves, even to the
extent of having features altered by plastic surgery. He
could have done all this, dyed his hair, grown a moustache,
undergone the most radical physical changes for the sake of
the cause, but how on earth would they have overcome his
six feet four inches?

He had, after all, been held captive a second time, subjected
to God knows what fearful torment in his last days, and
there came again that temporal sense of death I had
experienced as a child. Indescribable, yet connected in
some way to the cloying warmth of my own bed, the stars
and a fearful silence; not frightening but crushing in its
aftermath of desolation. For the second time in my life I

had been abandoned by the man I loved and trusted above all others.

In this broken-hearted reverie I went back over the last months to that fateful October day. Melancholy autumn, the dying of summer. 'Season of mists and mellow fruitfulness' we had learnt at school. 'Harvest Thanksgiving' we had sung in Church. The end of a love affair! And in my mind's eye I saw a troop of soldiers - twelve men in sinister grey uniforms, obediently standing to attention, ready to discharge their obscene duty. I heard that final, outrageous command to shoulder arms and fire as one man in that last, murderous cracking fusillade - eleven bullets, only, as a salve to each man's conscience - into the heart of a patriot, a lover! *The coup de Grâce!* The last – merciful blow as the life and love were blasted from his beloved body; his tenderness and smile extinguished forever; my dreams shattered with the smell of gunpowder lingering in the air as the sun broke through to reassure the startled birds. Judged and condemned in his own country by those who had not one scrap of right to be there. Was it punishment? If so, what had been his crime? Too much love? Enough to last me the rest of my life and some to spare, nobly, for that tiny corner of Europe which had been a battlefield more often and more savagely than any other. God forgive them.

My nightmare did not evaporate with the dawn. It haunted me night and day incessantly.

***

SEPTEMBER 1944

Monsieur Gobeaux was triumphant when news of the liberation of Brussels came through, and with visions of himself going home as the conquering hero, began to make plans for his return. There had been a gradual exodus of all other Belgians soon after D-Day. My mother started up business again in a small way. That rich, modish oyster world had gone forever. I became an art student.

We had never been officially informed of the exact fate of Jean. Whether or not the War Office had really not known and did not like to admit their ignorance was never clear. Espionage and counter-espionage can become a complex issue with both sides convinced they had the other outwitted. When Jean had been caught, perhaps the Germans had gone on using his transmitter to dupe the British and that is why his imprisonment and execution were kept secret. It might have accounted for the cryptic messages and the nasty moments the Captain had spoken of. Almost certainly he would have been given the option of life by turning coat and working for them. One day I promised myself, I would go to Belgium to try and fathom the truth. But what my mother and I were to discover, however, was that Jean was not the only one.

The months following the Christmas with Captain Peter proved to be a particularly black period in the annals of the S.I.S. (Secret Intelligence Service). Out of three hundred agents sent into Belgium only one hundred and eighty survived. Pierre had been shot in the back trying to escape a German ambush, one of his brothers too. Some were brutally tortured. Roll, on the other hand, whom they all derided over his obsession with the 'Piano', proved to be a most successful agent and was awarded the Military Cross by a grateful Britain.

What about Bunny? No-one had heard of Bunny.

During the Summer of '45, just as we were packing to go on holiday, the first we had taken since the outbreak of war, there was an unexpected knock on the front door. On opening it my mother was taken aback to see a familiar figure standing there, although thinner and the face had aged a little.

"Bunny," she cried out with all the warmth she could muster. "Bunny, my dear boy - come in. "Marjorie!" she called to me, "Look who's here!"

"Mam'selle Marjorie," he said gently as I came hurrying in.

"Bunny it's wonderful to see you," she said, quickly getting down to business. "What a tragedy about Spider. What happened - can you tell us anything?" Moved at seeing the two of us again, he shook his head slowly in an effort to free the thoughts and words which were obviously painful to him.

"Yes - for me - it was also a tragedy. He was my friend - a good friend," he stressed in slow English, his gaze straying up and around the picture rail, and I thought I detected the faintest wisp of a smile on his lips for the room was redolent of happy times.

"Can you - tell us - anything about Spider?" my mother tried him again more slowly. He made an attempt to reply in English but soon reverted to French. My mother listened serious-faced as he spoke and every now and then translated

340

the relevant points for my benefit. Although I understood most of what he told us, I liked hearing it twice, it was confirmation.

"Oh how terrible! Poor Spider," she said making clicking noises with her tongue. "He says he was caught at the transmitter and hadn't a chance. He says he had nearly completed his mission too. He was only there six weeks - poor dear Spider," tears were coming into her eyes, "When he was tracked down by one of the detection vans the Germans had to locate secret radio sets. He says," she continued, "He was supposed to have someone on the lookout for him but there is a bit of a mystery, whether he did or whether he didn't or, whether the man, once he saw the Germans coming, took fright and ran off, it isn't known. He was just finishing his transmission," she clicked again "When the Germans walked in and arrested him on the spot, still with the ear-phones on! He might have been betrayed."

"Weren't they together?" I asked, and my mother put this into French.

"No, apparently they weren't - they went together - but once they got there they separated and never met again. Poor Bunny," she said sympathetically, looking into his face. "It was sad for you too."

"It was difficult to believe. He was asking to be recalled when the mission was terminated," he replied.

"Was he able to see his mother?" I suggested, to break the silence following his last pronouncement, and Bunny shook his head.

"No!" exclaimed my mother in great astonishment. "Oh God! His mother was dead!" she repeated in some agitation. "Oh, how sad. She died just before he got back!" This fact touched her deeply and she put both hands up to her face and covered all but her glasses. "Poor boy, poor dear boy - no mother!" She took out her handkerchief to wipe the corners of her eyes. "Perhaps it was a blessing - how could she have borne to see the son she had given life to - executed?" she argued more chastenedly.

We sat talking and Bunny spoke of his own experience. Although he had been caught too, or denounced as he suspected, he had fared better in that he had been sent to work in a forced labour camp in Germany. I avoided asking the question uppermost in my mind - if Jean had been tortured in prison. I was not ready to take it.

Finally, he stood up to go.

"Well," said my mother, "It is really good of you to come, you are the only one so far - I do appreciate it."

"It is nothing - I make the promise to Jean in the aeroplane that I shall come to see you - after one unlucky moment. He ask it from me - it is my duty to him - Madame, Mademoiselle," he bowed respectfully.

"It seems such a long time ago since you were here with all the boys," My mother replied. "I never had another lot like you. That Christmas and the party - do you remember the party? Poor dear Spider and Jefke and Roll - and of course old Gobbo! Did you know he went back in the uniform of a British Captain and he could hardly walk. They rigged him out in battledress, three pips on each shoulder, and he went by plane, a soldier either side to hold him up!" she

342

chuckled but quickly pulled herself together. "War is a very terrible thing," she said, blowing into her hanky. "It never did come off - you and me. The dark woman - remember?" She looked at him askance. "And old Peter - God I wonder what happened to him. We still have some of his belongings here. I don't suppose we'll ever know the truth. I have a feeling he was using Dinah to get secrets out of you all. Oh well, life has to continue," she stated, seeing him to the door.

***

Some months later I received an official buff envelope through the post containing a letter I was surprised to see, headed by a firm of solicitors dealing in international affairs. It was to inform me that I had been left the personal effects of Lieutenant Jean Cornez of Brussels who had been killed on active service and to invite me to call at their address at my earliest convenience. I was overwhelmingly touched and rang at once to make an appointment to go the following afternoon.

While travelling to the city I wondered if any new light would be thrown on the fate of my hero. Would I see his will, which might give a clue to his thoughts and emotions at the end? It was as I began to walk through the streets around St. Paul's, where the bombing had left some of the greatest devastation, that the war was brought back to me in all its force. Large areas haunted by the ghosts of those who had once lived here through birth and death, now grassed over making sanctuaries for the birds again in the heart of London, were a sea of fiery willow-herb reflecting those two holocausts from which this great Cathedral had risen vulnerable yet strangely impregnable.

I climbed the stairs in a block of drab offices and knocked on the appropriate door. A clerk showed me into a room where an ancient elf of a man in gold-rimmed spectacles was sitting behind a desk. He stood up briefly to shake my hand before resuming his seat to give an explanation of how it all came to be left to me.

"Well, Miss Rae" he said. "I was in Brussels last week where I saw the last Will and Testament of your fiancé which he made - er, in prison." It was the first time anyone had referred to him as my fiancé, no-one, ever before, having accorded such respect to our relationship. I glowed with belated pride. Suddenly what might have been rushed into mind and as the man went over to his filing cabinet, mumbling some pleasantries as he passed, so the dingy room seemed incongruous, Dickensian almost. The cracked lino on the floor, the blistered varnish on the woodwork seemed years removed from the tall, courageous Lieutenant on whose account I was here today.

The lawyer brought over a pink folder which he set down in front of him and began to sort fastidiously through the contents, his mouth working continuously. Presently he regarded me over the top of his glasses.

"Lieutenant Cornez's stipend was paid into his London bank account until - er - the day of his decease," he said, unwilling to offend, and it occurred to me, who had authorised the stopping of it? No-one was supposed to know of the execution until it was in the papers more than six months afterwards! He picked up an envelope and held it downwards, away from his eyes. "Now let me see - we have a letter here - addressed to you Miss Rae which, on your fiancé's instructions, is to be handed to you after the liberation," he read out slowly. "Well, I think we can say that has been successfully accomplished," he added to be pleasant. A letter! My heart nearly stopped. I had not expected a letter but now it seemed most natural. I was bewitched. I grew excited. What seemed like a series of sparks pricked my stomach. He handed me the envelope which was bulky. It contained more than a letter. It felt like a small book. I was so happy to have it. A lump began to form in my throat. The man went on talking monotonously about the technicalities of having the money transferred to me but I was barely listening. Both hands were around that precious package which I longed to investigate. The lump grew more painful as I furtively stole a glance to reassure myself it was the familiar handwriting. A haze began to form over my eyes and I glimpsed the gaunt prison in that distant capital from where he would be taken to his execution, where there might be trees and grass, and some birds singing. Where Edith Cavell had taken her last look at the sky nearly thirty years before and where a part of my own heart had been murdered and lay buried with my love.

The advocate stopped talking and offered me his pen to sign the papers and, glad of this participation, I did everything as instructed. Finally, he picked up the folder and our interview was at an end.

"If I may be allowed to say so, Miss Rae, he was a very brave man, your fiancé, one of the many to whom we owe so much."

I tried to swallow my grief in order to smile for I could not speak.

On the way downstairs, through the streets, right until I reached home, I clutched my relic. The book was a copy of the 'Imitation of Christ'. With it was a much handled envelope containing a letter. I picked up the little book printed in French and opened it reverently. On the fly-leaf was inscribed:

TO MARJORIE
The letters had been pressed deeply into the paper several times so that they stood out proudly in large capital letters. I turned it over and read the message written in pencil in English.

Dear Marjorie

You must forgotten Spider, he has been a good friend of yours. But he has gone, for ever. Darling I hope you will forgive me.

This is my last night. You are present in my brain and my soul.

Remain always in the love and respect of God when you will be older.

You will have to marry a good boy and love him. I wish you a lucky life. Take always care of your mother, she is the greatest trésor you can have.

I love you darling.

Jean

And over the page...

I send you this book. It is my last present for you. But it is not the last time I shall think of you.

From the Paradise I shall protect you.

Good luck Darling. I hope see you again, there.

Jean

With trembling hands I unfolded the letter, written in French on two sides of plain prison writing paper.

St. Gilles, Bruxelles le 2e octobre 1942

Bien chère petite Marjorie,

Je t'écris en français car j'ai beaucoup de choses à te dire, et que mon anglais ne suffirait pas.

Bien chère petite fiancée, Dieu n'a pas voulu que nous soyons heureux plus longtemps sur cette terre. Et cependant, j'ai la conviction qu'il nous réserve à l'un et à l'autre un plus grand bonheur. Moi je vais partir, Il me rappelle. Toi tu auras probablement encore une longue vie. Tu dois m'oublier, complètement. Je n'ai d'ailleurs pas toujours été fair play avec toi. C'est là une des fautes de ma vie qui me songe le plus de remords. Toi, tu étais si gentille, si faible aussi, et moi! Pardonne moi chérie et prie Dieu qu'Il me pardonne. Oh, j'étais bien résolu à réparer tant que je pouvais, à te chérir et à t'aimer comme le veut la loi de Dieu, à te protéger aussi contre moi-même. Bien chère Marjorie, oublie-moi, car si tu conserves de moi des souvenirs agréables, il y en a d'autres qu'il faut effacer à tout prix.

Chérie, ma pensée, cette nuit, la dernière de ma vie, est pleine de toi, je te revois charmante comme tu l'étais à la Xmas dernière, douce et gentille, pleine d'amour pour moi. J'ai beaucoup perdu en te quittant et malgré tout je ne regrette rien. Mon devoir m'imposait de partir, et Dieu le voulait aussi. Ensuite, lorsque mon caractère faible n'écartait de lui a permis que je sois arrêté, prisonnier pendant cinq mois pour que j'aie le temps de me repentir et de m'apprêter à mourir. De quoi me pliendrai-je? Je n'ai certainement pas mérité mieux, et c'est pour moi une grande faveur que mourir en Chrétien.

Prie Le pour le repos de mon âme.

Ensuite ma chérie, tu dois te fonder un foyer, un foyer solide, avec un jeune homme qui t'aimera et que tu aimeras sincèrement. Tu es jeune, et tu peux encore aimer, tu dois encore aimer.

Je te souhaite un mari Chrétien et honnête, qui te rende heureuse ici-bas et qui veille sur ton Salut Éternel. Du Ciel je

347

veillerai sur toi et j'espère pouvoir te protéger toujours, comme j'aurais souhaité le faire ici-bas.

Bien chère Marjorie, aime bien fort ta maman, toujours, c'est le plus trésor que tu possèdes ici sur cette terre. Lorsque je revins à Bruxelles j'ai appris la mort de ma Maman! Ce fut très pénible pour moi. C'est alors que je vis combien j'avais manqué à mes devoirs filiaux. On n'est jamais assez prévenant, assez aimable, assez câlin pour sa maman. Et ce n'est lorsqu'il est trop tard que l'on regrette sa conduite. Ta maman est si bonne, si gentille, elle vous aime tant, Robin et toi, que jamais vous ne lui rendrez assez de gentillesse assez d'amour. Songe aux grands sacrifices qu'elle fait pour vous deux. N'est elle pas admirable.

Ma Chérie, dis lui, à ta maman, que je l'aime beaucoup et que je songe à elle, ainsi qu'à Robin. Fais mes amitiés à ton oncle, et à mes amis et connaissances que j'ai laissés là-bas en Angleterre.

Adieu, Darling, c'est la dernière lettre que je t'écris ne la conserve pas, il faut m'oublier.

Je n'ai été pour toi qu'un bon camarade qui est parti pour un grand voyage. Oublie mon amour, oublie les heureux moments que nous avons vécus ensemble, oublie tout. Ne pleure surtout jamais, je suis au Ciel.

Ton fiancé qui t'aime beaucoup.

s. Jean.

(Translation)

Bien Chère Marjorie

I write to you in French because I have many things to say and my English would not suffer it.

Bien Chère petite fiancée, God did not want us to be happy any longer on this earth and therefore, I am convinced he has greater happiness in store for both of us. I am leaving, He is calling me back. You will probably have a long life to live still. You must forget me completely. Besides, I have not always been *fair to you and that is one of the mistakes I made which causes me the greatest remorse.*

You were so lovely and also so weak and what about me! Forgive me darling and pray that God will forgive me too. Oh, I was well resolved to make everything good as far as possible, to cherish you, to love you according to God's holy law and also to protect you from myself. Dearest Marjorie forget me because even if you have happy memories of me there are others you must obliterate. Darling, tonight, the last of my life, my thoughts are full of you. I remember how charming you were last Christmas, sweet and kind, full of love for me. I have lost much in leaving you. Nevertheless I have no regrets. It was my duty to go and it was God's wish too. Later on when my weak human character separated me from Him, he allowed me to be arrested, held prisoner for five months thus giving me time to repent and to prepare myself to die. Why should I complain? I certainly didn't deserve more. It is a great favour for me to die a Christian. Pray for the repose of my soul.

And so my darling you will have to make yourself a home, a solid one together with a young man who will love you and whom you will also love sincerely. You are young, you can love again, you must love again. I hope you will find a good husband who is upright and honest, who will make you happy and who will protect you. I will watch over you from Heaven and I hope to be able to protect you always as I had hoped to do here on earth.

My dearest Marjorie love always your Mother, she is the greatest treasure you have got on this earth. When I returned to Brussels I learnt of the death of my mother. It was very hard for me. Only then did I realise how much I had neglected my duties as a son. One is never helpful or nice and loving enough to one's mother. Only when it is too late do we regret our shortcomings. Your mother is so good, so sweet, she loves you and Robin so much that you will never be able to show her enough kindness and affection. Think of the great sacrifices she makes for both of you. Isn't she admirable? My darling tell your mother I love her very much and that I am thinking of her and Robin. Give my regards to your uncle and to all my friends and acquaintances I leave in England.

There was no hesitation, no faltering in the writing. I had expected some miraculous ray of hope but there was nothing. No regrets, no recriminations. He had done with his earthly life and, with characteristic optimism, was already looking forward to his life hearafter. His words came through fluently in his mother tongue as I heard him speaking again and they saddened me deeply. Not so much because they were his last but because he died feeling remorse for his love and because he wanted me to forget him. We were not weak – our love was strong. It could not be denied. I hoped the German Army Chaplain had been some comfort at the end and not too harsh an accuser. I read on.

Goodbye Darling, this is my last letter, don't keep it, you must forget me. I have only been a good companion to you who has left on a long journey.

Forget me, forget my love, forget the happy times we spent together.

Forget everything, and don't ever cry. I am in Heaven.

Your fiancé who loves you very much.

Jean.

"Never! Never-ever!" I found myself speaking through my tears. Perhaps if he had concentrated more on the Morse, the other intricate exercises he had to master, instead of spending time with the dictionary perfecting his beautiful letters to me - so I might have been able to forget! In one last protest I took his photograph and wrote across the back, in French, so it would be quite easy for him to understand, *'Je ne t'oublierai jamais.'* - I will never forget you.

'Oublié! mot terrible! Qu'une âme ait peri dans les âmes!'
MICHELET.

***

And so it was not until many years later that I came to Brussels, to cry again, and to live through the romance of that spring I was not allowed during its time. Even now I was half-hoping for a miracle.

Occasionally Rose would dab her nose or sniff away a tear and offer a word of comfort or lament. Our meeting, just as moving an experience for her, had quickly established our friendship.

I made a start at putting everything back inside the box with that same love and respect which had seen to it all being stored away in the first place. The old photographs, of a surprisingly young man, still preserved that proud and eloquent nature, and the tiny ones of myself, smiling, trusting and adoring. I picked up the prayer book and rosary of polished wooden beads and hoped his indifferent faith had helped him in the end, the citation to the rank of Captain which had come too late and the two crosses awarded posthumously for gallantry. My only consolation today was that I had been there when he needed me. To make promises forever had only been to create for himself the illusion of a future. I knew it was a dangerous job. The real risks, the sacrifice, how could I have really understood at fifteen? My job should have been to prevent him going. Made him choose between his country and me! And if I'd won? He would only have deplored it as the gravest symptom of his own weakness. Tears started in my eyes, tears of regret. We had been of no lasting comfort to one another.

I sorted through the letters again to refresh my memory of those passages I could understand best and which touched me most.

> *There remain a few more hours to live. Condemned to death I am going to be executed tomorrow morning at eight o'clock.*
>
> *Dear little sister I have done my duty, the end may seem hard, to me it doesn't seem too heavy...*
>
> *One of my regrets is never to know my dear nephew. Later on, when he is older you will tell him about me...*
>
> *On the invasion of my beloved Belgium I was stationed at Binche. We suffered our first serious encounter on the Gette. It was then that I remarked on the helplessness and the frailty of man. The end of the campaign proved very severe for the regiment, we fought for several days without stopping.*
>
> *I was thankful never to feel myself not up to the ordeal...*
>
> *One of my proudest moments came after the capitulation when one of my Corporals said to me on behalf of my men 'Sir we are proud and happy to have served under your orders' but I mustn't let vanity get the better of me.*
>
> *Keep this anecdote for you and your little son...*
>
> *After the capitulation I spent several months at home looking for some way of getting to England to continue fighting and also to find Anita ...*
>
> *After many adventures of which four and a half months were spent in captivity in Spain, I finally reached Gibraltar where I embarked for England only to find some big disappointments awaiting me...*
>
> *In a very distressed condition I met a little girl who consoled me truly and with whom moreover I was counting on making a home ...*

I love her very much and regret being unable to keep the promise I made to her, but at that time I was already engaged for the mission I came back to fulfil in Belgium...

I was parachuted here in March and caught by wireless detection apparatus in April...

I await death steadfastly and hope to remain master of myself to the end...

I do not regret what I have done, what led me here or who I am. To be shot is a quick death, each man must die. It is not a punishment...

Presently I shall face the twelve guns of my executioners. I bear them no ill-feeling, they are doing their duty as I have done mine...

I die content and without fear ...

Long live Independent Belgium.

"It was already too late when he met you!" his sister said and shook her head. "The family did everything. They wrote to the Queen Mother - to everyone who had any influence at all - to try to get a reprieve, but his 'crime' had been too serious."

I had left until last the little lace bundle to investigate. I could tell by the shape exactly what it contained. I had been half afraid of finding them, for they were such an integral part of our love. Rose saw me hesitate.

"You keep that," she encouraged, pressing the little parcel more firmly into my hands. She spoke in French but I had no difficulty in understanding every word she said. "The lace will be a souvenir for you of our mother," she added kindly.

I tentatively drew apart the delicate layers of handworked lace to reveal that relic which had been part of him more than any other. Once more I held in my hands those precious dark-framed glasses. They had shared his life and love. They had enhanced the sparkle in those soulful eyes and overrated that air of casual confidence. They had never minded being cast aside in his more tender moments.

"He refused a blindfold." My friend spoke out. The lenses were smeared and dirty, in all likelihood the residue of that infernal moment when they had ceased to be of any further effect. They would have known his despair and probably contained his tears. They may have even glimpsed heaven before coming back to me. I was so pleased to have them and somehow they gave me the courage to ask the question that had niggled at the back of my mind for years.

"W-was your brother - tortured in prison?" Rose fixed me with her beautiful, sad eyes and gently shook her head in that ingenuous, trusting manner I had known and loved.

"No, he was an army officer - detained in a military prison. It was against the Geneva Convention to torture prisoners of war."

"Are you certain? So many of them —" I began with that scepticism which comes with age.

"I am sure - it was the civilians, who were not classified as prisoners of war, who suffered. My aunt saw him for a quarter of an hour after his condemnation - he was so happy to see her - much thinner, but there was no mark of violence on him." I was thankful that there had still been some chivalry amongst fellow officers, even on opposing sides.

"At his trial the Germans honoured him - they stood to attention and saluted him as he left the court, and said his sentence would in no way be a stain on his honour," she informed me proudly, and I realised there was no need to try to force secrets from him. He had been caught red-handed with British equipment and no chance to deny it. His capture had been final and uncomplicated involving no-one else as he would have wished.

"Some of his letters which he wrote on lavatory paper were smuggled out of prison by German guards who could be bribed. In none of them does he describe being physically maltreated," she assured me - "He had not much food in prison but he was not tortured."

I wondered, hunger, or calculated starvation could be a particularly insidious form of torture.

"Poor Jean - I think he had no fear of danger. He was too easy-going. He was transmitting for too long and the house was unlocked," she despaired. "It was impressed on them to stay only a short time on the transmitter - that was imperative so that the Germans would not have time to track them down once they had picked up the signal (it took about twenty-five minutes to get a man once they had pin-pointed the location) and also, to keep every door locked save their escape route, to delay the Germans and give themselves a chance. He had nearly finished his mission too - it was as if he was in a hurry to get it over! Some months after the war, he was exhumed and reburied with full military honours."

In the afternoon on the hottest day we drove out to one of the military cemeteries on the outskirts of Brussels of which that tiny country has more than her fair share. A peaceful, tree-bordered sanctuary on the edge of that old and vibrant city. As we walked along the gravel paths between the uniform lines of well-kept turf the past and present, life and death, heaven and earth, became inextricably interwoven. His sister's eyes, her smile and friendliness helped. Christmases would come and go forever, and the spring, summer and melancholy autumn. From the mouldering would begin fresh green life, eager and exposed. The echoes resound in sweet new words to soothe and sadden, and nightly the skies would be filled with stars to remind us of those dear departed souls to whom we owe in part ourselves.

Tears mingled with sweat and streamed down my face as we came to rest beside one white cross, inscribed with the proud initials J.C., amongst hundreds marking so much love and sacrifice. I envied my rival her snug earth-womb to cradle my lover's long, brave bones but I could not help feeling that the best of him had remained with me; that he had kept his promise and become my guardian angel. He was very near, youthful and elegant; spared for all time the pain of infirmity and the indignity of old age, forever twenty-eight. And for half an hour amongst the trees and the birds, the sun warm on my bare arms and nothing between myself and Paradise, I was fifteen once more.

I loved you then, when love was Spring and May.
Eternity is here and now, I thought.
The pure and perfect moment briefly caught
As in your arms, but still a child I lay.

VITA SACKVILLE-WEST